Anti-Fascism in Britain

Anti-Fascism in Britain

Nigel Copsey
Lecturer in History
University of Teesside
Middlesbrough

© Nigel Copsey 2000

Published by
PALGRAVE
Houndmills, Basingstoke, Hampshire RG21 6XS and
175 Fifth Avenue, New York, N. Y. 10010
Companies and representatives throughout the world

PALGRAVE is the new global academic imprint of
St. Martin's Press LLC Scholarly and Reference Division and
Palgrave Publishers Ltd (formerly Macmillan Press Ltd).

Outside North America
ISBN 0–333–69636–0

Inside North America
ISBN 0–312–22765–5

This book is printed on paper suitable for recycling and made from fully managed and sustained forest sources.

A catalogue record for this book is available from the British Library.

Library of Congress Cataloging-in-Publication Data
Copsey, Nigel, 1967–
Anti-fascism in Britain / Nigel Copsey.
   p. cm
   Includes bibliographical references and index.
   ISBN 0–312–22765–5
1. Great Britain–Politics and government–20th century. 2. Anti
-fascist movements–Great Britain–History–20th century.
3. Fascism–Great Britain–History–20th Century. I. Title.

DA566.7.C64   1999
320.53'3'09410904—dc21   99–33827
                                                     CIP

10   9   8   7   6   5   4   3   2
09   08   07   06   05   04   03   02   01

Printed and bound in Great Britain by
Antony Rowe Ltd, Chippenham, Wiltshire

Contents

Acknowledgements

I would like to express my gratitude to the following people for their assistance with this project: Morris Beckman, Jenny Bourne, Monty Kolsky, Henry Morris, Dave Renton, Len Rolnick, David Turner and Mike Whine. I am especially indebted to my colleague Graham Ford for reading the draft manuscript and for his critical comments. I would also like to thank other colleagues within the History section at the University of Teesside for providing me with both financial support and relief from teaching commitments. A special thanks must go to Geoff Watkins whose practical help proved invaluable in enabling me to finish this book.

More generally, I would like thank the Board of Deputies of British Jews, Brynmor Jones Library at the University of Hull, the British Library, the Learning Centre at the University of North London, the London School of Economics Library, the National Museum of Labour History, the Newspaper Library at Colindale, the Public Record Office, the University of Sheffield Library and the Wiener Library for granting me access to materials.

Finally, I would like to thank those people close to me for all their support and encouragement over the years namely Maureen and the late Bill Copsey, as well as my brother Rick. Last, special thanks go to Clare.

NIGEL COPSEY

List of Abbreviations

AFA	Anti-Fascist Action
AFCs	Anti-Fascist Committees
AFL	Anti-Fascist League
AJEX	Association of Jewish Ex-Servicemen
ALCARAF	All Lewisham Campaign Against Racism and Fascism
ARA	Anti-Racist Alliance
ARAFCC	All London Anti-Racist Anti-Fascist Co-ordinating Committee
ANL	Anti-Nazi League
BBC	British Broadcasting Corporation
BDP	British Democratic Party
BF	British Fascisti, British Fascists
BM	British Movement
BNP	British National Party
BoD	Board of Deputies of British Jews
BUF	British Union of Fascists (and National Socialists)
CARF	Campaign Against Racism and Fascism
CARM	Campaign Against Racism in the Media
CPGB	Communist Party of Great Britain
GLC	Greater London Council
ILD	International Labour Defence
ILP	Independent Labour Party
IMG	International Marxist Group
IS	International Socialists
ITV	Independent Television
IWA	Indian Workers' Association
JACOB	Jewish Aid Committee of Britain
JC	Jewish Chronicle
JDC	Jewish Defence Committee
JPC	Jewish Peoples' Council Against Fascism and Anti-Semitism
LAC	London Area Council of the Board of Deputies
LSI	Labour and Socialist International
MUJEX	Manchester Union of Jewish Ex-Servicemen
NAFL	National Anti-Fascist League
NCCL	National Council for Civil Liberties

NF	National Front
NMP	Newham Monitoring Project
NSM	National Socialist Movement
NUCF	National Union for Combating Fascismo
NUJ	National Union of Journalists
NUS	National Union of Students
NUWM	National Unemployed Workers' Movement
NWF	New World Fellowship
PDF	People's Defence Force
PNL	Polytechnic of North London
POA	Public Order Act
RAR	Rock Against Racism
RCP	Revolutionary Communist Party
SWP	Socialist Workers' Party
TUC	Trades Union Congress
TUFS	Trade Union Friends of Searchlight
TWAFA	Tyne and Wear Anti-Fascist Association
UCAR	United Campaign Against Racism
WRP	Workers' Revolutionary Party
YCL	Young Communist League
YSM	Yellow Star Movement

Introduction

This book seeks to provide both an accessible and critical analysis of the history of British anti-fascism. It is a full-length study which means our starting point is the 1920s. To be precise, our account opens in October 1923, over a decade before the most celebrated episode of popular anti-fascism in British political history – the 'Battle of Cable Street'. From beginnings which many will be unfamiliar with, this book charts the course of anti-fascism throughout the twentieth century and concludes in the present day. The first two chapters have a pre-1945 agenda and relate the origins and development of anti-fascism from the initial responses to the precursors of Oswald Mosley's British Union of Fascists, through the early origins of opposition to Mosley's Blackshirts before proceeding to Cable Street and beyond. The final three chapters cover the postwar period. Chapter 3 starts with attempts to prevent the resurrection of fascism in the period from 1945 to 1950 before moving on to explore under-researched responses to a renewal of fascist activity in the late 1950s and early 1960s. Chapters 4 and 5 have a more contemporary focus. In Chapter 4, opposition to the National Front between 1967 and 1979 is investigated. In Chapter 5, we examine the fight against fascism in the 1980s and 1990s. What therefore is distinctive about this book is that it is the first attempt to write a broad history of British anti-fascism as a continuous phenomenon from the 1920s.

The historical literature on British anti-fascism is thin and mainly comprises several local studies, autobiographical accounts written by former anti-fascist activists and specific chapters in books where usually the radical Left or fascism is the main issue under consideration. In a brief survey of what historiography exists, recent local studies on the inter-war period, including Todd's work on anti-fascism on Tyneside, Turner's study of fascism and anti-fascism in the Medway Towns, and Renton's study of fascists and anti-fascists in Oxford can now be added to Kibblewhite and Rigby's local study, published in 1978, of fascist and anti-fascist street politics in Aberdeen in the 1930s.[1] As for autobiographical accounts, the key works are recollections on the struggle against Mosleyite fascism in the East End of London by Joe Jacobs, a former Communist Party member; and Morris Beckman's account of the 43 Group, an anti-fascist organisation formed immediately after the Second World War of which Beckman was a founder member.[2] Where the extreme Left occupies the centre of attention, Noreen Branson's *History of the Communist Party of Great Britain 1927–1941* provides the standard Communist Party view of anti-fascism in the 1930s.[3] Where the central issue under consideration is fascism, substantive material on anti-fascism can be found in Benewick's *The Fascist Movement in Britain,* in *Illusions of Grandeur: Mosley, Fascism and British Society, 1931–81* authored by Lewis, and in Taylor's volume on the National Front.[4] However, there is no work that has yet attempted to synthesise this literature into an extended national perspective of the type produced by Thurlow in his commanding twentieth-century history of British fascism.[5]

In fact, by comparison, anti-fascism is a little studied area. A voluminous body of literature has been published on the protagonists of British fascism yet very little has appeared on its antagonists. In part, it was in response to this imbalance that *Anti-Fascism in Britain* was first conceived. However, the function of the historian is not merely to fill gaps in existing literature. Clearly there must be a rationale for why anti-fascism is historically important. On this point, it is the scale of popular participation in anti-fascist activity that first and foremost makes anti-fascism significant. In cumulative terms, from the 1920s to the present day, the figure extends to hundreds of thousands of people. It is an undeniable fact that anti-fascism has impacted on many ordinary lives and this alone makes anti-fascism worth considering in its own right. To reinforce this point, we should never lose sight of the fact that even in relative terms, far more people supported the anti-fascist cause than ever supported fascist organisations. The membership of the Oswald Mosley's British Union of Fascists, the largest fascist organisation in Britain, peaked at under 50,000 in 1934; in that year, possibly between 100,000 and 150,000 people attended a rally against Mosley in London's Hyde Park where the *Manchester Guardian* estimated that Mosley's contingent was outnumbered by around 20:1. In more recent times, where the membership of the

National Front – Britain's largest postwar fascist party – reached 17,500 at most, the Anti-Nazi League, formed to oppose the Front in 1977, could boast support in excess of 40,000 members within the first year of its existence.

Numerical significance aside, another aspect to anti-fascism's historical importance is the part it has played in the failure of British fascism. Naturally anti-fascist groups are keen to stress the influence of popular anti-fascism usually to the exclusion of all other factors. Thus we are faced with statements from present-day anti-fascist groups such as 'Mass mobilisations like Cable Street stopped Mosley' and the presence of the Anti-Nazi League on the streets 'meant it proved impossible to turn out Front members. Recruitment slumped and their vote collapsed'.[6] But even if anti-fascist activists overstate their case, accounts from disinterested historians usually accord anti-fascism a place in multi-causal explanations of why British fascism failed. For instance, in his study of Mosley's fascism, Lewis identifies three groups of reasons that prevented its success, one of which was anti-fascist opposition.[7] As for the decline of the National Front, Thurlow believes that this 'was partially due to the successful undermining of it by the Anti-Nazi League'.[8] It has to be said, however, that some historians divest anti-fascist opposition of any real impact on its adversary. From a generic perspective, Griffin takes the view that fascism's revolutionary ideology appeals to only a small minority in modern pluralistic societies and so 'What marginalizes fascism, then, is the irreducible pluralism of modern society, and not the strength of liberalism as such, let alone the concerted opposition of anti-fascists …'[9]

From our extended perspective, we find ourselves in a position to re-examine how far anti-fascism was of consequence in the political marginalisation of British fascism, though this does not mean to say that fascism will occupy the centre of attention. Throughout, anti-fascism retains the focus and accordingly, the scope, strategy, organisation and operation of anti-fascism form the other major concerns of this book. It is through these concerns that linear traditions of anti-fascism emerge and, as we shall see, the overarching feature in this regard has been the historic divide between radical anti-fascism – with its emphasis on physical confrontation – and 'legal' forms of anti-fascism – a tactical division which has consistently influenced relations not only between but also within those forces actively engaged in opposing British fascism.

But what exactly is anti-fascism? Though admittedly not as problematic to define as fascism, we must nevertheless proceed with caution. There is a stumbling block – this relates to how far the term 'anti-fascism' should stretch. If we take anti-fascism to mean simply opposition to fascism, then should it include responses by the state and the media? Renton, in the most recent academic definition, opts to restrict its usage to 'activists, people who objected to the rise of fascism, who hated the doctrines of fascism and did something to stop their growth'.[10] Renton puts the emphasis on activism, and what follows from this is his additional defining feature – organisation – where 'Almost every anti-fascist shared the belief that fascism could not be beaten by individuals, but only by an anti-fascist group or campaign.'[11] It is thus activism and organisation that separates anti-fascists from 'non-fascists'. The latter term is reserved for those who may have found fascist ideas 'objectionable' but who did nothing to actively stop fascism.

The approach adopted in the following study departs from Renton. Here, anti-fascism is defined as a thought, an attitude or feeling of hostility towards fascist[12] ideology and its propagators which may or may not be acted upon. In other words, anti-fascism can be both active and passive. It can take numerous forms, its sources therefore vary and so conceivably encompass responses by both the state and the media. In Chapter 2, for instance, it is argued that the Public Order Act, seen as the answer to public disorder resulting from fascist and anti-fascist conflict in the 1930s, was a piece of anti-fascist legislation. In Chapter 4, where opposition to the National Front is examined, a section is devoted to anti-fascist responses by the national and local media. The problem with Renton's definition is that it is too narrow. By stressing the importance of activism and organisation, Renton seems to restrict anti-fascism to non-governmental groups. This clearly raises a problem when describing the action of a democratic state that proscribes a fascist organisation. Indeed, what of a newspaper feature that takes a hostile line towards, and exposes, fascist activity? How do we define the action of a local council that denies a meeting hall to fascists? Surely a culture can be defined as 'anti-fascist' even if the vast majority of society refrain from active expressions of hostility towards fascism? Although this gives us a harder furrow to plough, our approach to anti-fascism is more flexible and far-reaching. In the end, it is hoped that this will leave an impression of anti-fascism as a mosaic, a variegated phenomenon which, when pieced together, provides a rich picture of a neglected yet important part of British political history.

1
The Origins and Development of Anti-Fascism, 1923–35

I

The origins of anti-fascism in Britain can be traced back to 7 October 1923, when the inaugural meeting of the 'British Fascisti' (BF) was disrupted by Communists. This meeting of Britain's first fascist organisation, attended by some 500 people, ended in 'pandemonium'. Two further meetings, both held in November 1923 in London's Hammersmith, were also disrupted.[1] These opening remarks indicate that the very birth of British fascism encountered opposition and suggests that anti-fascism in Britain pre-dates the more widely known hostility that was directed towards Oswald Mosley's British Union of Fascists (BUF) in the 1930s. Yet there has been a marked failure by historians even to consider the possibilities of antagonism towards the precursors of the BUF given that Britain's early fascist organisations have been dismissed by most historians as irrelevancies, unimportant both in ideological and organisational terms.[2] Whilst clearly in the 1920s there was no equivalent to the anti-fascist mass mobilisations that occurred in the 1930s, such as the celebrated 'Battle of Cable Street', it remains that antecedents of anti-fascism can be found in this preceding decade. This first section will therefore consider opposition to British fascism in the 1920s, for the most part instigated by the militant Left, who regarded British fascism as a real threat, despite its apparent 'innocuousness'.

The formation of the British Fascisti in 1923 raised concerns on the militant Left that British fascists would try to mirror the violent activities of fascist squads in Italy, which during 1920–2 had employed violence against left-wing opponents to such devastating effect. This period had seen the emergence of Italian fascism as a mass movement.

Italian fascism was accordingly interpreted by left-wing militants in Britain as inherently anti-working class, a 'tool of reaction', a violent, 'strike-breaking' instrument of the bourgeoisie. For the narrow circle of grassroots left-wing militants who disrupted the earliest meetings of the British Fascisti, the founding of an Italian-style fascist organisation in Britain (the imitative name 'Fascisti' made the British Fascisti's link with Mussolini's movement explicit) was deeply provocative. What is interesting, therefore, is that even in the pre-Nazi era, evaluations of foreign fascism were important in shaping responses to domestic fascism. Those left-wing militants who opposed the British Fascisti in Hammersmith were clearly propelled by hostility towards Italian fascism.

However, since mainstream opinion paid modest attention to Italian fascism, the founding of a domestic equivalent was largely ignored. Typically, Italy was portrayed in the mainstream press as a minor 'Mediterranean land' and Mussolini's fascism therefore attracted little in the way of detailed analysis. Fascism came across as specifically Italian, 'theatrical' and 'dramatic', and although it was inclined towards violence, Italian fascism was widely praised for having saved Italy from the anarchy of the Left. Conservative opinion generally applauded Mussolini for restoring order to Italy and this evaluation was even echoed in the Labour press, which acclaimed Italian fascism for a 'bloodless revolution'. Surprisingly, despite Italian fascism's assault on the Left, Labour declared that 'we must welcome Fascism half-way' and concluded that left-wing militancy had brought about Italian fascism by engendering disorder and political confusion.[3] Labour was keen to stress democratic, legalistic credentials and was anxious to dissociate itself from the 'irresponsible' revolutionary agitation of 'continental' socialism. Altogether, the effect of the mainstream response to events in Italy was that initial opposition to the British Fascisti did not attract wide interest or support.

Whilst mainstream opinion devoted little attention to either Italian fascism or its domestic counterpart, left-wing militants alive to the fascist threat in Britain quickly perceived a need for specific anti-fascist organisations. It has been suggested that this was a response to the Fascisti gaining the upper hand in initial confrontations.[4] The earliest initiative came in January 1924 when an attempt was made to launch a defensive 'anti-Fascisti' organisation known as the People's Defence Force (PDF). The PDF issued a statement from the 1917 Club in Soho, London on 26 January 1924 which maintained that the 'existence of a militant body calling itself the British Fascisti obviously inspired by the example of the Italian reactionaries … calls for a corresponding force pledged to resist any interference with the due operation of the constitution.' The PDF cast itself as a non-aggressive, legalistic organisation and even commended the police as a model to all its members. It declared itself formally independent, but nevertheless aligned to the 'workers' movement', pledged to 'keep a watchful eye on the activities of the Fascisti' and 'resist any attempt to breakup meetings'.[5] Special Branch reported that it was not known whether this body had any official connection with the Communist movement, although key personnel appeared to be closely linked. One of the organisers, H. Martin, was Secretary of the London District Council of the National Unemployed Workers' Committee[6] and another PDF official, H. Johnstone, was identified as the probable organiser of the West London local branch of the Communist Party of Great Britain (CPGB).[7]

Alongside the PDF, a second anti-fascist organisation was formed in 1924. This was known as the National Union for Combating Fascismo (NUCF) and was initially organised by E. Burton Dancy. The NUCF aimed to check the influence and growth of the British Fascisti, declared itself ready 'to meet Fascist outbreaks' and would pursue 'vigorous Socialist propaganda'.[8] The primary objective of the NUCF, which anticipated endeavours to create a 'united anti-fascist front' in the 1930s, was to end left-wing factionalism and provide a common platform for all socialists to unite in order to 'launch a concerted attack' on fascism.[9] The NUCF may have had pretensions to national significance but there is little evidence to suggest that the NUCF, or indeed the PDF, progressed beyond 'paper' organisations. In this respect, it is instructive to note that the first time that the BF appeared to have been aware of the existence of the NUCF was through the letters page of the *Daily Herald* in June 1925, when Alfred Holdsworth, a NUCF member from Hebden Bridge in Yorkshire, called on all socialists to unite against 'Fascist reaction'.[10]

Even allowing for the attempted initiation of these early anti-fascist organisations, and minor confrontations between left-wing militants and British fascists during 1923–4,[11] it appears that majority opinion on the Left was not unduly concerned by British fascism and this would account for the failure of the PDF and the NUCF to become established as substantive anti-fascist organisations. By 1924, general impressions of the British Fascisti, led by Rotha Lintorn Orman, a woman with a Girl Guide background, viewed it as an adult extension of the Scout movement, an eccentric and amateurish pressure group whose public activities were largely innocuous. Even on the far Left, this view of British fascism was widely received. The Marxist 'Plebs League',[12] in a booklet published in October 1924, dismissed the BF as 'a glorified Boys' Brigade' and proceeded to ridicule it as a 'laughing stock', an unsophisticated caricature of the Italian fascist movement.[13] Indeed, rather than engaging in Italian-style anti-communist aggression, the British Fascisti seemed to be more concerned about the party's name, which was subsequently changed to the English-sounding 'British Fascists' in 1924.

Nevertheless, for those few on the militant Left who had taken the threat of fascism more seriously, the kidnapping of Harry Pollitt, a leading figure in the Communist Party, by a group of British Fascists in March 1925 brought vindication. Where, previously, concerns about domestic fascism were restricted to a minority of 'on the ground' activists in London, the kidnapping of Pollitt from a train at Edgehill, Liverpool, prompted the highest echelons of the CPGB, to focus on the possible dangers of fascist provocation in Britain. The Political Bureau of the CPGB disturbed by incipient fascist activity, subsequently urged the Labour Party and Trades Union Congress to launch an enquiry into the strength of the fascist movement and suggest possible anti-fascist counter-measures. The Marxist press in Britain issued repeated warnings about fascism. However, these were met with derision from the mainstream Left, which judged the Communist Party unnecessarily alarmist. The Labour Party interpreted the kidnapping of Pollitt as nothing more sinister than a publicity-seeking stunt and all the more unusual because BF activities ordinarily revolved around political meetings and relatively 'innocuous' social and leisure pursuits, such as dances, dinners and the like.[14]

In the event, the fascists charged with kidnapping Pollitt were acquitted following claims that they merely wanted to take him away for a weekend in north Wales (!); but where this acquittal met with a vacant response from the Labour Party, the CPGB continued to sound the alarm. In July 1925 the CPGB's leading theoretician, Rajani Palme Dutt, called for urgent preparations against fascism. He stressed that the prevailing tendency of the labour movement to 'laugh at the Fascists in this country' was 'stupid'. According to Palme Dutt, fascism in Britain was not an 'isolated freak phenomenon', but part of a wider and deeper social movement rooted in the petty bourgeoisie and unorganised proletariat. Ominously, for Palme Dutt, fascism was developing in two directions: 'guerilla escapades' against the Left (i.e. the Pollitt incident) and 'strike-breaking' preparations. He then predicted that this developmental process would continue and warned that, given its potential support base, fascism constituted a significant threat to the entire labour movement. Moreover, for Palme Dutt, the Pollitt case confirmed the close connection between the state and fascism, and it was now clear that the working class could not put its trust in the state for protection. Therefore, rather than relying on 'bourgeois legality', Palme Dutt called on the working class to organise against the fascist danger. He suggested 'publicity and exposure of fascist movements and plans of the enemy; and second, local defence organisations of the workers to prevent disturbance'.[15]

Shortly afterwards, Palme Dutt's call was given added urgency by the formation of the Organisation for the Maintenance of Supplies (OMS). The OMS, launched towards the end of September 1925, was ostensibly a 'non-political' organisation sponsored by the government to ensure the delivery of essential supplies in the event of a General Strike. Yet it was interpreted by the CPGB as 'the most definite step towards organised Fascism yet made in this country'.[16] The Communist Party accused the OMS of being violently anti-working class, a 'strike-breaking' organisation with direct links to the government. Hence it was denounced as a 'fascist-type' operation. But this view of the OMS was not widely shared. The official Labour leadership accepted the OMS despite a belief that 'fascists' were 'more or less associated with Conservative politics'.[17] Labour leaders retained faith in official assurances that the OMS was neither 'political' nor 'aggressive', nor did it have any connection to the British Fascists. In this respect, it was further reassured when the government refused the offer made by the British Fascists to assist the OMS. Indeed, soon after, the BF split with many conservative 'loyalists' leaving the movement whilst the remaining group, having failed to become an approved ally of the state, rapidly disappeared into obscurity.[18]

With the Labour Party and TUC rejecting the Communist Party's analysis of the fascist danger inherent in the OMS, the CPGB decided to 'go it alone' and create an anti-fascist 'Workers' Defence Corps'. Consequently, small groups of men, especially in London, formed a Defence Corps which was activated during the General Strike in May 1926.[19] Then, following the General Strike, there were calls for the revival of a workers' defence organisation, a move encouraged by the Executive Committee of the Communist International (Comintern) which had met in Moscow between November and December 1926. This had directed the CPGB to work towards 'the preparation of the workers to repel a new development of Fascism'.[20] Efforts were made thereafter to revive the Defence Corps, which now became known as the 'Labour League of Ex-Servicemen'. It was envisaged that a key function of this organisation would be defensive response to fascist provocation.[21] According to Home Office files, however, the Labour League of Ex-Servicemen remained a skeleton organisation and it was never numerically significant. In December 1927 Home Office sources claimed that the League's total membership in London was only 300 with a mere third described as active members.[22] An extract from the British Fascists' organ, *British Lion*, from 1928 also testifies to the organisational insignificance of the Labour League of Ex-Servicemen when it remarked that this Workers' Defence Corps could be 'individually troublesome' but the organisation was 'too loose and widespread to be very dangerous collectively'.[23]

Although set up during the General Strike principally to defend workers from the OMS and the British Fascists, the Workers' Defence Corps also pledged to defend workers from other allied organisations, such as the 'National Fascisti'. Formed in 1924, when it was estimated to have had just 60 members, the National Fascisti was an offshoot from the BF. It was inclined towards street activism and was more radical and violent than its parent organisation. The National Fascisti was vehemently anti-Communist and its literature was accordingly inflammatory:

Communism and Bolshevism is the creed of wild beasts.... Wild beasts cannot be met with bare hands or gloves, they require more forceful and stronger weapons. So to work Fascisti, let us band together and pitch this hell's spawn into the sea, and Britain will be all the sweeter and cleaner by their removal.[24]

Essentially, this 'clean-up' operation involved National Fascisti activists holding sorties into Hyde Park from their offices in Edgware Road in order to disrupt left-wing meetings. This resulted in sporadic disturbances and crude, *ad hoc* anti-fascist retaliation: a National Fascisti meeting in Hyde Park in February 1926 was interrupted by a crowd of 60–70 left-wing militants, a National Fascisti meeting held at Marble Arch in November 1926 was sabotaged by Communists who rushed the platform, and in January 1927, following attempts by National Fascisti activists to disrupt a meeting in Trafalgar Square, where 1,500 people had gathered to protest against a refusal to grant an amnesty to those imprisoned during the General Strike, some 150–200 Communists were reported to have chased after a group of Fascisti in retaliation. Communists had taken offence at the Fascisti demonstrating from the tops of passing buses and, in order to avoid a fracas, the organiser of the Paddington local branch of the CPGB was arrested by police.[25]

Low-key retaliatory disorder was the typical response to National Fascisti provocation; the one notable exception to this was the reaction to the hijacking of a *Daily Herald* delivery van at gun-point by four National Fascisti activists in October 1925. This episode briefly widened interest in British fascism and gave rise to broader opposition. Following an exposé of the National Fascisti in the *Daily Herald*, a van containing some 8,000 copies of the pro-Labour newspaper was hijacked en route to Euston Station in London and then 'driven furiously' until it crashed into the railings of a church, whereupon it was abandoned.[26] The National Fascisti claimed that it wanted to draw attention to the *Daily Herald's* 'subversive nature' and delay circulation. The fact that the hijackers were merely charged with a breach of the peace and not larceny was met with consternation on the Left, and taken as clear evidence of the government's 'class' prejudice. The *Daily Herald* received hundreds of supporting letters calling for a firmer anti-fascist line by the government. Labour (and Liberal) MPs subsequently pressed the Tory Home Secretary, William Joynson-Hicks, for an explanation, the Independent Labour Party (ILP) held a series of protest meetings, and the Secretary of the Trades Union Congress, Walter Citrine, sent a letter of protest to Joynson-Hicks which spoke of a 'disquieting feeling' arising within the trade unions that the authorities were not dealing firmly enough with fascists.[27]

Since fascist provocation had hitherto been carried out solely against Communists, the Labour Party had remained silent. Following the *Daily Herald* incident, concern over domestic fascism started to be expressed in mainstream Labour Party circles. But this development should not be overstated. What was more noticeable was the way that mainstream Left (and Liberal) opinion appeared primarily disturbed by Conservative political prejudices interfering with the impartial administration of justice, especially since the *Daily Herald* case followed on from the acquittal of the fascists involved in the kidnapping of Pollitt. As far as the official Labour leadership was concerned, judicial leniency towards fascism was far more significant than these provocative displays which, after all, hardly invited comparison with Italian fascism.

By the late 1920s, British fascism had suffered acute regression and consequently the British Fascists and the National Fascisti were no longer capable of sustaining any real opposition. The National Fascisti quickly disappeared from public view following a damaging internal rift in March 1927 over alleged misappropriation of funds and the British Fascists had also effectively collapsed by the late 1920s. By this time, Home Office figures suggest that the BF's following had fallen to a mere 300–400 members from a peak in 1924–5 when two public demonstrations by the British Fascists in London had attracted 2,000 and 5,000 members respectively.[28] Benewick has argued that the 'influence of the British Fascists and the National Fascisti on public order, policy and opinion, was negligible.... The political forces on neither the right nor the left took them seriously.'[29] Benewick's standard conclusion does have validity: the mainstream Right generally viewed fascism as an eccentric foreign import of little real consequence and excluding a fleeting concern following the *Daily Herald* case, this view of British fascism was also shared by the mainstream Left. It is worth emphasising, however, that the extremist wing of the labour movement paid fascism more attention, a consequence of events in Italy where fascism had been interpreted by the CPGB as a 'violent' and 'lawless' anti-working-class phenomenon.

Prior to 1925, a narrow circle of left-wing radicals actively opposed the British Fascists. Meetings were disrupted and attempts were made to create specific anti-fascist organisations. Moreover, following the kidnapping of Pollitt and with the formation of the OMS, the leadership of the Communist Left did begin to take British 'fascism' seriously. The CPGB leadership focused on the dangers of fascism in 1925 and through the means of a Workers' Defence Corps, greater effort was directed towards establishing a functioning anti-fascist organisation. However, the fact that these various anti-fascist organisations did not develop beyond the 'paper' or 'skeleton' stages and flourish into substantive national movements with mass support, and the fact that oppositional confrontations with the British Fascists and the National Fascisti involved small numbers of people, geographically restricted to London, confirms that anti-fascism in the 1920s failed to achieve national significance. In this respect, the extent of anti-fascism in the 1920s was merely proportional to the political insignificance of domestic fascism. Yet it is an important consideration that fascism did not go unchallenged in the 1920s and this point clearly deserves recognition.

II

If anti-fascism was born in the 1920s, it was in the 1930s when it came of age, appearing to reach maturity at the 'Battle of Cable Street' on

4 October 1936. This well-documented mass mobilisation of between 100,000 and 300,000 people against a planned march by Oswald Mosley's British Union of Fascists through the East End of London, is frequently celebrated as one of the most dramatic mass mobilisations in Britain's modern political history.[30] The 'Battle of Cable Street' has certainly left an enduring mark on the history of anti-fascism and has assumed legendary status as a particularly impressive illustration of popular, spontaneous anti-fascist opposition. However, this depiction is unfortunate as it tempts historians to focus on Cable Street as the principal event in the inter-war period, without giving due consideration to preceding events. Indeed, by focusing on Cable Street, anti-fascism does not appear to possess any developmental dynamic. The emphasis on the 'popular' and the 'spontaneous' obscures anti-fascism's organisational features, neglects the causal factors in the strengths and weaknesses of different anti-fascist organisations, and fails to draw out different anti-fascist analyses and strategic positions. In short, it underestimates the structure and complexity of anti-fascist opposition. Furthermore, because Cable Street was such a spectacular event, its contribution to the failure of British fascism is typically exaggerated. And, even amongst those historians that have avoided preoccupation with Cable Street and have discussed the importance of earlier anti-fascist opposition, a number have fallen into the additional trap of either viewing events from a skewed 'metropolitan' perspective which focuses on incidents in London and neglects local dimensions, or have viewed events from a local perspective without reference to other parts of Britain.

It is interesting that Skidelsky begins his account of confrontations between anti-fascists and fascists before the founding, in October 1932, of the British Union of Fascists. Skidelsky argues that as early as 1930–1, the CPGB identified Mosley as a 'potential fascist'.[31] In due course, New Party[32] meetings were subjected to frequent disruption and it was common for hecklers to accuse Mosley of 'fascism'.[33] It seems reasonable to speculate that these hecklers were Communists since it was the CPGB's paper, the *Daily Worker* which labelled the New Party 'fascist'.[34] This indictment of Mosley and the New Party can either be seen as a reflection of the CPGB's prophetic powers or, alternatively, as political opportunism in so far as the New Party now competed with the Communist Party for the support of the disaffected working class. Skidelsky tends towards the latter reading, arguing that the Independent Labour Party received similar treatment by the Communists.[35] The irony in this, of course, is that the ILP became a leading participant in the later struggle against Mosley's British Union of Fascists from 1933.

According to Skidelsky, harassment of Mosley and the New Party was orchestrated by the Communist Party. Yet Skidelsky overlooks the fact that Mosley's final departure from the Labour Party in 1931 engendered considerable hostility within Labour's ranks and it is clear that significant opposition also came from Labour Party supporters. This was especially the case at the Ashton-under-Lyne by-election in April 1931, contested by the New Party and previously a safe Labour seat. Labour animosity was exacerbated when the Conservative Party candidate won the seat, a victory which Labour supporters felt had resulted from a split in the working-class vote caused by the intervention of Mosley's New Party. John Strachey, later to become a leading anti-fascist, but at the time a key figure in the New Party,[36] famously remarked that it was at this point, with the incensed crowd expressing its anger, that Mosley embraced fascism. Mosley reacted to his antagonists by creating an activist youth movement with semi-fascist trappings before moving progressively towards outright fascism following the abysmal failure of the New Party at the general election in October 1931 and his visit to Mussolini's Italy in January 1932. Notwithstanding the oversimplification of Strachey's comments, it is certainly another irony that 'anti-fascism' may well have played a role in Mosley's turn towards fascism.

If the Left's opposition to Mosley and the New Party was driven entirely by 'anti-fascism', then one would have expected the formation of the categorically fascist BUF in October 1932 to have triggered a much more animated response from the labour movement as a whole. But according to BUF sources, between October 1932 and March 1933 fewer than 3 per cent of BUF meetings resulted in disorder.[37] Between the New Party's farcical failure at the polls in October 1931 and the formation of the BUF a year later, Labour Party opposition to Mosley, born more from betrayal than anti-fascism, subsided. Active Labour Party hostility was not sustained into the first few months of the BUF; instead, Mosley faced isolated opposition from a small group of Communists who were presumably responsible for the more visible interruptions of BUF meetings in London, at Memorial Hall and Battersea Town Hall in October and December 1932 respectively.[38] Thus, when comparing the New Party phase with the very opening BUF phase one can point to a downward trend in the level of conflict between Mosley and left-wing opponents. Yet it is significant that this trend did begin to reverse from March 1933. The decisive factor here was the rise of Nazism. The appointment of Adolf Hitler as Chancellor of Germany in January 1933 and the Nazi victory at the polls in March focused the attention of the Left on the British Union of Fascists, allowing anti-fascism to gather momentum. By violently attacking the German Social Democratic and Communist Parties, Nazism inflamed emotions on the Left and, in due course, as Skidelsky puts it, 'Transnational passions were thus inevitably concentrated on national movements.'[39]

Following close upon Hitler's rise to power, the Communist Party approached the Labour Party, trade unions and the Co-operative Party in March 1933 with a proposal for joint activity in a 'United Front against Fascism'. Instructions had been issued from Moscow through the Comintern directing Communist Parties to seek co-operation with social-democratic parties in the fight against fascism, the clear consequence of events in Germany where the victory of Hitler had demonstrated the futility of left-wing sectarianism. The Communist Party in Germany, locked into the Comintern's 'class against class' doctrine, had denounced Social Democracy as reformist capitalism and had castigated Social Democrats as 'class enemies' or 'social fascists'. The resulting Communist–Social Democrat disunity had allowed room for the Nazis to seize power and subject the Left to immediate persecution. The 'class against class' principle had been officially adopted by the British Communist Party in 1928, but its adoption had generated considerable opposition from within the CPGB's ranks. Consequently, when the call came in March 1933 for a united front there was little disagreement amongst the CPGB, especially given the gravity of the situation in Germany.

The Communist Party's approach to the labour movement on 10 March took the form of official correspondence substantiated by visible displays of anti-fascist activity. On 12 March 1933, at a BUF meeting in Manchester's Free Trade Hall, the local branch of the CPGB distributed an anti-fascist manifesto entitled 'Unity Against Fascist Reaction', which was addressed to all members of the Labour Party, trade unions, Co-ops and ILP. As well as distributing this manifesto, Communists disrupted Mosley's meeting by chanting in unison, 'Up with Russia! Down with Mosley!' and by singing the 'Red Flag'.[40] The objective was to impede the speaker's audibility, thereby preventing the BUF from getting its message across to the audience. As a tactic it had ample potential. Opponents acting in groups could disrupt even the largest meetings but the BUF had reacted quickly by creating a 'Fascist Defence Force', comprised of strong-arm stewards who would try to eject offenders, frequently leading to violent disturbances. This Defence Force was activated at Manchester and not surprisingly fighting ensued. The clash at Manchester was hailed by the CPGB as a victory over the BUF and undoubtedly provided inspiration for small groups of Communists to lay siege to a BUF branch office in Walworth Road in London for over a fortnight in March 1933. On 28 March, an organised raid damaged fixtures and fittings and, according to BUF sources, an attempt was made to set fire to the staircase.[41]

The CPGB's call for the 'United Front' ran concomitantly with a corresponding call made by the Independent Labour Party which had followed a resolution by the ILP's international co-ordinating body, the Labour and Socialist International (LSI) in Paris. The ILP, which had disaffiliated from the Labour Party in 1932, was around twice the size of the Communist Party in 1933 with some 11,000 members.[42] These two groups essentially comprised the militant wing of the labour movement, but whereas the Communist Party was staunchly revolutionary, the more pragmatic ILP contained a spectrum of opinion from revolutionary to reformist. The leadership of the ILP, centred on Fenner Brockway and James Maxton, was deeply critical of Moscow's control over the Communist International and was uneasy about collaboration with the CPGB. Nevertheless, prompted by the LSI and pro-Comintern elements, the ILP decided to co-operate in anti-fascist activities and accepted the CPGB's invitation for joint action despite further fears that the Communists were intent on hijacking the ILP's membership.

However, the Labour Party, Trades Union Congress and Co-operative Party all rejected the CPGB's proposals. The National Joint Council, which represented the Labour Party, the TUC and the Parliamentary Labour Party defended their refusal in a manifesto entitled 'Democracy versus Dictatorship' issued on 24 March 1933. In this manifesto Labour argued that that it was fear of communist dictatorship that had led to the rise of fascism. Therefore, radical action by the Left, of the type proposed by the CPGB, would only encourage fascist reaction. This manifesto not only incriminated communism for being responsible for fascism, it also accused communism of dictatorship. It maintained that since both communism and fascism obliterated parliamentary democracy, communism was commensurate with fascism. In contrast, the Labour Party was constitutional, it stood for the defence of democracy and freedom, therefore it could not possibly countenance co-operation with the Communist Party. Besides, the Communists had previously attacked the Labour Party and TUC especially during the 'class against class' phase and the CPGB's disruptive tactics had hardly fostered an atmosphere of mutual respect and co-operation. Moreover, the Labour Party had little to gain from collaboration with the CPGB, given that 'the sheer disparity of size between the Labour Party and the T.U.C. on the one hand, and five or six thousand Communists on the other, made the idea of a "united front" between these organisations seem ludicrous'.[43]

Instead of militant action, the anti-fascist policy of the Labour Party stressed moderation. It maintained that the British state was deeply democratic boasting a liberal-democratic tradition that would in normal circumstances act as a barrier against fascism. However, in the event of economic collapse, the political system could be undermined and if, in this situation, the Labour Party joined forces with the Communists in militant action against fascism, there was a real danger of a fascist upsurge. Thus, the Labour Party warned against working-class militancy, hoped for economic recovery and anchored its anti-fascism to the democratic state. The result of this analysis was that the Labour Party's anti-fascist policy developed from 1934 onwards in a 'twin-track' direction. First, stress was placed on educating workers to the dangers of both fascism and communism; second, this was combined with calls for the democratic state to legislate against fascism, which ultimately culminated in Labour Party support for the Public Order Act in 1936.[44]

The Labour Party's discouragement of anti-fascist militancy was intended to send a clear message to potential backers of fascism that the labour movement did not constitute an ultra-Left threat. Furthermore, Labour's attachment to constitutionalism also ensured that the existing liberal-democratic consensus was not challenged from within the mainstream. Thus, political space for the illiberal and anti-democratic ideology of the British Union of Fascists was restricted. In this way, the anti-fascist policy of the Labour Party contributed to the marginalisation of British fascism by reinforcing the prevailing consensus behind political moderation and parliamentary traditions. As Griffin has explained, where liberal democracy enjoys general acceptance, 'viable' space for radically alternative ideologies is necessarily restricted.[45] The situation in inter-war Italy and Germany was entirely different. Here, socio-economic crisis shattered a very weak liberal consensus and this opened up space for extremist ideologies whilst also making political violence by fascists more socially acceptable. The CPGB, however, mistakenly assumed that the situation in Britain in 1933 replicated that in Germany before the Nazi acquisition of power. Accordingly, it wrongly attacked Labour's position as analogous to the German Social Democratic position which, it claimed, had facilitated the Nazi victory by rejecting the possibility of mass action.

The CPGB's reply to Labour's anti-fascist policy took the form of a scathing pamphlet entitled 'Democracy and Fascism' authored by Rajani Palme Dutt. Refusing to accept that communism could take the blame for fascism, Palme Dutt returned the charge. Rounding on the Labour Party, he denigrated its attitude as insidious and reprehensible. According to Palme Dutt, Labour's position was a mirror-image of the policy of the German Social Democrats, a recipe for disaster and for the victory of fascism:

> The line of the Labour Party is the line of German Social Democracy, the line of bidding the workers trust in capitalist 'democracy,' which has led to the disaster of the working class in Germany and the victory of Fascism. This same line will lead to the victory of Fascism in Britain, if the workers do not correct it in time. The workers must be warned in time of the lying and hypocritical character of the Labour Party's propaganda of 'democracy' in the abstract, which covers in reality betrayal of the working class, servitude to capitalism, and, finally, surrender to Fascism.[46]

Palme Dutt implored all militant workers in every trade union branch and local Labour Party to agitate for joint action and disregard the instructions of the official Labour leadership. And, in due course the Communist Party's appeal to the rank and file within the labour movement did meet with considerable receptivity. Although Labour's official leadership rejected joint action, such was the fervency of reaction to Hitler's accession to power and subsequent persecution of the Left, that there was unofficial co-operation between both militant and moderate wings of the labour movement in the fight against domestic fascism. This co-operation occurred at grassroots level either through loose association or through support for various local 'united front' committees. For all the rivalry, the distrust and antagonism between the Labour Party and the Communist Party, the emotive issue of fascism did foster significant degrees of collaboration at local levels.

As anti-fascism gathered pace from March 1933, Labour Party members began to participate in anti-fascist activities, frequently acting on their own initiative in the absence of an active lead from either the Labour Party or the TUC. Local studies of anti-fascism corroborate this point. Renton details the creation of the anti-fascist Oxford Council of Action in May 1933. Albeit short-lived, this was a broad-based group, with around 100 members representing some 40 organisations, including the local Labour Party and trade unions. In a similar study of the Medway Towns, Turner notes the launching of a local Anti-Fascist Campaign Committee in May 1933 which had the support of leading figures in the Chatham Labour Party, as well as support from the ILP and CPGB; though co-operation with the radical Left in this particular United Front did trigger factional conflict leading to its eventual rejection by the local Labour Party. And, according to Todd's local study of anti-fascism, despite the Labour Party's official line, a number of Labour councillors in Sunderland supported an anti-fascist united front committee, formed in 1933 by the Communist Party, ILP and the militant National Unemployed Workers' Movement.[47]

Since the mainstay of anti-fascism was localised 'united front' action, such action tended to be strongest in large urban, industrial areas with the most vigorous left-wing traditions. It should not be forgotten, however, that the anti-fascist opposition also embraced support from non-Left elements, as Mullally notes: 'though it suited Mosley to label them all "Reds", they were made up of Communists, Socialists, trade unionists, Liberals and – to their credit – a sprinkling of honest anti-fascist Tories.'[48] And with the emphasis on local activity, the general organisational character of anti-fascism was naturally loose-knit and ill-defined. Again according to Mullally, it was therefore obvious that:

> ... such an opposition completely lacked organisation or an integrated plan of action; it was made up of far-sighted individuals who were alive to the menace of fascism right from the start and who had the courage to demonstrate their faith whenever a Blackshirt meeting was held in their districts.[49]

In fact, despite wide involvement in various locally based initiatives, anti-fascist activity by Labour Party members in 1933 was at its most visible in opposition to Nazism. The Labour Party leadership had given official backing to such activity by making calls for a boycott of German goods. But one association, the Relief Committee for the Victims of German Fascism, was giving cause for concern precisely because of its links with the Communist Party. At its first conference in May 1933, a Labour peer, Lord Marley, was in the chair and a number of high-profile Labour Party members, including Ellen Wilkinson and Dorothy Woodman, were on the platform. The platform was shared with leading Communist and ILP speakers, which was also the case at further meetings, attracting audiences of some 2,500 and 4,000. The Communist Party had taken a leading role in the campaign to assist the victims of Nazism through its ancillary organisation, the International Labour Defence (ILD), and was now focusing its efforts on the Relief Committee. This prompted the Labour Party to publish a pamphlet entitled 'The Communist Solar System' in September 1933, which was a list of proscribed Communist 'auxiliary' organisations. This included the Relief Committee for the Victims of German Fascism to the obvious annoyance of Labour Party supporters such as Ellen Wilkinson, who criticised the Labour leadership for having no regard for the anti-fascist feelings of its ordinary rank and file.[50] In theory, the Labour Party reserved the right to expel any member that belonged to, supported or even appeared as a speaker at any meetings of Communist 'auxiliary' organisations; but in practice, the authority of the Labour Party over its members was more a 'moral' authority, which came to depend largely upon persuasion rather than compulsion.

With the Labour Party refusing to provide a strong lead for anti-fascism, the radical Left began to establish itself at the forefront of physical opposition to the British Union of Fascists. From March 1933, confrontations between left-wing militants and the BUF showed signs of increasing frequency, especially in London, although this trend was denied by the BUF, which insisted that opposition in the 'old New Party days' was much more pronounced.[51] Arrests were made at a BUF march through the West End in May 1933, disturbances occurred at BUF meetings at Edmonton in May and June 1933, there was disorder at Kilburn, Deptford and Wood Green in October, with further disturbances at Wood Green in November 1933. Moreover, the BUF's own paper, *The Blackshirt* (17 April 1933) reported that four members of the BUF were attacked following an anti-fascist demonstration in Trafalgar Square, and also reported violence at meetings in Brixton and Battersea.[52]

Yet other disturbances in London in 1933 point to the existence of specific Jewish opposition, which interestingly pre-dates the BUF's turn towards hardline anti-Semitism in the mid-1930s. The *Daily Worker* (2 May 1933) reported a disturbance in Piccadilly Circus when cinema crowds, with a significant Jewish element, 'jostled' BUF paper-sellers on to the steps of the Eros statue. Surrounded by a large crowd, missiles were thrown and fighting ensued. A further disturbance occurred a week later in similar circumstances in Coventry Street, when a crowd of around 200 people witnessed a fracas between Jews and 12 BUF members selling papers.[53] These confrontations between Jews and BUF newsvendors appear to have been largely spontaneous responses, undoubtedly induced by Jewish persecution in Germany. Angered by events in Germany these Jews failed to distinguish between the BUF's brand of fascism which at the time harboured anti-Semitism, and Hitler's variety which propagated it to the extreme.[54] The proportion of Jews involved in these disturbances who were also Communist Party supporters is difficult to determine with any precision, but there was certainly an overlap with the militant Left: the ILD later held protest meetings in the East End in support of those arrested in connection with these disturbances. This demonstrated the eagerness of the Communist Party to arouse anti-fascist feeling amongst the Jewish population in the East End and confirms the existence of anti-fascist attitudes in this area long before the BUF's penetration in the mid 1930s.

Unlike the 1920s, when confrontations between fascists and anti-fascists were restricted to London, already in 1933 conflict between Mosley's BUF and anti-fascist opposition had extended beyond London into provincial areas. The events at Manchester have been mentioned, but other notable clashes occurred at Stockton-on-Tees in September and Oxford in November. According to one former BUF member, the small branch at Stockton-on-Tees had faced considerable hostility from the local Communist Party in 1933, with individual members being attacked and meetings disrupted. This had led the BUF to bus in activists from Manchester and Tyneside, to march alongside the Teesside contingent in a show of force to Stockton's Market Square on 10 September 1933. As the BUF's speakers addressed the meeting, they were continually heckled and booed by a group of left-wing militants, leading the Defence Force to weigh into the crowd, resulting in serious hand-to-hand fighting. One BUF activist sustained a serious eye injury; it was claimed that another was struck from behind with an iron bar.[55] The meeting was subsequently closed by police and the fascists were escorted to buses followed by an angry crowd of some 1,000 demonstrators, a far larger number than the initial anti-fascist antagonists.[56]

This incident is an early illustration of the BUF's predilection to violence. As later events at Olympia in June 1934 were to confirm, the BUF's irresponsible use of force played directly into the hands of anti-fascism. The fact that the BUF's lack of restraint carried the potential to broaden hostility was recognised at an early stage by anti-fascists who looked to use fascist violence as a way of denying the BUF political and social respectability. With this in mind, it has even been suggested that on occasions anti-fascists deliberately overstated the extent of BUF violence. It has been argued by Cullen[57] that one such occasion was the response to Mosley's meeting at Oxford Town Hall in November 1933. At a protest meeting subsequently called by prominent Oxford dons to expose the violence used by the Blackshirts at Oxford Town Hall, anti-fascists alleged that fascist stewards thrust fingers up noses wearing gloves with metal rings and knuckledusters. As Cullen points out, however, a local police report in the Home Office files makes no mention of any fascist stewards wearing knuckledusters and where this report remained private, the anti-fascist version of events was heard publicly in a 'packed' meeting and was reported in the press. Not surprisingly, the adverse publicity that this generated did not do much to enhance the BUF's local reputation.

III

Despite the negative publicity surrounding the incidents in Oxford, in January 1934 the BUF secured the support of Lord Rothermere's *Daily Mail* and other Rothermere papers, such as the *Sunday Pictorial, Sunday Dispatch* and the *Evening News*. Rothermere had already praised both Mussolini and Hitler for strident anti-communism and youthful dynamism. What he saw in Mosley was a radical Conservatism which he hoped would break the grip of 'Old Gang' politicians and infuse Britain with fascist-style vitality. Rothermere's influential backing allowed the BUF's membership to increase substantially from 10,000–15,000 in 1933 towards 50,000 by June 1934.[58] The infamous 'Hurrah for the Blackshirts!' article in the *Daily Mail* on 15 January 1934 opened the campaign, supplemented by generous publicity in other titles. The *Evening News* offered 500 seats at Mosley's rally at the Albert Hall in April 1934 as prizes to readers in a Blackshirt competition, and the *Sunday Dispatch* even ran a beauty contest for Blackshirt women. Rothermere's support for the BUF and the advent of the hard-line Dollfuss regime in Austria provided further impetus for anti-fascism with the Communist Party and Independent Labour Party renewing attempts to establish a 'united front' with the labour movement in February 1934. Once again, their advances were rejected. Whilst willing to provide humanitarian relief for workers in Austria, the Labour Party leadership remained steadfastly opposed to direct action against fascism in Britain. So without organisational backing from the Labour Party leadership, anti-fascist opposition still lacked broad structural cohesion. The official line of the Labour Party leadership, as Lewis recognises, meant that 'the united front was prevented from expressing itself as a nation-wide campaign' leaving by default, a loose patchwork of local anti-fascist organisations.[59]

Within this organisational mosaic, anti-fascism during early 1934 became increasingly focused on the British Anti-War Movement, especially in Communist Party circles in London. The British Anti-War Movement was a Communist Party 'satellite' organisation, included in Labour's list of proscribed organisations and thus considered 'out of bounds'. Renaming its monthly bulletin 'Fight War and Fascism' in March 1934, the British Anti-War Movement drew on a perceived convergence between anti-fascism and pacifism. Its declared aim was to fight simultaneously both war and fascism, interpreting fascism as the means by which the ruling class in the capitalist state subjugates the working class through militaristic organisation. Notably, the Chairman of the British Anti-War Movement was John Strachey. Since his break with Mosley, Strachey had gravitated towards Communist circles and had recently authored a polemical work, *The Menace of Fascism*, which had gone on to sell close to 5,000 copies.[60] Strachey had written this work in order to maximise opposition to the Labour Party's refusal to form the 'United Front'. From his leading position in the British Anti-War Movement, Strachey looked towards steering the developing anti-fascist movement which had, by the spring of 1934, already widened to include industry-specific groups as well as non-Left groups.

In response to Rothermere's support for fascism, the pro-Communist Printing and Allied Trades Anti-Fascist Movement was established at a meeting in Kingsway Hall in London in March 1934 with over 500 volunteers signing membership forms. This group, which included machine-minders from the *Daily Mail* and *Evening News*, pledged itself to the defence of all printing workers who refused to print or handle fascist propaganda.[61] Other anti-fascist groups active in London during early 1934 were the Green Shirts and New World Fellowship. The first of these followed the economic doctrine of Social Credit pioneered by Clifford Hugh Douglas.[62] His most enthusiastic followers in Britain were led by John Hargrave who formed the Green Shirts in 1932 as the 'militant' wing of Social Credit. At the opening of the National Headquarters in London in July 1932, Hargrave had announced that the Green Shirts stood opposed to both fascism and communism. This anti-fascist stance was substantiated as early as January 1933 when disorder followed a fascist meeting in Crouch End in London after Mosley refused to reply to dogged questioning by a Green Shirt activist. In April 1933, some 80 Green Shirts had participated in an anti-fascist demonstration in Hyde Park and in June 1933, a group of Green Shirts had demonstrated outside BUF offices in London's Regent Street only to be dispersed by police. In February 1934, at a time when the Green Shirts claimed 2,000–3,000 followers,[63] the BUF took matters into their own hands when two Green Shirts chalked anti-fascist slogans on the shutters of the BUF's office at Grosvenor Place in London and were subsequently 'arrested' by BUF members and subjected to a violent assault.[64]

New World Fellowship (NWF), an organisation that has left little historical record, protested outside Mosley's first large meeting at London's Albert Hall on 22 April 1934. NWF activists had attempted to distribute anti-fascist leaflets but had been dispersed by police.[65] Significantly, at this meeting it had been noted that despite the additional presence of small groups of left-wing militants, opposition to Mosley had been low-key and noticeably ineffectual. There was no visible opposition inside the hall and, given the relative meagreness of the opposition outside, a need for greater organisation and planning of anti-fascist activities in London was now manifestly clear. This was accepted by the London Communist Party, which resolved to organise much more effectively against Mosley's next large meeting, to take place at Olympia on 7 June 1934.

In the months preceding Olympia, the main focal points of anti-fascist activity outside London were Edinburgh, Bristol, Plymouth and Newcastle upon Tyne. The BUF press reported that a hostile crowd had broken up a fascist meeting at the Mound in Edinburgh in February 1934.[66] Disturbances involving Communists were recorded outside a BUF meeting at Colston Hall, in Bristol on 28 March 1934. Fighting also occurred at a BUF meeting at Plymouth Corn Exchange on 26 April where chairs were used as weapons. This had come in the wake of a BUF meeting on 16 April where, according to Home Office sources, a 'rowdy communist element' had been present.[67] Indeed, as early as February 1933, there had been considerable heckling of BUF speakers in the Market Square at Plymouth.[68] But by far the most significant events, involving substantial numbers of ordinary people, occurred in Newcastle. Events in Newcastle demonstrate that although anti-fascism lacked broad organisational structure, 'united front' activities could find more distinctive anti-fascist form and additionally encourage wide public participation. The events in Newcastle have been documented in a local study by Todd[69] and therefore require only a brief summary.

In May 1934, a 'united front' Anti-Fascist League was established on Tyneside which immediately recruited some 200 members. These anti-fascists were also known locally as 'Grey Shirts' and drew their support in the main from the ILP and the Communist Party.[70] On 13 May 1934, local BUF organiser and former Labour MP for Gateshead, John Beckett,[71] was confronted by a large hostile crowd at an open-air meeting in Newcastle where Beckett was lambasted for his 'treachery'. Apparently inspired by the AFL, though the causal relationship is not clear, the crowd rushed the BUF platform. Anti-fascists then lay siege to the BUF's local headquarters, attacking it with missiles. The next day, Beckett attempted to address a meeting at Gateshead Town Hall but was subjected to anti-fascist heckling. Outside, he faced yet another antagonistic crowd but this time it was estimated that the crowd had grown to an imposing 10,000 people. Beckett was subsequently escorted back to the local headquarters by mounted police where once again the BUF's local offices were subjected to a hostile siege. Todd identifies these anti-fascist counter-demonstrations as the 'turning point' in the local fortunes of the BUF on Tyneside. Beckett bid a hasty retreat to London, Mosley postponed an open air rally on the Town Moor, and the local BUF was forced to shift activities away from Newcastle and Gateshead towards other areas in a fruitless search for new recruits. Clearly these events at Newcastle anticipate other popular anti-fascist mobilisations in the 1930s, but unfortunately in Todd's otherwise detailed account, the dynamics of the relationship between the AFL and popular anti-fascism on Tyneside remain largely unexplored.

Parallel to events in Newcastle, the Communist Party in London became actively engaged in preparations for Olympia. According to a Special Branch report, two or three leading members of the CPGB had made a 'tour of inspection' of Olympia's surrounding neighbourhood in order to familiarise themselves with the layout. It noted that the CPGB had a prearranged plan to sit groups in different parts of the hall, with each group shouting slogans in turn. The report concluded that the Communist Party was 'making every effort to bring off a spectacular coup against the fascists' and 'in order to counteract the loss of prestige the Party has suffered in recent by-elections' also revealed more hidden reasons for this cause of action. A further report noted that, in addition to making frequent announcements in the *Daily Worker*, the London District Secretariat had sent out a circular to all 'street and factory cells', had issued an invitation to the trade unions, Labour Party and Independent Labour Party to co-operate in the proposed counter-demonstration, and had distributed leaflets. Furthermore, the Young Communist League (YCL) had distributed a pamphlet, *Ten Points against Fascism*, and had issued special invitations to the Labour Leagues of Youth and the ILP Guild of Youth.[72] Unsurprisingly, the Labour Party and the London Trades Council rejected the invitations, but local Labour Leagues of Youth pledged support in defiance of the Labour Party leadership. This refusal to conform to the strictures of the Labour Party's anti-fascist policy was not as surprising as it first seems given that the Labour Party's League of Youth had been the target of considerable Communist 'entrism' since 1933 and a group of League of Youth activists had already distributed anti-fascist leaflets outside Mosley's meeting at the Albert Hall.[73] Aside from the League of Youth, support for the Olympia mobilisation also came from the ILP, the ILP Guild of Youth, furnishing trade unionists, busmen, the catering branch of the Transport and General Workers' Union, building workers, and the Printing and Allied Trades Anti-Fascist Movement.[74]

In the immediate approach to Olympia, the Communist Party had been especially active amongst the Jewish community in the East End and, on 7 June, the largest contingent numbering some 150 gathered at a pre-Olympia meeting in Stepney Green led by Ted Bramley, who was Secretary of the London Communist Party. The other rendezvous points were Mornington Crescent, Battersea Park Road and Harrow Road. Contingents from these four meeting places descended on Olympia and were joined by Communists and other anti-fascists who made their way independently. A Special Branch report noted that by 7.45 pm, around 1,000 people had gathered outside, with slogans being shouted and anti-fascist literature distributed. It also noted that a motor car was being used by Communist leaders in order to direct operations.[75] Inside Olympia, several hundred anti-fascists were scattered amongst an audience numbering some 12,000, many of whom had forged tickets. As Mosley began to speak he encountered heckling. He paused, the spotlight shone on the offenders who, hopelessly outnumbered by fascists stewards, were forcefully ejected. This pattern was repeated throughout the meeting. Crowds outside, subjected to charges by mounted police, witnessed anti-fascists being ejected. Many were bleeding, their clothes were torn and some victims were said to be verging on collapse. Special

Branch reported that those ejected received particularly fierce treatment by Blackshirts in the foyer and it was further reported that one doctor had treated between 50 and 70 victims.[76]

Significantly, Mosley had invited many influential people to the Olympia meeting. As many as 150 MPs were present; the press was also there in force. Given the composition of the audience, the dramatic events at Olympia were set to make front-page headlines. With the notable exception of the Rothermere press, the events were generally reported in hostile or 'disdainful' terms.[77] Mosley claimed victory over the 'Reds', but leading politicians, establishment figures and the press were generally shocked at the brutality of the Blackshirts and subsequently condemned the disturbances. Notwithstanding a vocal minority from the Conservative right wing who rallied to the defence of Mosley, reaction to Olympia was far from positive and confirmed the extent to which, even in the depths of economic depression, the British establishment remained attached to liberal-democratic procedures and values. Indeed, Olympia was widely interpreted as a great success for anti-fascism despite Labour Party claims that the Communist Party had damaged the anti-fascist cause and had given Mosley unnecessary publicity. Although the BUF experienced an overnight surge in recruitment (presumably by those attracted to the prospect of violence), it is clear that by revealing the BUF's sinister side, the overall effect was to alienate potential support from within the establishment in particular and from within society in general.

It has been further argued that events at Olympia led Rothermere to drop his backing for British fascism, thereby breaking the BUF's base of support, leaving Mosley isolated and 'beyond the pale'. Clearly Rothermere's decision to withdraw his endorsement of the BUF in July 1934 was a decisive factor in reversing the fortunes of British fascism, but arguably Olympia did not sever this relationship. Even following the violent scenes at Olympia, the *Daily Mail* remained unapologetic: 'The crime of the Blackshirts, it appeared on maturer investigation, was that they had protected themselves in very difficult circumstances…. There was no other course if free speech was to be maintained and the right of public meeting. The Red hooligans have not the faintest claim to public sympathy.'[78] Mosley claimed in his autobiography that it was withdrawal of Jewish advertising revenue that determined Rothermere's break with the BUF, although violent events in Germany, where the 'Night of the Long Knives' on 30 June had established a clear link between 'foreign' methods of violence and the BUF, probably proved most decisive.

As a consequence of Olympia, the Communist Party became widely recognised as the leading force in the struggle against Mosley's BUF and this brought significant financial rewards. In June 1934, Joseph Maggs, a director of United Dairies, gave the CPGB a donation of £1,000 for its anti-fascist work.[79] Initially, the CPGB looked towards forming a 'United Anti-Fascist League' with the YCL, ILP, Labour League of Youth and the Green Shirts in preparation for Mosley's next scheduled meeting at White City on 5 August 1934. It was planned to bring transport and catering workers out on strike in order to prevent the transportation of fascists to the meeting and to stop refreshments from reaching the venue. However, Mosley's meeting was cancelled, with the Metropolitan Police Commissioner, Lord Trenchard, foreseeing even more serious disorder than Olympia as White City could potentially hold 80,000–90,000 people.[80] The Metropolitan Police had requested the Chairman of the White City Board to demand a bond from Mosley to cover possible damage costs, but this was deliberately set so high that Mosley was forced to cancel the booking.

As the idea of the United Anti-Fascist League was apparently being forwarded, an 'Anti-Fascist Special' was published by the CPGB, which claimed that 'the nucleus' of a United Front Anti-Fascist Movement already existed in the British Anti-War Movement.[81] This claim, which points to a rather confused organisational strategy, was also made by the Secretary of the British Anti-War Movement, Neil Hunter, in an article in the *Daily Worker* on 19 June 1934. In the aftermath of Olympia, various attempts were made by the Communist Party to give anti-fascism more organisational coherence, but although the Communist Party had emerged from Olympia as the leader of anti-fascism, organisation still remained vague and uncoordinated. The Anti-Fascist Printers declared that they had 800 members ready to affiliate to a national anti-fascist movement should one be formed; other independent groups were being launched, such as the Kings Cross Railwaymen's Anti-Fascist Group and some groups were still active, such as New World Fellowship.[82]

But if the organisational structure of anti-fascism continued to be uncertain, the exposure of fascism at Olympia undoubtedly acted as a mainspring for street-level anti-fascist activities, inspiring a surge of anti-fascist feeling throughout London and elsewhere. In the days following Olympia, a BUF meeting in Hackney was abandoned, BUF meetings were also stopped at Edmonton, Southall, Hammersmith and St Pancras, and two fascists had to be escorted ignominiously from Finsbury Park by park-keepers when surrounded by a hostile crowd. In

June 1934, confrontations between fascists and anti-fascists also occurred at meetings at Regents Park, Notting Dale, Woolwich and Lewisham.[83] Outside London, the BUF experienced a particularly vigorous anti-fascist challenge in Plymouth and Glasgow, indicating the presence, as in Newcastle, of strong local cultures of anti-fascism. In Glasgow, a crowd of 2,000 anti-fascists lay siege to the local BUF office and 13 fascists were reportedly trapped inside.[84] In Plymouth, anti-fascist activity was sustained over the course of several days, with local Communists and the National Unemployed Workers' Movement the driving force behind these activities. The immediate spark was a BUF meeting on 12 June and the arrest of a leading anti-fascist. When the anti-fascist was subsequently released, it was reported that he led a march of 1,000 workers through the streets. The following day, an antagonistic crowd, reported to number some 2,000, processed to the BUF's offices in Lockyer Street. Although later dispersed by police, anti-fascist activities continued into a third day when there was a 'barrage of heckling' at a BUF meeting with anti-fascists throwing missiles.[85] Given the wave of anti-fascist feeling after Olympia, even fascists in rural middle-class areas were not immune to the occasional missile attack: in Melksham in Wiltshire, on 21 June, a car was overturned and stones, eggs and fruit were thrown by anti-fascists at an unfortunate group of Blackshirts.[86]

Anti-fascist demonstrations also followed in June 1934 at Leicester and Swansea, but there were no reports of disorder. At Leicester, where a leading BUF figure, A. K. Chesterton, addressed a meeting at Oriental Hall a counter-procession of anti-fascists brought a donkey along dressed in a blackshirt.[87] The largest counter-demonstration in the immediate aftermath of Olympia occurred during Mosley's visit to Sheffield City Hall on 28 June. This was organised by the CPGB and the ILP, under the auspices of the 'Sheffield United Action Committee' and set out to be the 'mightiest working-class demonstration ever known in Sheffield', attracting a crowd variously estimated at between 5,000 and 15,000. It was reported that anti-fascists 'paraded' the streets with banners reading 'Down with Mosley', 'Fight Fascism and War Now!' and distributed pamphlets urging people to demonstrate against 'Mosley and his thugs'. Increasingly conscious of Labour Party claims that the radical Left was too fond of causing disturbances, the focus of CPGB and ILP activity was on peaceful demonstration outside the hall, where speakers 'talked solidly' for over three hours.[88] The examples of Leicester, Swansea and Sheffield suggest that after Olympia, especially where 'mass action' was planned, the CPGB was keen to present itself as non-violent, responsible and law-abiding. The idea behind this tactic was to break the anti-CPGB rhetoric of Labour leaders which repeatedly accused Communists of encouraging disorder. The object was to further extend the United Front to the rank-and-file of the Labour Party and trade unions and ultimately attract disaffected leftists into the Communist Party or, at the very least, into one of the CPGB's satellite organisations.

IV

In order to assist this strategy and consolidate non-Communist involvement in anti-fascist activities, a meeting was held on 25 July 1934 at Conway Hall, Red Lion Square in London where a 'Co-ordinating Committee for Anti-Fascist Activities' was established. This meeting, attended by some 50 people, appears to have been instigated by the British Anti-War Movement with John Strachey delivering the keynote speech. Strachey drew specific attention to the anti-fascist work of the British Anti-War Movement which had, only three days earlier, organised a large anti-fascist rally in Victoria Park in East London, distinguished by the contribution of the Artists' International which had prepared effigies of fascist dictators, much to the delight of the crowds.[89] Strachey identified a spontaneous movement against fascism emerging in diverse industries and trade unions in London, from printers, busmen, railwaymen, shop assistants through to workers in Spitalfields Market. Strachey argued that this movement needed to be given coherence and that it should direct all its efforts towards breaking down the refusal of the Labour Party, TUC and Co-operative Party to form a united front against fascism. He considered that the ideal way of achieving this was through a massive counter-demonstration against Mosley's rally in Hyde Park, scheduled for 9 September 1934.

Thus, the central task of the Co-ordinating Committee for Anti-Fascist Activities, born essentially as an offshoot from the British Anti-War Movement, was to wreck the Labour Party's refusal to co-operate in a united front anti-fascist activity through appeals to various anti-fascist trade union groups, industry-specific groups and disaffected leftists in local Labour Party branches and Co-operative Guilds. It was not conceived as a national body; its remit was initially confined to London.[90] At the inaugural meeting, Strachey was elected Secretary, with amongst others, D. N. Pritt (a left-wing lawyer), W. Gallacher (elected CPGB MP for West Fife in 1935), W. Elliot (Men's

Co-op Guild), H. Adams (Building Trade Workers) and Professor H. Levy agreeing to serve on the initial Committee. In due course, they were joined by the support of Lord Marley, James Maxton, Fenner Brockway, Ellen Wilkinson, Dorothy Woodman, Harry Pollitt and Leah Manning (President of the National Union of Teachers).[91]

An internal CPGB memorandum dated 13 August, reveals how central the Hyde Park counter-demonstration was to the CPGB's strategy of breaking the Labour Party's ban on the United Front. It states that the 'whole energy' of the CPGB must be put into preparations for Hyde Park over the next four weeks, the United Front with Labour organisations being the 'central task running through all the preparations .... If we are not able to get TU branches, Trades Councils and Labour Parties to participate we shall have failed in our main task.'[92] With the CPGB interpreting Olympia as a great success for anti-fascism, the main priority now was to direct popular anti-fascist feeling, aroused in the wake of Olympia, towards victory over the 'reformist' Labour Party. In a somewhat disingenuous letter to the London Labour Party, the Co-ordinating Committee maintained that the workers would inevitably turn out in force against Mosley in Hyde Park if left to their own devices, therefore it had decided to organise and co-ordinate the Hyde Park demonstration in order to safeguard the workers from the violence of the BUF. Clearly the Co-ordinating Committee was trying to convey the impression of responsible behaviour, answering a legitimate call to protect workers from the 'calculated brutality' of the Blackshirts and ensure that 'peace can be kept on September 9th'. Pointing to the success of Olympia, 'which everyone now admits was the greatest setback which Fascism has had in this country', the Co-ordinating Committee maintained that if 'the co-operation of all London working class organisations is secured, the Fascist Rally can be drowned in a sea of working class activity'. The Co-ordinating Committee also stated that it would press the London trade unions to consider the use of one-day strikes on the days of fascist demonstrations, following the example of workers in Madrid and Paris.[93] On 15 August, a copy of this letter was published in the *Daily Worker*.

Predictably, the Labour Party, TUC and Co-operative Party once again rejected the proposals. The official Labour leadership understood the more Machiavellian intentions behind the Hyde Park counter-demonstration and besides, by August 1934, the Labour Party's interest in British fascism had waned as a result of the withdrawal of Rothermere's support for the BUF. In a circular from the National

Council of Labour (formerly the National Joint Council), signed by Walter Citrine and Labour Secretary Arthur Henderson, it was made clear that most of the signatories to the Co-ordinating Committee for Anti-Fascist Activities 'are either known as Communists, or are associated in one form or another with Communist activities'. Unconvinced by the Co-ordinating Committee's stress on orderly conduct, the circular concluded that the Hyde Park proposals would 'inevitably' lead to widespread disorder and this type of activity 'would merely be playing the game of those who desire to see a restriction, if not the abolition of the rights of public meeting and freedom of speech'.[94]

Yet it would be unwise to decry Labour's passive response to the Hyde Park proposals as indicative of aloof complacency towards British fascism. In early 1934, the National Council of Labour forwarded a serious plan of action to counter fascism, concerned that youth was being led astray by the generous publicity provided by Rothermere. First, a national educative campaign was planned, which would involve meetings, demonstrations, supply of notes for speakers, leaflet and pamphlet distribution. Through explicit reference to the disastrous effects of fascism in other countries, these leaflets and pamphlets would continually expose BUF policy and its anti-working class character.[95] Second, alongside this educative campaign, an investigation was to be pursued into the legal status of fascist organisations, and whether new legislation should be enacted in order to safeguard democracy. As part of this campaign, a deputation on behalf of the National Council of Labour visited the Home Secretary, Sir John Gilmour, on 26 June. At the meeting, the dangers of allowing the 'militarisation' of politics were 'impressed' on the Home Secretary, who responded that the government was determined not to tolerate disorder and was engaging in a review of existing legislation. The Labour Party also sent out a questionnaire to its local district parties on 12 June 1934 in order to ascertain the nature and extent of BUF activities, relations with other political parties and local press reaction. But given Rothermere's break with Mosley, the semi-positive response of the government, the findings of its own questionnaire (which hardly forecast an impending fascist takeover) and the end of economic depression, the urgency behind Labour's anti-fascist campaign abated. By August 1934 the National Council of Labour was satisfied that public opinion had turned against fascism and that without the support of Rothermere, the BUF was left with 'hollow teeth'. Nevertheless, it still warned against complacency.[96]

On the radical Left, Communist Party preparations for Hyde Park carried on regardless of Labour's response. These preparations were classified by Special Branch as follows: appeals for support, propaganda in the Party press which had, since 15 August, promoted the Hyde Park counter-demonstration in virtually every issue of the *Daily Worker*, circulation of literature, instructions to groups and members, public meetings and propaganda from a motor van. It was also reported that from a secret source, the Communist Party had received further financial contributions – some £2,000 was donated towards financing anti-fascist activity, especially activity connected with 9 September.[97] But these early arrangements were not going according to plan: news of the proposed protest was met with silence from the mainstream press. A train entering King's Cross station, with the words 'March Against Fascism on September 9' painted on the boiler in large letters failed to attract press coverage, as did the delivery of crates to numerous factories with the same call written on the sides. The CPGB claimed that this press silence was intentional, orchestrated by the National Press Association, an organisation of the large newspaper proprietors which controlled all newspaper trains and which refused to allow these trains to be used by the *Daily Worker*. Frustrated by the paucity of media coverage the CPGB worked relentlessly to overcome the purported 'press ban' through an innovative publicity campaign, which appears to have been largely directed by an *ad hoc* group based around the CPGB's propaganda chief, Bert Williams.[98]

On 3 September, the front page of the *Daily Express* reported that three anti-fascists had interrupted a BBC outside broadcast and had succeeded in calling on London workers to demonstrate against fascism on 9 September. This was followed by further attempted broadcasts from what the *Daily Mirror* termed 'microphone bandits'; one such 'bandit' having seized the microphone at Romano's restaurant in the Strand where dance music was being broadcast on a powerful new transmitter. Thousands of anti-fascist leaflets were dropped on a busy Oxford Street from the roof of Selfridges on 3 September and leaflets were also thrown down from buses and from other buildings over the course of the next six days. These included leaflets issued by the London District Committee of the CPGB, the Young Communist League and the Co-ordinating Committee for Anti-Fascist Activities.[99] As many as one million leaflets may have been distributed.[100] In accordance with standard practice, walls and pavements were also chalked, but audacious anti-fascists also dared to elect Nelson's Column as the place to paint a call for 'workers to do their duty' in large letters. Other ostentatious deeds included the unrolling of a banner from the roof of the BBC's Broadcasting House at midday on 7 September, which remained in position for over half an hour before it was removed. Additional banners were unfurled from the top of the Law Courts and Transport House.[101] Not surprisingly these various publicity-seeking measures, with their emphasis on the unorthodox and sensational, attracted press coverage and ultimately proved very effective in publicising the Hyde Park counter-demonstration.

On the day of the Hyde Park counter-demonstration, as with Olympia, contingents of anti-fascists assembled at various points in London. Some 1,300 gathered at the junction of Edgware Road and Marylebone Place to form the North and North West London contingent. Various local Communist Party branches were represented here, but there was also support from the Portsmouth Workers' Movement, the Leicester and Sheffield Youth Anti-War Council, the YCL, ILP, Transport and General Workers' Union, the National Amalgamated Furnishing Trades Association, local branches of the NUWM, the Artists' International and the Kings Cross Co-operative Society. An estimated 1,000 met at Stepney Green and were led by Harry Pollitt. Some 50 banners were carried by this East London contingent which represented local CPGB branches and various trade union bodies, such as the Hackney Electricians. Special Branch noted this East London contingent seemed well supported by the local Jewish community, further evidence that ahead of the BUF's turn towards hardline anti-Semitism the CPGB had recruited Jewish elements in the East End. Elsewhere, the West, South West and South East London contingents, numbering approximately 2,700, gathered near Exhibition Road. Once again various local CPGB, NUWM branches and trade unions were represented. Finally, a group of some 300 anti-fascists from the Printers', Busmens' and Railwaymens' Anti-Fascist Groups met separately at Lambeth Palace Road. Thus, according to Special Branch estimates, approximately 5,000 organised anti-fascists marched to Hyde Park.[102] Again acting in open defiance of the Labour Party leadership, these marchers were also joined by 30 sections of the Labour Party's League of Youth.[103]

On arrival at Hyde Park, the four processions of anti-fascists met a vast crowd, estimated from a very conservative 60,000 by Special Branch through to between 100,000 and 150,000 according to various newspapers. The size of this crowd indicated the extent to which popular anti-fascist feeling amongst ordinary Londoners had been mobilised by the events at Olympia and by the Communist Party's unorthodox publicity campaign. Explicit instructions on the anti-fascist side were issued to avoid violence and make for the four anti-fascist platforms, but large numbers uninterested by the speakers left the anti-fascist platforms and congregated around the fascists as they marched into Hyde Park behind Mosley. There was much booing, heckling and ridicule from anti-fascists but there was no serious disorder despite fears that the propaganda which had appeared in the *Daily Worker* and in the various leaflets was 'violently phrased' and could be interpreted as incitements to violence.[104] According to a Special Branch report, the 'demeanour of the majority of the persons' in this crowd 'was distinctly hostile to the fascist speakers', yet the report qualifies this point with the observation that 'many thousands were present merely out of curiosity or in anticipation of seeing a clash between the two factions, or with police'. This was apparent 'by the little interest taken in the objects of the proceedings and the manner in which large numbers rushed to the scene of any unusual activity'.[105] But notwithstanding these observations, the CPGB clearly succeeded in mobilising unprecedented numbers of ordinary Londoners to Hyde Park, leading Harry Pollitt to later describe the Hyde Park anti-fascist demonstration as 'the biggest breakthrough ever made against the ban on the United Front imposed by the Labour leaders'.[106] Unsurprisingly, the Labour Party minimised its importance. The next day the *Daily Herald* declared that 'the Mosley fiasco was mainly owing to splendid police organisation and the good sense of London workers, who observed the direction of the TUC and took no part in the counter-demonstration'. Angered by this version of events, one Communist organiser recollects that the *Daily Herald* was publicly burnt in Brighton by local Communists and the ashes returned to the *Daily Herald* offices in a large envelope.[107]

V

The scale of the anti-fascist mobilisation at Hyde Park clearly presented an opportunity to launch a national anti-fascist organisation, and indeed, membership forms for the (British) Anti-War and Anti-Fascist Movement were distributed on the day. Yet Strachey later warned against this initiative, insisting that if a national organisation was launched before the rank-and-file of the labour movement fully understood the nature of fascism, then a divide between informed anti-fascists and misinformed sections of the working class would result. The CPGB protested that the Labour Party 'would have us believe that Mosleyism is Fascism, that at its best it is a foreign importation entirely unsuited to the British climate, an importation that will wither away if it is ignored'.[108] For Strachey and the CPGB, this perspective was naive, indifferent to the fact that fascism was more than a case of Mosley and the Blackshirts. In fact, according to the Communist Party's 'class' analysis, fascism was the 'open dictatorship of capital' – its source was the capitalist system and in particular, finance capital. By late 1934, the CPGB's theoretical position had hardened to an 'ultra-leftist' critique: finance capital backed the National Government as the main weapon of 'Fascisation'. The capitalist class used the existing state to enforce anti-working class legislation (for example, Incitement to Disaffection Bill) but also backed Mosley as a 'subsidiary weapon' to be used against the working class if the force of the National Government proved insufficient in time of crisis. Thus fascism had a 'two-fold' character and this character implied that the struggle against fascism could not rely on the state or 'bourgeois democracy' to defend the working class. For Strachey and the CPGB, the Labour Party's analysis which encouraged workers to trust 'bourgeois democracy' and which subsequently pointed to the weakness of Mosley in Hyde Park in order to reject the need for special anti-fascist activities, was seriously flawed:

> It is essential to make clear to the workers this twofold character of the Fascist offensive, at once through the official State machine and through the open Fascist forces.... The understanding of this necessarily destroys the 'democratic' illusion, the illusion of the possibility of the legal bourgeois democratic opposition to Fascism.[109]

Accordingly, the only way to oppose and defeat fascism was through proletarian revolution. Strachey, therefore, insisted that following Hyde Park, the anti-fascist struggle should concentrate on liberating workers from the reformist chains of the Labour Party's narrow interpretation of fascism, inculcating revolutionary zeal and broadening the appeal of the Communist Party. This demanded 'untiring and unceasing work in every Trade Union branch, in every Labour Party, and in every Co-operative Guild'.[110] But this did not imply an end to 'mass action' because 'by far the most effective method of converting workers to our point of view is by example rather than precept'. Strachey concluded that this strategy would encourage the development of anti-fascist organisations at local levels, leaving the Co-ordinating Committee at the centre to 'maintain contact and give general direction and cohesion to all these organisations as they come into being'.[111]

Thus, the continuation of the Co-ordinating Committee for Anti-Fascist Activities relied on the sustained growth of militant anti-fascist movements 'from below', but without local-level organisations providing necessary momentum, the Co-ordinating Committee faced stagnation in the long term. The success of the CPGB's strategy, therefore, required incisive penetration of the labour movement, but Labour leaders quickly took measures to resist Communist influence: in October 1934 the TUC issued a Black Circular which pressured trade unions to exclude militants from office and forbade trades councils from accepting militants as delegates – only 18 out of 381 Trade Councils failed to execute this circular. Already in December 1934, it was noted in the CPGB's monthly that there had been 'a noticeable slowness to penetrate into working-class organisations'.[112] Yet for Strachey and the CPGB, the success of the 'anti-fascist front' could only be made certain by fighting 'fascism' on all its fronts and this required broad mobilisation of rank-and-file Labour supporters not only against the BUF, but also against the 'fascisation' of the National Government, and ultimately the 'reformism' of the Labour Party and TUC leadership. But the CPGB's analysis of fascism ran counter to the core ideology of the Labour Party, which committed the Party to democratic socialism and interpreted the state as a neutral entity. Conversion to the Communist Party position, which essentially saw anti-fascism in terms of proletarian revolution, would have meant Labourites repudiating both the leadership and the entire consensual basis of Labour ideology. This was an unlikely prospect, and although ideological differences between the militant Left and the moderate Left did not prevent local co-operation in the common fight against Mosley's fascism, it effectively blocked co-operation with the militant Left in what the CPGB perceived as a revolutionary struggle against a wider 'fascism'.

Even though revolutionary mobilisation within working-class organisations proved unattainable, further activities against the British Union of Fascists continued in the wake of Hyde Park as the Communist Party also looked to convert the rank-and-file of the labour movement through example. Towards the end of September 1934, the Communist Party orchestrated opposition to a rally held by Mosley at Belle Vue Gardens in Manchester. Calling on workers to follow the lead of London, an estimated 5,000 anti-fascists responded and opposed around 1,000 Blackshirts. Once again the *Daily Worker* declared that Mosley had been swamped by a 'sea of working class activity', drawing explicit, albeit forced parallels with the much larger mobilisation in Hyde Park. In fact Belle Vue had a further dimension. Acting inconsistently with the CPGB's official line, which stressed police indulgence towards fascism, Maurice Levine, a prominent local Jewish Communist, called on the Chief Constable of Manchester to ban the BUF's rally.[113] Presumably this approach followed indications that the Chief Constable was hostile to the BUF given that on previous occasions Manchester police had removed Blackshirt stewards from the Free Trade Hall meeting in March 1933 and had imposed a curfew on a BUF meeting in October 1933.[114] What Levine's approach to the authorities does reveal is that ideological concerns did not prevent pragmatism and variation in anti-fascist strategy at a local level, even for an organisation like the Communist Party which was so closely attached to its ideology. More in keeping with Hyde Park, however, was the absence of serious disorder at Belle Vue and this also appears to have been the case at a large BUF meeting held in Plymouth Market Place on 11 October. But violent disorder had followed Mosley's visit to Worthing on 9 October despite the CPGB's attempts to minimise physical confrontations at large BUF meetings.[115]

In October 1934 the Co-ordinating Committee for Anti-Fascist Activities received notification that Mosley intended to hold a further meeting at the Albert Hall. It called a counter-demonstration in Hyde Park, but in the event managed to attract a crowd of just a few thousand at most. Support came from the ILP, various branches of the CPGB, YCL, Labour League of Youth, as well as industry-based anti-fascist groups.[116] Joe Jacobs, in his autobiographical account of East End militancy and the rise of fascism, concedes, 'I don't remember why this meeting was not opposed in any real strength.'[117] Perhaps Jacobs was embarrassed that complacency, born from the perceived success of Hyde Park, had set in. Indeed, discussions about launching a new anti-fascist newspaper in November 1934, inspired by the Co-ordinating Committee, came to nothing. The proposed editor, CPGB reporter Claud Cockburn, complained of being overworked and Strachey became increasingly frustrated with what he perceived as lacklustre management of the CPGB's anti-fascist policy. Both Pollitt and Palme Dutt informed Strachey that it was his responsibility to overcome these administrative problems, but Strachey replied that he was no 'leader', and instead of providing the Co-ordinating Committee with much needed direction, Strachey took up the invitation to give a lecture tour in the United States and left Britain in December 1934 and did not return until mid-April 1935.[118] Without Strachey to provide stewardship, the Co-ordinating Committee lost momentum, although it did manage to organise relatively small demonstrations against a meeting held by Mosley at the Albert Hall in March 1935.[119]

According to the picture gleaned from Home Office sources, the scale of anti-fascist activity noticeably declined in 1935. As Cullen has noted, for the first part of 1935 the CPGB concentrated its efforts on anti-Jubilee activities.[120] Clearly a contributory factor behind this decline in anti-fascist activity and the CPGB's corresponding shift in agitational focus was the departure of Strachey who, prior to his visit to the United States, was insisting that the 'most urgent task of Communism' was 'to save human civilisation from Fascism'.[121] A further factor was the failure of the CPGB to develop an offensive struggle against 'fascism' on the widest possible front. Anti-fascist counter-demonstrations in 1934 had been primarily 'defensive', triggered by announced BUF activities. Mobilisations had been particularly significant when a high profile visit by Mosley was given public notice, sparking the creation of local united front anti-fascist committees. However, once a counter-demonstration had been organised, activity often lapsed. There were exceptions, such as Manchester, which was noted for frequent low-level street confrontations between hardline fascists and anti-fascists. But as a general rule the problem, noted in the CPGB's monthly, was apathy and lack of direction. It was, as one comrade remarked, a case of 'now that Mosley has gone there seems to be nothing for us to do'.[122] For the CPGB, this inactivity was the direct result of the prevailing 'reformist' position which defined fascism solely in terms of the fight against Mosley and the BUF.

This 'reformist' mode of anti-fascist opposition also meant that levels of anti-fascist activity mirrored levels of BUF activity and as the frequency of BUF activity decreased in 1935, so too did anti-fascism. The adverse publicity which the BUF attracted at Olympia resulting from anti-fascist exposure, combined with the loss of Rothermere's support, helped undermine the BUF's membership base which had fallen to a mere 5,000 by October 1935.[123] The number of BUF meetings recorded in the Home Office files, tabulated by Cullen, correspondingly fell from 89 in 1934 to 53 in 1935.[124] Yet whilst this decline in the BUF's fortunes did reduce general levels of activity, the BUF remained active in certain regional pockets, such as Lancashire where from November 1934 to April 1935, in an attempt to revitalise the BUF, a cotton campaign was launched, though this was promptly countered by the CPGB which held a series of public meetings and distributed some 10,000 pamphlets entitled 'Mosley and Lancashire'. Mosley did continue to make the occasional high-profile visit to provincial centres, but in May 1935 he was forced to close a meeting at Newcastle City Hall when faced with continual heckling from the audience which made it impossible for him to continue.[125] None the less, fascist activities generally fell during 1935 as a consequence of the BUF's contraction and subsequent preoccupation with internal re-organisation. Noticeably, the BUF failed to contest the 1935 general election and it was not until the autumn before the BUF was fully reactivated in London where the decisive factor, as Thurlow identifies, was 'the discovery that anti-Semitism was a good recruiting tactic in the East End'.[126]

Looking back over the early development of anti-fascism in the 1930s, it is clear that in sharp contrast to the 1920s anti-fascist activities did engage significant numbers of people. Where in the 1920s a narrow circle of precocious anti-fascists countered Britain's first fascist organisations, in the early 1930s thousands of people opposed Mosley's British Union of Fascists. Unlike the 1920s, anti-fascism was not restricted to London; it had extended into provincial areas as early as 1933 and grew to national significance. It is worth reiterating that the rise of Nazism, the early growth phase of the BUF and the willingness of the militant Left to take the lead in organising opposition through locally based united fronts were the key factors behind this wider development of anti-fascism. Local activities raised anti-fascist consciousness and on a number of occasions encouraged large-scale participation. The refusal of the Labour Party leadership to support direct confrontations with the BUF did not prevent anti-fascist co-operation at local levels, but without the organisational resources of the Labour Party to support the 'United Front', anti-fascism was deprived of broad structural cohesion.

The development of anti-fascism in the early 1930s was therefore loosely defined and variegated. In 1934 the Communist-sponsored Co-ordinating Committee for Anti-Fascist Activities attempted to impose coherence from the 'centre', but following the Hyde Park counter-demonstration it lost momentum, and as the CPGB's revolutionary struggle to proselytise the workers against a wider 'fascism' met little tangible success, the activities of the Co-ordinating Committee petered out. Nevertheless, the *modus operandi* of disruptive tactics employed by anti-fascist activists did succeed both in restricting the BUF's operations and limiting its capacity to disseminate fascist ideology. Most importantly, these tactics invited the BUF to employ violence against opponents and this served to discredit fascism, denying the British Union of Fascists political and social respectability at a most critical stage in its formative development. At the same time, Labour's official refusal to engage in militant anti-fascism reinforced the strength and stability of the prevailing liberal-democratic consensus, hence restricting political space for the BUF. So ironically, although Labour's anti-fascist policy was attacked by the CPGB, it actually worked in tandem. Labour's commitment to political moderation and liberalism helped marginalise and delegitimise both the violence and ideology of British fascism. Isolated, and with very little room to manoeuvre, the BUF had no real alternative but to descend into the sewers of anti-Semitism.

2
Opposition to British Fascism, 1936–45

The forcible injection of militant anti-Semitism into the BUF's campaign towards the end of 1935 marked a turning point in the fortunes of British fascism and correspondingly heralded a second wave of anti-fascist activity which peaked at the 'Battle of Cable Street' on 4 October 1936. This famous episode should be firmly located in a chronology of anti-fascism which recognises that events at Cable Street proceeded from a relative decline in anti-fascist activity during 1935. The perception that Cable Street was the dramatic climax of an uninterrupted sequence of ascending conflicts between fascists and anti-fascists starting in 1932 and culminating in October 1936 may be widely shared, but it has little foundation in fact. It should additionally be noted that any satisfactory chronology must also recognise that anti-fascist responses from early 1936 became increasingly defined in terms of opposition to anti-Semitism. Indeed, the greater prominence afforded to anti-Semitism by the BUF led to more substantive involvement by the Jewish community in anti-fascist activities, thereby widening the base of opposition to domestic fascism.

It is common knowledge that the BUF's campaign against Jewry was concentrated in the East End of London where the Jewish community was estimated to number over 100,000 in a national Jewish population of 330,000. Combining a generous supply of street meetings with increasing levels of anti-Semitic intimidation, harassment and violence, the BUF's campaign began in Bethnal Green in late 1935 before being widened out to other East End districts during 1936. Menacingly, this new departure procured significant numbers of new recruits for British fascism in an area already infused with an anti-Semitic tradition that originated in hostility to the migration of large numbers of Jews to East London from Eastern Europe between 1870 and 1914. In trying to capitalise on local successes in the East End and attract wider national interest, Mosley announced a high-profile meeting at the Albert Hall scheduled for 22 March 1936. After the dip in anti-fascist activity during 1935, this announcement served to reanimate the Communist Party. Alarmed by the political advantage that the BUF was gaining from its East End campaign it resolved to bring Mosley's progress to an abrupt halt and accordingly pressed for a mass demonstration against Mosley's Albert Hall meeting. This was seen as an opportunity to repeat the Hyde Park 'victory' of September 1934 and, following its example, the Co-ordinating Committee for Anti-Fascist Activities was resurrected, albeit temporarily.

Returning to political activity, John Strachey once more assumed the mantle of anti-fascist figurehead and, under the auspices of the Co-ordinating Committee for Anti-Fascist Activities, issued a circular calling for a demonstration outside the Albert Hall. In line with the Hyde Park counter-demonstration, Strachey's call was publicised by the *Daily Worker* and was joined by an appeal from the CPGB for all working-class organisations in London to give their full support. As many as 250,000 leaflets were distributed. These were mainly directed towards East London Jews where local events were linked with the repression of Jews in Germany. Informed by a 'class analysis', the CPGB attacked anti-Semitism on socio-political rather than racial grounds, insisting that anti-Semitism was an instrument used by capitalists to scapegoat the ills of capitalist society. The Communist Party castigated Mosley for following the example of Hitler who, according to the CPGB, was turning the Jew into a scapegoat for capitalism. Lebzelter has argued that by analysing anti-Semitism in this way, as a socio-political problem specific to capitalist societies, the Communist Party was 'in fact less concerned about the lot of unfortunate Jews than about the principle involved'.[1] Nevertheless, by stressing that it was leading the active opposition against fascist-related anti-Semitism, the CPGB succeeded in drawing into the Communist movement East London working-class Jews offended by the passivity of both the local Labour Party and the leaders of Anglo-Jewry.

Although sections of the East End Labour Party were sympathetic towards anti-fascism, the local hierarchy was dominated by Irish Catholics, who tended to hold greater hostility for atheistic communism than fascism. Moreover, the Jewish communal leadership as represented by the Board of Deputies of British Jews (BoD) and defended by the *Jewish Chronicle* (JC), continuously advised Jews to avoid anti-fascist demonstrations and maintain a low profile in order not to publicise Mosley or give substance to the claims of anti-Semitic propaganda that Jews were pro-communist. The Board of Deputies appeared convinced that British traditions of liberalism and tolerance would resist anti-Semitism. Yet to working-class Jews in the East End, the Board was indifferent and distant, whereas the Communist Party, dominated locally by Jewish leaders appeared pro-active and more in touch with everyday concerns. The CPGB's strident opposition to fascism undoubtedly appealed to many East End Jews, but it is impossible to quantify how many Jews actually joined the Communist Party in the 1930s. The impression of contemporaries was that many Jews were attracted to the CPGB not because of communist ideology, but because the Communist Party appeared to be the only organisation willing to fight fascist-related anti-Semitism.[2]

In the approach to Mosley's Albert Hall meeting, the *Daily Worker* reported that the East End was being chalked and whitewashed every night and that mobilisation 'on the ground' was being led by the Young Communist League and Labour Party's League of Youth. The *Daily Worker* also reported that a protest letter had been sent to the management at the Albert Hall, signed by a number of leading literary figures, including Aldous Huxley, Virginia Woolf and H. G. Wells.[3] In spite of their protestations, the Albert Hall meeting received the go-ahead from the Corporation of the Royal Albert Hall, the body responsible for the Albert Hall's management. A crowd reported by the *Daily Worker* to number 10,000 attempted to assemble outside the Albert Hall, but the police had cordoned off the hall in line with a directive issued by the Metropolitan Police Commissioner, Sir Philip Game. This had stated that no counter-demonstration should be allowed to take place within half a mile of the Albert Hall.[4] Consequently, the crowd was dispersed by foot and mounted police. One section of the crowd was directed towards Hyde Park, another to nearby Thurloe Square where an impromptu, tightly packed meeting took place chaired by John Strachey. The crowd in Thurloe Square reportedly numbered between 3,000 and 5,000 and was, without apparent warning, subjected to repeated baton charges by police forcing it to disperse. The police alleged that the anti-fascist meeting in Thurloe Square was 'provocative', 'disorderly' and fell within the declared exclusion zone. This was contested by the National Council for Civil Liberties (NCCL) which, having set it up its own commission of inquiry, concluded that the baton charges were unprovoked and listed some 46 complaints of police brutality against anti-fascists. The fact that the NCCL amassed some 113 witness statements that contested the police version of events suggests that Home Secretary, Sir John Simon's insistence that the police did not use undue force was somewhat disingenuous.[5]

The actions of the police at Thurloe Square reinforced the common perception on the Left that the police were prejudiced in favour of Mosley's fascists. This view originated partly from the radical Left's ideological analysis of the relationship between fascism and the state, and partly from observing the extent of police protection afforded to fascists – at the 1934 Hyde Park demonstration for instance, 7,000 police had provided a safety cordon for 3,000 fascists. Appalled by allegations of police partiality against anti-fascists, the NCCL, led by Ronald Kidd, having originally formed in February 1934 to protest against police treatment of hunger marchers, now anchored itself to the anti-fascist cause. The NCCL claimed to be 'non-political', but was said to be close to the Communist Party, providing the CPGB with observers to monitor police behaviour at meetings and demonstrations. This connection discredited it in official circles, where the NCCL was construed as a front organisation for the CPGB.[6] Not surprisingly, the government refused to cede to pressure for a public enquiry from a perceived Communist-controlled body.

This refusal gave credence to the line of the radical Left which stressed collusion between the police and fascism, but otherwise the CPGB gained little from the Thurloe Square demonstration. In comparison with the Hyde Park mobilisation of 1934, the numbers involved were disappointing. Despite a Jewish presence there were still complaints that not enough Jewish people attended.[7] The mainstream press generally ignored the demonstration and consequently there was little exposure of Mosley's virulent anti-Semitism.[8] The demonstration at Thurloe Square also marked the end of the Co-ordinating Committee for Anti-Fascist Activities, with John Strachey now directing his energies towards the Left Book Club. Launched in May 1936, Strachey saw this venture as a much more effective way of broadening the appeal of communism and raising mass anti-fascist consciousness. The Left Book Club was an idea imported from the United States and had been suggested to Strachey by the publisher Victor Gollancz. Members could purchase left-wing books cheaply and already, by the end of May 1936, the Club could boast 11,500 members, eventually rising to an impressive 60,000 with some 1,200 discussion groups by the end of the 1930s. Undoubtedly, the Left Book Club became an important vehicle for promoting anti-fascism. Indeed, Club members would often use the 'discussion groups' to organise concrete political agitation rather than merely discussing abstract ideas raised from current volumes.[9]

The BUF's concentration on East London was not exclusive and it should not be forgotten that it also targeted provincial cities such as Manchester and Leeds where there were sizeable Jewish communities. In Manchester, the Jewish community numbered 35,000 and was spatially concentrated on working-class Cheetham. As the BUF closed in on Cheetham in the first six months of 1936, anti-fascist opposition was galvanised by the local Communist Party, especially the predominantly Jewish branch of the Young Communist League. Known locally as the 'Challenge Club', this had some 150–200 members and was said to be probably the largest YCL branch in the country.[10] Employing strong-arm tactics, the Young Communist League continually opposed the BUF's physical presence in Manchester with Jewish Communists at the forefront of street-level confrontations. Communists also came together with other left-wing organisations to form an umbrella, 'united front' committee known as the North Manchester Co-ordinating Committee Against Fascism in order to organise protest through more formal channels, such as raising petitions against the letting of municipal buildings to fascists. Although dominated by the CPGB, this local anti-fascist co-ordinating committee also included wider representation from trade unions, the Jewish-based Workers' Circle and members of the Labour Party.[11]

Fascist activity in Leeds, where the Jewish population numbered 30,000, peaked in September 1936 when a provocative march through the City's Jewish areas to Holbeck Moor was announced. Official channels were used by local anti-fascists to try to prevent the march and it was subsequently re-routed. According to a Leeds Police report, the CPGB organised an opposition meeting on Holbeck Moor which attracted a crowd of 1,000 people but it appears that as the Blackshirts marched across Holbeck Moor, the crowd grew to anything from an estimated 20,000 (*Manchester Guardian*) to 50,000 (*Daily Worker*).[12] In due course, Mosley's platform was attacked, stones were thrown and Mosley was struck in the face, sustaining a gash underneath one eye. As the Blackshirts left Holbeck Moor, they were subjected to a well-orchestrated ambush by members of the CPGB, Labour Party and perhaps the ILP, resulting in about 40 fascists receiving injuries. In drawing our attention to events at Leeds, Cesarani reminds us that the

BUF's anti-Semitic campaign wasn't just confined to London and that the violence at Holbeck Moor was, in relation to Cable Street, 'just as nasty in its own way – in fact far more bloody than what occurred in Cable Street'.[13]

It is also worth emphasising that the BUF ran into opposition in those isolated areas where anti-Semitism was not employed as the prime means of enlisting support. In South Wales, the BUF, under the local leadership of Tommy Moran, markedly failed to win over disaffected miners. The industrial valleys of South Wales proved impervious to the BUF's appeal as the Left was deeply entrenched, this area being one of the few Communist strongholds in Britain.[14] In June 1936 the BUF organised a large open-air meeting at Tonypandy in the Rhondda Valley, attracting a hostile crowd of 2,000 people mobilised by an anti-fascist ringing a bell and calling on locals to 'give the Blackshirts the welcome they deserve'.[15] The fascist platform was stoned and the meeting was brought to a swift close with 36 anti-fascists arrested. Similarly at Hull, Mosley's parade at Corporation Field in July 1936 was subjected to a barrage of missiles. A local police report concluded that opposition was 'very strong' and 'apparently organised with the intent of breaking up the meeting'.[16] The former BUF branch organiser for Hull, John Charnley recalls:

> Newcastle was rough but the roughest and toughest meeting that I ever attended was on the Corporation Field, Hull, in 1936. After this meeting, which I had organised, the police collected bicycle chains, brush staves with 6-inch nails in the end, chair legs wrapped with barbed wire and thick woollen stockings containing broken glass in the heels. We had 27 hospital cases and the Communists had over a hundred. It was at this meeting that a bullet was put through the windscreen of Mosley's car.[17]

Although official reports accused the Communists of being responsible for the violence, to Charnley's consternation, the press later alleged that the crowd had been initially attacked by fascists using steel-buckled belts which doubtlessly confirmed popular impressions that British fascism was intrinsically violent.[18]

Disparities between official reports and media reports were also apparent following violence that flared at an indoor meeting held by Mosley in 1936 at the Carfax Assembly Rooms in Oxford. This meeting descended into a 'riot' following the ejection of an anti-fascist heckler. Skidelsky and Cullen have contended that opposition to this meeting, organised by the Communist Party (but also with local Labour Party support), was determined on fomenting violence and thus anti-fascists were primarily responsible for the resulting disorder. Yet it became, for Cullen, 'something of a propaganda coup' for anti-fascists with the opposition using the involvement of fascists in the violent altercation to full advantage in order to further blacken the BUF's image.[19] Indeed, Renton likens the local impact of this meeting to the delegitimising effect of Olympia, playing 'an identical role in Oxford to the Olympia meeting in the wider history of British fascism and anti-fascism'.[20]

The examples of Leeds, Tonypandy, Hull and Oxford all confirm that during 1936 anti-fascist opposition turned increasingly violent. The geographical spread of disturbances, as Webber has pointed out, had much to do with the regional strength of anti-fascism – in conservative areas in the South, fascist meetings could still be conducted 'in an orderly and even gentlemanly fashion'.[21] According to Charnley, the severity of the opposition that the BUF experienced in Hull was due to the sizeable presence of the Communist Party. With support concentrated in the docks, he believed that the CPGB had more influence in Hull 'than anywhere else outside London, with the possible exception of Glasgow'.[22] The BUF claimed that increasing violence resulted from the realisation on the anti-fascist side that peaceful tactics, such as those deployed at Hyde Park in September 1934 when the BUF was ridiculed, were no longer capable of checking the advance of a reinvigorated fascist movement. Certainly the adoption of a more forceful and provocative style of fascism, symbolised by the addition of 'National Socialists' to the BUF's title in 1936, reinforced identification with Hitler's Nazism and radicalised opposition. Another factor was increasing awareness by anti-fascists that violence proved disadvantageous to the fascist cause. Olympia had established that physical confrontations between fascists and anti-fascists served to delegitimise fascism by denying the BUF respectability. Skidelsky maintains that in this respect, since it favoured anti-fascism, the general context of fascist and anti-fascist violence was all-important: as 'it proved all too easy to portray the situation as one in which 'single' and 'innocent' hecklers were brutally manhandled by fascist 'bullies' or in which whole neighbourhoods rose 'spontaneously' against deliberate fascist provocations'.[23] Finally, the demise of the Co-ordinating Committee for Anti-Fascist Activities confirmed a lack of central co-ordination over anti-fascist activities and allowed anti-fascist militants relative freedom to implement local strategies determined independently of a

Communist Party leadership that remained intent on forging closer links with the rest of the labour movement.

In fact, in line with policy emanating from the seventh congress of the Comintern held in the summer of 1935, attempts by the CPGB to secure closer relations with the Labour Party were revived. At this congress, Georgi Dimitrov had defined the defeat of fascism as the overriding objective of Communist Parties and this had led to a common strategy which, in Communist parlance, became known as the 'Popular Front'. The idea behind the 'Popular Front' was an alliance of anti-fascists across all classes, thereby drawing the entire nation, not just the working class, into the revolutionary struggle. The theoretical line established by Dimitrov was that fascism was not synonymous with 'capitalist democracy', but was the last stage of capitalism: the dictatorship of the 'most reactionary elements' of finance capital. It followed from this definition that Communists should ally with all 'democrats' – even bourgois democrats – in the struggle against fascism. Accordingly 'ultra-leftism' was dropped and attacks on 'capitalist democracy' were muted.

In Britain, the CPGB argued that since the industrial workers formed the 'decisive majority' of the population, then an essential precondition of the 'Popular Front' was establishing working-class unity through the 'United Front' which, given the strength of the industrial working class, would then act as an 'irresistible magnet' for all other progressive forces.[24] Thus, the CPGB had called on its supporters to vote Labour in all but two constituencies at the 1935 general election and following this approach had launched a campaign seeking affiliation to the Labour Party in early 1936 which was supported by the Labour Party's Socialist League.[25] However, with the Labour Party leadership repeating the charge that the rise of fascism abroad had been encouraged by Communist tactics, CPGB leaders were becoming increasingly anxious that anti-fascists should eschew physical confrontations with fascists. The CPGB leadership continued to press for greater trade union activity in the struggle against fascism and this position was frequently restated by Communist Party officials at local levels. But as the violent episodes show, this strategy was often rejected by militant elements in the rank and file. And, since the early development of anti-fascist opposition had relied on local initiative where activists had considerable autonomy, moves to impose a non-confrontational policy 'from above' led in some cases to resentment and division 'below'.

Phil Piratin, the former Communist MP for Stepney, has drawn attention to tactical divisions within the Stepney branch of the CPGB between those that said 'Bash the fascists whenever you see them' and those who advocated alternative ways of opposing fascism.[26] Following the Party line, Piratin held that the way to defeat Mosley was not through physical confrontations. Instead, he proposed workplace or residential initiatives which would serve to 'cut the ground from the under the fascists' feet'.[27] On the opposite side, the case for combative battles was supported most vociferously by Joe Jacobs, Secretary of the Stepney Branch. Jacobs complained that trade union work was ineffective, it was typically thwarted by Labour's right-wing moderates and did not produce concrete anti-fascist results. Moreover, residential initiatives demanded access to fascist strongholds and these areas were often impenetrable. Over the short term, Jacobs convinced a majority within the Stepney Branch to favour a physical response to fascism and this position was then justified on the grounds of self-defence. Although the example of Stepney is revealing, it would be a mistake to assume that tactical divisions affected all local CPGB branches. The work of Gewirtz on Manchester shows that local Communists engaged an anti-fascist strategy that combined physical opposition, spearheaded by the YCL, with more conventional trade union and 'united front' work without apparent conflict.[28]

Significantly, intensification of the BUF's anti-Semitic campaign also caused divisions within Anglo-Jewry, firing debate in the *Jewish Chronicle*. In January 1936, the JC noted increasing dissatisfaction with the BoD's passive position within the Jewish community, especially amongst working-class Jews facing anti-Semitism close at hand. In June 1936 the JC responded to grassroots opinion by running a section entitled 'Jewish Defence', reporting anti-Semitic incidents and publishing readers' letters that were deeply critical of the BoD's perceived inactivity. Majority opinion coalesced around urgent demands for a Jewish defence organisation, a view endorsed by the *Jewish Chronicle* which had hitherto been a staunch defender of the BoD's more cautious approach. Facing mounting pressure from within the Jewish community and concerned that Jews were being drawn into the CPGB, the BoD responded in July 1936 with the announcement that it was establishing a defence co-ordinating committee responsible for directing communal responses to anti-Semitism.

This was greeted enthusiastically by the *Jewish Chronicle*, which called on the community to rally in support of the Board's new initiative.[29] But this 'new' initiative was merely an extension of existing defence policy. Neville Laski, President of the Board, remained resolutely opposed to violent action against fascism and again repeated the line that Jews should ignore fascist meetings. For Laski, 'anti-fascism' amounted to the confrontational politics of the radical Left, which he believed only served to exacerbate anti-Jewish feeling. Besides, any anti-fascist position would compromise the Board's traditional policy of political neutrality. Laski refused to accept that fascism and anti-Semitism were integrally connected and even declared at one point to be unconcerned with fascism. The solution to the problem of anti-Semitism was not 'anti-fascism', but educating the public through anti-defamatory campaigns. Hence, the primary function of the Co-ordinating Committee (which in 1938 became known as the Jewish Defence Committee) was to add strength to the Board's existing anti-defamation work. At the outset, this involved distribution of literature countering the charges of anti-Semitic propaganda and an open-air speaking campaign initially undertaken by teams of speakers from the Jewish Ex-Servicemen's Legion and the Association of Jewish Friendly Societies. Not surprisingly, given the volatility of the situation in the East End, the Board's conservative message fell on stony ground. According to Metropolitan Police files, meetings organised by the Board in 1936 tended to attract small audiences and it was noted that at one meeting held in Stepney 'a good deal of hostility was shown towards the speakers'.[30]

II

Notwithstanding divisions within both the militant Left and within Anglo-Jewry, there was a notable rise in active anti-fascist responses as the BUF's anti-Semitic campaign in East London intensified. Anti-fascism was then imparted with additional momentum by the outbreak of the Spanish Civil War in July 1936 which, as Newton says, 'crystallized many people's political ideas into a neat black and white, Fascist versus anti-Fascist pattern'.[31] During June and July 1936, anti-fascist rallies were held in Victoria Park, the BUF's favourite East End pitch. Violent scenes were recorded as anti-fascists demonstrated against Mosley's first large East End rally in Victoria Park on 7 June. Special Branch put the numbers present at 1,500 although, some London newspapers went as high as 50,000. This counter-demonstration was organised by the East London Section of the CPGB, joined by a contingent of Green Shirts.[32] A further demonstration against fascism was held in Victoria Park on 12 July, but this time it was organised by the Labour Party under the auspices of the Trades Councils of

North and East London. Chanie Rosenberg has already noted that this was not related to a BUF rally and was therefore a largely symbolic and 'tame affair'.[33]

More significant than these planned demonstrations were everyday 'street-corner' meetings which typically resulted in physical confrontations between fascists and anti-fascists. In the period August–October 1936, it was reported that East London police attended an average of 600 political meetings a month. Special Branch estimates suggest that in the London area, anti-fascists disrupted at least 60 per cent of BUF meetings during August 1936.[34] In Hackney, for instance, frequent clashes between fascists and anti-fascists occurred throughout the summer, especially at Ridley Road, John Campbell Road, Stamford Hill, Lower Clapton Road, Mare Street and Reading Lane.[35] Yet it is worth bearing in mind that the BUF did not meet with significant levels of physical opposition in every East London district. Mullally records that the BUF claimed 4,000 members in Bethnal Green, with the fascists particularly well implanted in the areas of Green Street and Essian Street.[36] According to Linehan's study of the BUF in East London, such was the strength of the fascist presence in its 'fiefdom' of Bethnal Green that anti-fascists found it largely inaccessible.[37]

A Metropolitan Police report confirms that the majority of anti-fascist activity in East London during the summer of 1936 was undertaken by the CPGB, YCL or NUWM; but the widening of anti-fascist opposition was also noted with reference to specifically Jewish anti-fascist organisations formed independently of the BoD, such as the British Union of Democrats.[38] In September 1936, Laski dismissed these independent initiatives as 'Jewish mushroom organisations', organisations that had sprung up in the past six months and described by Laski as little more than unscrupulous money-making 'rackets'.[39] Eager to discredit rival organisations, Laski refused to recognise that such organisations were legitimate representatives of the Jewish community.

However one organisation, the Jewish Peoples' Council Against Fascism and Anti-Semitism (JPC) stood on much firmer ground and can be interpreted as a popular vote of no confidence in the defence policy of the Board of Deputies. Essentially an offshoot from the Jewish Labour Council,[40] the JPC was established at a delegate conference in July 1936, attended by some 179 delegates representing 86 organisations, from trade unions, local Workers' Circle branches through to synagogues and ex-servicemen's organisations. Of working-class origin, the JPC condemned the Board as 'bourgeois' and 'obsolete', unresponsive to the needs of working-class Jews. It was particularly disparaging of the Board's separation of fascism and anti-Semitism and insisted that since anti-Semitism was being used by fascist movements instrumentally in order to achieve power, anti-Semitism could not be isolated from fascism. Thus, a *sine qua non* of the fight against anti-Semitism was anti-fascism.

Despite popular underpinnings, Laski maintained that the Board would have nothing to do with the JPC because it was explicitly 'anti-fascist' as well as being a suspected tool of the Communist Party, which the Board suspected was 'exploiting the natural resentment of the Jews against fascist attacks for political purposes'.[41] On the face of it, the suspicions of Laski and the Board were well grounded. A substantial element of the JPC's leadership was comprised of Communist Party members, such as Jack Pierce and Julius Jacobs, and the CPGB also provided the JPC with much needed organisational support. Moreover, Smith has cited oral evidence suggesting that the East London Communist Party held a series of meetings to discuss the founding of the JPC but remains convinced that the JPC 'conducted its anti-fascist campaign independently of the Communist Party'.[42] Although close to the CPGB, little concrete evidence exists to verify claims that the JPC was a CPGB front organisation – in fact, the Jewish Peoples' Council never affiliated to the Communist Party.

Even so, resources provided by the CPGB did enable the JPC's anti-fascist campaign to assume wide dimensions: thousands of leaflets were distributed exposing the fascist motives of the propagators of anti-Semitism and countering anti-Semitic defamation, an anti-fascist monthly was published, indoor and outdoor meetings were held, calls were made for active involvement in public demonstrations against fascism, there was co-operation with other anti-fascist organisations, especially the NCCL in an attempt to construct a popular front of both Jews and non-Jews in the fight against fascism, deputations were sent to local mayors to protest at cases of Jew-baiting and fascist activities, and pressure for a ban on the wearing of political uniforms and for the passing of a Racial Incitement Act was organised. Most impressively, the JPC gathered a petition of 77,000 signatures in just 48 hours calling for a ban on the planned march by the BUF through East London on 4 October 1936.[43]

Closely associated with the JPC (and CPGB) was the Ex-Servicemen's Movement Against Fascism. This was formed in July 1936 and claimed 1,000 members, the vast majority of whom were Jewish, including its chairman, Alexander Harris. Though predominantly Jewish, the

Ex-Servicemen's Movement Against Fascism claimed to have support from all religious denominations as well as from Conservatives, Liberals, Labourites and Communists. It committed itself to the defence of democratic government and pledged to 'destroy the evil of Fascism'.[44] This organisation was described in a Metropolitan Police report as 'probably one of the largest movements outside the CPGB, on the side of the anti-fascists', and though it claimed to be 'non-partisan' and 'non-sectarian', the report notes that the 'prime movers in this organisation are Jews and it is an established fact that most of them are in close contact with the Communist Party'.[45] In September 1936, the Ex-Servicemen's Movement Against Fascism convened an anti-fascist meeting and procession through Victoria Park. Home Office sources estimated that 3,000 people were in attendance, with the procession being joined by contingents from the YCL and Green Shirts.[46]

By the autumn of 1936, an active Communist-Jewish anti-fascist bloc had been established in East London from a plurality of groups, including the East London Communist Party, YCL and NUWM, the JPC, the Ex-Servicemen's Movement Against Fascism and the British Union of Democrats. An adjunct to this anti-fascist alliance was a small quantity of Green Shirts whose contribution has been overlooked by historians. This alliance comprised the anti-fascist 'movement' in East London and provided the organisational mechanism for anti-fascist expression. It was led by the Communist Party, held together both by its opposition to passive line of the Labour Party and the leaders of the Anglo-Jewry, and a common strategy based on the active disruption of fascist meetings and shows of numerical strength.[47] Nominally outside this anti-fascist alliance stood the BoD's Co-ordinating Committee, the Jewish Ex-Servicemen's Legion (which later became known as the Association of Jewish Ex-Servicemen) and the Association of Jewish Friendly Societies, which campaigned against anti-Semitism and hence countered BUF propaganda, but refused formally to classify themselves as 'anti-fascist' with speakers specifically instructed not to be drawn into 'political controversy'.[48] Additionally, one should not forget the contribution made by certain individuals who were not tied to any anti-fascist organisation, such as Father Groser, an Anglican priest who, by addressing crowds at fascist meetings along with a number of helpers, effectively countered Blackshirt activity in his East End parish.[49]

The solidity of the anti-fascist alliance in East London was put to the test by the announcement, made on 26 September 1936, that Mosley and the BUF intended to march through the East End on 4 October in order to celebrate the BUF's fourth anniversary. Initial efforts by anti-fascists were directed towards pressing the authorities to impose a ban the march. On 29 September a letter was sent from the Mayor of Stepney, Helena Roberts, to the Home Secretary, Sir John Simon, requesting that the march be prevented. This was followed by a deputation of East London mayors who visited the Home Office on 1 October. On 2 October, the Jewish Peoples' Council's petition was handed in to the Home Office by a further deputation led by James Hall, Labour MP for Whitechapel. These various approaches maintained that Mosley's proposed march through an area containing a large Jewish population was deeply provocative and would inevitably lead to large-scale disorder.[50] The Home Office refused to ban the march because such a course of action might be interpreted as a restriction on freedom of speech. It was all too aware of Mosley's fondness for seeking legal redress and feared negative publicity would result with Mosley claiming that he was a victim of discrimination.[51]

In the meantime, Joe Jacobs approached Willie Cohen, Secretary of the London YCL, regarding Communist Party preparations for Mosley's march. To his dismay he found the Communist Party unwilling to cancel a planned rally in aid of Spanish workers in Trafalgar Square on 4 October and was 'horrified' when Cohen declared Spain to be of greater importance than Mosley. On 30 September, the *Daily Worker* instructed workers to attend the main rally in Trafalgar Square and only afterwards proceed to East London to demonstrate against Mosley. In communications from the CPGB's London District Committee, it was stressed that there should be no disorder and 'If Mosley decides to march let him'.[52] For Jacobs, the stance of the London District Committee epitomised the 'supine' position held by minority elements within the Stepney Branch. Furthermore, Jacobs believed that if the Communist Party in Stepney followed orders from above and avoided physical confrontation with the BUF, then it would be finished as a political force in the East End. With other anti-fascist organisations, such as the Ex-Servicemen's Movement Against Fascism clearly determined to oppose Mosley under the Spanish Republicans' slogan 'They shall not pass!', Jacobs held that the local Communist Party would lose all credibility as the leader of popular anti-fascism.

In the event, the situation on the ground forced reluctant CPGB leaders to alter their policy: the YCL meeting was cancelled and eleventh hour calls were made to organise opposition against Mosley. What emerges from Jacobs's testimony is that the Communist Party leadership calculated that disengaging from the active struggle against

Mosley would alienate grassroots party activists in the East End and would trigger a local crisis of confidence in one of the CPGB's emerging strongholds. Figures supplied by Piratin suggest that the Stepney Branch had seen its membership double from 115 in 1934 to 230 by 1936.[53] Consequently, on 1 October, the CPGB's London District Committee issued a bulletin communicating an 'Urgent Alteration to Sunday's Plans'[54] and on 2 October, the *Daily Worker* carried the announcement that the demonstration against Mosley should be the largest anti-fascist mobilisation yet seen in Britain. That same day, the CPGB organised a 'warm-up' anti-fascist demonstration from Tower Hill to Stepney Green, attended by 2,000 people.[55]

At an Institute of Contemporary British History seminar on Cable Street, held in the 1990s, Piratin re-opened old wounds and accused Jacobs of exaggerating the conflict between anti-fascist militants in the East End and the London District Committee. Piratin maintained that the London District Committee's initial reluctance came not from opposition to militant anti-fascism but from other considerations, such as the long-term booking of demonstrations in Trafalgar Square which required police support – if the YCL rally was cancelled then future access would be blocked. There was also concern that cancellation of YCL's annual rally would hinder the progress of the YCL whose membership had increased to over 2,000 by 1935, three times the 1934 figure.[56] All the same, this still fails to account for why the London District Committee issued explicit instructions to East End radicals to avoid clashes with fascists and why it declared that the 'They shall not pass' policy amounted to a 'harmful stunt'. It was noticeable, moreover, that in relation to other mobilisations against Mosley, publicity in the *Daily Worker* appears to have been relatively low-key.[57] This all suggests that the CPGB's backing was less than whole-hearted and confirms the existence of reservations over anti-fascist policy within the Party's leadership circles.

According to Fenner Brockway, the main responsibility for publicising the 4 October mobilisation consequently 'fell on the shoulders' of the Independent Labour Party, even though ILP branches were relatively weak in the East End.[58] Since disaffiliating from the Labour Party, the ILP's membership had declined rapidly and already by 1935, plagued by debilitating splits, membership had fallen to a mere 4,400. This compared unfavourably with a Communist Party membership that had grown steadily to 11,500 by October 1936.[59] Ironically, by intensifying divisions between reformists and revolutionaries, 'united front' activity with the Communist Party proved a decisive factor in triggering the ILP's disintegration. Moderate ILP members disillusioned by CPGB collaboration had turned back to the Labour Party whilst more radical elements, receptive to the CPGB switched to the Communist Party. Yet despite the ILP's contraction, it retained influence through the *Star* newspaper with a circulation still surpassing that of the *Daily Worker*.

On 3 October, the *Star* ran a front-page which appealed to workers to resist Mosley in their thousands by blocking the route of Mosley's intended march through East London. Brockway claims that every newsagent shop in the East End displayed an ILP poster calling on workers to stop Mosley.[60] ILP leaflets were issued as duplicated sheets and thousands were distributed. A loud speaker van hired by the ILP toured East London, and a mass meeting was convened by the ILP at Hackney Town Hall to further publicise the call for workers to demonstrate against fascism.[61] This call was supported by the Ex-Servicemen's Movement Against Fascism which issued posters and leaflets calling on all ex-servicemen to oppose Mosley. Meanwhile, the Communist Party printed over the existing leaflets for the Trafalgar Square demonstration with details of a new location at Aldgate and the YCL distributed leaflets which called on East London Youth to 'bar the roads to fascism' and 'block the roads around Aldgate at 2 pm'.[62] Streets and walls were chalked and whitewashed with slogans such as 'Bar the road to fascism', 'All out on 4 October' and of course, 'They shall not pass', the symbolically charged slogan inspiring Spanish Republicans in the defence of Madrid against Franco's forces.

Conforming to now standard procedure, the joint call issued by the Communist Party and Independent Labour Party was spurned by the Labour Party. Rather than promoting unity on the Left, the Labour Party urged people to ignore the intended demonstration, a position loyally defended by the *Daily Herald*. On 1 October 1936, the *Daily Herald*'s editorial faithfully repeated the Labour Party's line that if fascism was ignored it would wither away: the 'only attraction is the prospect of disturbances. Withdraw that attraction, and fascist meetings would die on the organisers' hands.' Elsewhere, the liberal *News Chronicle* called on its readers to boycott the anti-fascist counter-demonstration, declaring that the 'Communist has no more right to break up a fascist meeting than the fascist has to break up a Communist demonstration'.[63] The Jewish communal leadership, through the Co-ordinating Committee of the Board of Deputies, also issued advice which subsequently appeared in the form of a prominent notice in the *Jewish Chronicle* on 2 October directing Jews to keep away from the demonstration: 'Don't go. Shut your doors. Don't be involved.' Through its Association of Jewish Youth, the BoD even targeted Jewish youth clubs in East London instructing members to keep away from the Aldgate demonstration and deliberately organised an unscheduled programme of football on 4 October as a distraction.[64] On 3 October, Labour mayors in the East End and a number of rabbis made a final appeal to people to stay away.

III

The anti-fascist mobilisation on 4 October 1936 was undoubtedly successful both in terms of forcing the abandonment of Mosley's march and in terms of obtaining large-scale popular participation. The numbers involved, estimated at anything between 100,000 according to police estimates, through to a reported 300,000 in the *News Chronicle* were impressive and do underline its significance as a striking example of popular anti-fascism. Romantic accounts by the militant Left hold that the entire East End came together in working-class solidarity and inflicted a crushing defeat on Mosley's forces, driving his movement into a spiral of decline from which it never recovered. Accordingly, Cable Street has assumed legendary status as an historic victory for radical anti-fascism and has provided later generations of anti-fascist activists with rich inspiration. Sustaining the myth, Chanie Rosenberg writes, 'The decisive battle to smash the fascists was the Battle of Cable Street, which has rightly passed into history as a crucial victory for the British working class.'[65] Yet it is worth bearing in mind that the 'Battle of Cable Street' was not a clash between fascists and anti-fascists, but between anti-fascists and the police. And most importantly, as Susser has stressed, 'Impressive as it was, important as it was, the Battle of Cable Street did not, in itself, stop Fascism in the East End.'[66]

Although the Communist Party played a secondary role in drawing public attention to the planned 4 October counter-demonstration, CPGB activists did assume prime responsibility for organisation of activities on the day, doubtless because the Communists, unlike the ILP, had the required strength in numbers at the local level. The principal assembly point was Gardiner's Corner at Aldgate where anti-fascists hoped to gather in sufficient numbers to block Mosley's intended route. An anti-fascist headquarters was established with lines of communication between the 'front' and headquarters maintained through cyclists and motor-cyclists. Anticipating violence, a number of first-aid posts were also established, and in the event of the fascists managing to get through, groups of anti-fascists were instructed to occupy the pitch at Victoria Park where Mosley intended to hold a rally to mark the end of proceedings. A number of anti-fascist loud-speaker vans also toured the area further encouraging local people to oppose Mosley. Some 6,000 police, including the entire Metropolitan Police Mounted Division, were drafted into the East End and add-itional police logistical support was provided by radio vans and an aeroplane.

By 2 pm, a vast crowd, estimated by Piratin to number at least 50,000 people,[67] had gathered at Gardiner's Corner, forming a human barri-cade with a number of trams deserted by their anti-fascist drivers providing additional obstacles. Meanwhile, anti-fascists had erected barricades along Cable Street and it was here that the most dramatic clashes between police and anti-fascists took place as the police attempted in vain to clear the only possible route through to the East End. The police made repeated baton charges on the Cable Street barri-cade and eventually captured it, only to be faced with more barricades and further militant opposition. In all, according to Home Office sources, some 79 anti-fascists were arrested.[68] Faced with the prospect of serious violence between fascists and anti-fascists, at 3.40 pm, Sir Philip Game, the Metropolitan Police Commissioner, instructed the 3,000 or so fascists who were patiently assembled along Royal Mint Street to abandon the march. They were escorted westwards to the Embankment where they subsequently dispersed. Surprisingly, there was very little fighting between fascists and anti-fascists although one incident, caught by a news cameraman and shown in cinemas across the country, did help create the myth of an epic confrontation. It has been suggested, however, that this news item backfired on anti-fascists. Richard Bellamy, the BUF's 'official historian', has contended that this incident, which involved Tommy Moran in a brawl with nine anti-fascists, 'inspired cinema audiences to applaud'. Bellamy further claims that this sympathetic response led to the newsreel being withdrawn.[69]

Even though Cable Street was the site of the most animated clashes between anti-fascists and police, the 'Battle of Cable Street' was arguably incidental to the main point of activity at Gardiner's Corner. Certainly, doubts remain as to whether the incidents in Cable Street alone convinced Sir Philip Game to call off Mosley's march. The more decisive factor, identified by Deakin[70] amongst others, was anticipa-tion of serious disorder given the size and determined nature of the crowd at Gardiner's Corner. This is supported by Brockway's account which states that following his arrival at Gardiner's Corner, he warned the Home Office by telephone of the possibility of serious disorder if Mosley was allowed to march, and subsequently informed the Press Association of his phone call. Once the decision had been made to stop the march, Brockway then contacted the Press Association and discovered that instructions had been given to abandon the march half an hour after he had originally telephoned the Home Office. Although Brockway doubts that his warning to the Home Office had anything to do with the decision to call off Mosley's procession, the Press Association certainly saw it as a decisive factor and it was reported as such throughout the world's press. In official Communist Party histories, Brockway's actions are never mentioned. Indeed, more generally, as far as the 4 October demonstrations are concerned, the ILP's role is noticeably minimised.

If Cable Street was merely an 'aside', then the events of 4 October 1936 have passed into anti-fascist legend under an entirely inappropriate name. It has even been suggested by one anti-fascist veteran, present at Gardiner's Corner, that we should 'forget' Cable Street altogether and instead call it 'October 4th' in the tradition of the peaceful mass action at Hyde Park on 9 September 1934. This designation would give greater prominence to the scale of popular involvement and would underline the extent to which it was a 'great popular victory' for anti-fascism.[71] Indeed, a key element of the Cable Street myth, identified by Deakin is the belief that 'it was the East End as a whole, and not merely the Jewish element that was the ostensible object of his hostility, that threw Mosley back'.[72] A constant theme running throughout oral testimony is reference to the 'exceptional' degree of working-class unity, where it is stressed that ethnic cleavages between the local Jewish and Irish communities in the East End were suppressed by common hostility towards Mosley. Piratin recollects:

> Never was there such unity of all sections of the working class as was seen on the barricades of Cable Street. People whose lives were poles apart, though living within a few hundred yards of each other; bearded orthodox Jews and rough-and-ready Irish Catholic dockers ...[73]

In the same vein, Charlie Goodman recalls:

> And it was not just a question of Jews being there on 4 October, the most amazing thing was to see a silk-coated religious Orthodox Jew

standing next to an Irish docker with a grappling iron – the docker had a grappling iron! This was absolutely unbelievable.[74]

On closer reflection, however, it becomes clear that the depth of anti-fascist 'unity' within the East End has been exaggerated. It is worth bearing in mind that the BUF recruited heavily from the working class in East London, and although the Irish community was generally hostile to the British fascism, Irish immigrants and Catholics were particularly attracted to, and over-represented within, the BUF.[75] Moreover, the events of 4 October were not an entirely East End affair. Groups of anti-fascists from other parts of London and from outside London came into the area, thereby inflating the numbers. Berkowitz has pointed to the presence of the entire London Communist Party as well as groups of Jewish ex-servicemen who travelled from Manchester and Leeds.[76] But equally, the extent of provincial involvement should not be overstated. The line traditionally advanced by fascists is that Cable Street was not a spontaneous uprising of local people against fascism but was organised by Communists, for the most part imported from outside London. Yet, of the anti-fascists arrested only one did not come from London. It is also reasonable to assume that an element of those present were not necessarily committed anti-fascists but either there out of curiosity or looking for an opportunity to engage in violence. None the less, putting these qualifications to one side, the presence of thousands of ordinary people participating in a mass anti-fascist demonstration cannot be denied. This, in itself, was an impressive achievement and underlines the scale of popular hostility towards fascism and fascist-related anti-Semitism in East London. And, since most of the anti-fascist opposition would have been comprised of traditional Labour Party supporters, the extent of the refusal to submit to the authority of the Labour Party (and leaders of Anglo-Jewry) is also abundantly clear.

Following the pattern of Olympia, the most immediate impact of the events of 4 October, was a short-term surge in active street demonstrations against fascism, though curiously this was more in evidence outside London. On 11 October, a fascist procession in Liverpool, from Mount Pleasant to Liverpool Stadium, met an angry riposte. Mosley had intended to lead the march from Lime Street, but the extent of opposition forced him to travel to the stadium by car, having already been attacked on leaving the Adelphi Hotel by one anti-fascist disguised as a tramp.[77] Local anti-fascists attempted to obstruct the march at various points along the route but were resisted by police who subsequently dispersed anti-fascists from the area around the stadium. Nevertheless, missiles were thrown as fascists made their way from the stadium at the end of the rally and altogether, some 12 anti-fascists were arrested. At Bedford, police also had to protect Blackshirts from a hostile crowd and at Tunbridge Wells, fascist speakers were bombarded with eggs, vegetables and tomatoes. In Edinburgh, fascist speakers were 'barracked' at the Mound and required a police escort to ensure their safety.[78] The work of Gallagher suggests that the BUF faced militant opposition in Edinburgh not only from the Left but also from sections of the Right, particularly Protestant Action. Although Protestant Action shared the BUF's anti-Semitism, it attacked the BUF for pro-Catholic tendencies as well as Mosley's long-standing sympathy for Irish nationalism.[79]

Yet surprisingly, the impression conveyed in Metropolitan Police reports is that in East London the fascists 'gained rather than lost prestige' in the week following Cable Street. Even though 10,000 anti-fascists marched in a victory parade from Tower Hill to Victoria Park on 11 October, large crowds were present at BUF meetings in Stepney, Shoreditch, Stoke Newington and Limehouse, where fascist speakers were said to have received an 'enthusiastic' reception and opposition was 'either non-existent or negligible'. Moreover, Mosley succeeded in holding a meeting attended by an estimated 12,000 people in Victoria Park Square on 14 October and was said to have been 'enthusiastically received'. The view of the Metropolitan Police was that attempts by the CPGB to consolidate the 'tremendous victory over fascism' had met with a 'very poor response'.[80] According to Special Branch reports, the BUF recruited some 2,000 new members in the aftermath of the 'Cable Street' events, presumably as a reaction to left-wing violence.[81] This is borne out by Linehan's study, which cites oral evidence indicating that membership of the Bethnal Green North East branch expanded to over 1,000 following the 'Cable Street' disturbances, and the Limehouse Branch recruited around 800 new members.[82]

Clearly the 'Battle of Cable Street' was not such a 'decisive' victory. It didn't 'smash the fascists' or put an immediate end to Mosley's anti-Semitic campaign. Ominously, on the day of the anti-fascist victory march from Tower Hill to Victoria Park, over 100 youths engaged in a pogrom in the Mile End Road where Jewish shop windows were smashed, a car was set on fire and individual Jews were attacked. One Jew and a seven-year-old girl were thrown through a window.[83] This anti-Semitic backlash was seen as retaliation for events a week earlier at Cable Street, but over the longer-term anti-Semitic incidents still persisted. A Metropolitan Police report from April 1937 was of the opinion that the frequency of anti-Semitic incidents had been steadily increasing;[84] and fascist meetings continued unabated. In November 1936, 131 fascist meetings were recorded by the Metropolitan Police in London, with only seven meetings resulting in disorder. By February 1937, the number of meetings had increased to 222.[85] At London County Council elections in March 1937, the BUF polled a respectable 23 per cent of the vote in Bethnal Green from a register that disadvantaged the BUF by allowing only householders to vote. A significant proportion of fascist support came from disenfranchised youth who, because of the housing shortage in the East End, tended to reside with parents.[86] Revealingly, the upsurge in fascist activity that immediately followed Cable Street was even admitted by Joe Jacobs, the leading exponent of physical opposition to fascism. Jacobs also refers to a renewal of tactical debate within the Stepney Branch after 'Cable Street' and this may account for the lack of organised disruption of fascist meetings in East London in the aftermath of 4 October.[87]

Following the 'Battle of Cable Street', the Communist Party leadership was becoming increasingly concerned that physical disruption of fascist meetings would lead the government to impose public order legislation that may well have an adverse effect on its activities.[88] Reflecting this concern, in mid-October 1936, the London District Committee circulated a policy document which outlined a number of proposals for future anti-fascist activities. Conspicuously absent from these proposals was a commitment to the physical struggle against Mosley, and this omission provides further evidence of the desire of CPGB leaders to avoid violent confrontations with fascists. Instead of disrupting BUF meetings, the London District Committee called, *inter alia*, for a petition demanding the banning of uniforms and Mosley's 'army', the launching of an anti-fascist newspaper, and mass distribution of anti-fascist literature. It did propose incursions into fascist strongholds such as Bethnal Green, but these were to be very cautious forays with the use of touring loudspeaker vans and the holding of anti-fascist meetings by invitation only thereby ensuring 'an audience of good quality'.[89]

Unquestionably, the CPGB's concerns over possible public order legislation were well founded with sustained political pressure being applied on the government to introduce some form of public order legislation in the wake of the events of 4 October 1936. Demands for a legal clampdown were led by the Labour Party. At its annual conference which opened on 5 October, the Labour Party called for legal action by the state in line with its belief that the use of the state against fascism was the most effective way of safeguarding democracy and curtailing fascist activities. The response of the Home Secretary indicated that any legislation introduced would have to apply equally to the Left as well as to the Right, and this prompted the CPGB to send a communication to the Home Secretary calling for government action to be directed exclusively against Mosley's fascists, a move by the CPGB that would have been improbable a few years earlier in its 'ultra-left' phase. Specifically, the Communist Party called on the government to prohibit all political uniforms, to close fascist barracks, to dissolve fascist semi-military organisation, to protect the population against all attempts at hooliganism and violence, and to ensure that there was no limitation of the CPGB's democratic rights of agitation and propaganda.[90]

As anticipated, legislation in the form of a Public Order Act (POA) was quickly introduced and came into effect at the beginning of January 1937. But, contrary to the wishes of the militant Left, the POA was not exclusively directed against fascism, although it did contain clauses which, by seeking to criminalise Blackshirt activity, were ostensibly anti-fascist. According to the terms of the Act, political uniforms and quasi-military organisations were banned, the police were given powers to re-route marches and could implement a three-month ban on marches in a given area; it was also made an offence to use threatening, abusive or insulting words or behaviour in a public place or meeting which would likely lead to a breach of the peace. Although the banning of uniforms and quasi-military organisations was interpreted favourably as a blow to the BUF, the radical Left attacked the POA both because it gave the police unprecedented powers to ban marches (including Communist ones) and secondly it did not make incitement to racial hatred illegal.

Despite charges that the Act might be used against the Left – criticisms made in particular by the NCCL and the Communist Party – the measures taken against the British Union of Fascists do raise the possibility of 'anti-fascism' by the state and this obliges us to consider the role of the state as an element within the mosaic of anti-fascist opposition. The relationship between the state and fascism in inter-war Britain has been most thoroughly researched by Richard Thurlow and it is not my intention to duplicate his material.[91] However, based on his research and that of others,[92] it is possible to arrive at some summary conclusions regarding the attitude of the state towards fascism in inter-war Britain.

From a left-wing perspective, Lewis has argued that the government opportunistically used the situation in the East End to introduce public order legislation in order to restrict the activities of the Left, in particular militant activity which had been associated with the NUWM's hunger marches. The suggestion here is that the state used 'anti-fascism' as a cover to introduce a series of 'repressive' and 'reactionary' anti-Left measures. Lewis does not go as far as classifying the National Government pro-fascist, but does interpret the POA as more 'anti-libertarian than anti-fascist'.[93] For Lewis, the POA was a reflection of the desire of the conservative Right to clamp down on any form of extra-parliamentary activity which threatened the stability of a society founded on class privilege and concludes that the POA was 'a high price to pay for a few morsals of anti-fascist legislation'.[94]

More convincingly, Thurlow offers an alternative analysis where the response of the state is interpreted within a 'liberal-democratic' framework. Thurlow sees the role of the state as protecting the liberal-democratic centre from both the extremism of the Right and Left.[95] This perspective allows us to define the state as 'anti-fascist' even though it attempted to curb radical anti-fascist activities. According to Thurlow, the state used a variety of methods to try to isolate Mosley prior to enacting public order legislation. Following Mosley's break with Rothermere in 1934, pressure was applied on the media to give Mosley and the Blackshirts the 'silent treatment'. Newspaper editors were instructed not to give British fascism undue publicity, newsreel companies were requested not to film mass demonstrations, and the BBC was pressed not to broadcast extremist views. Thus in the period before the Cable Street disturbances, 'behind-the-scenes' attempts were made to marginalise Mosley's Blackshirts without introducing formal methods of social control that would unnecessarily limit civil liberties. It was only after Cable Street had threatened a breakdown of public order in East London and with the support of opposition parties, most notably the Labour Party, that the National Government brought in legal restrictions curbing fascist (and anti-fascist) activities. Thus, rather than being an agent of 'encroaching fascism', the state moved cautiously to protect democracy from the extremes and, whilst hostile to left-wing militancy, it was nevertheless 'anti-fascist'.

At the forefront of political pressure for a Public Order Bill, the Labour Party greeted the POA as a great victory for anti-fascism. Herbert Morrison was later to declare that the '... Bill did the trick. It smashed the private army, and I believe commenced the undermining of Fascism in this country'.[96] Yet doubts remain as to whether the Public Order Act was such a potent weapon against Mosley's fascists. By banning processions in the East End, the POA did exert a degree of control over the East End situation, but fascist meetings continued and even increased in frequency in the approach to the London County Council elections of March 1937. No fewer than 150 BUF meetings were held during the election campaign.[97] The ban on processions may have impeded fascist recruitment in East London, but the BUF still held high-profile marches elsewhere in London as well as in provincial areas. The appeal of the BUF may have been further reduced by the ban on uniforms, but it simply adapted by adopting a new 'uniform' of polo-necked sweaters and trench-coats. And, although the POA strengthened the law against the use of insulting words at public meetings, there were many complaints that the police refused to arrest fascists who persisted with anti-Semitic provocation.

It would be wrong, however, to treat the POA too unfairly. As Linehan has shown, the provisions of POA prohibiting the use of insulting words and behaviour at public meetings did trigger internal division within the BUF. As anxieties over possible legal action mounted, leading anti-Semites, such as William Joyce and John Beckett, were cut adrift and forced out of the organisation. According to Linehan, these divisions led to a period of 'ideological confusion' which cost the BUF the support of more radical anti-Semitic elements in the East End. As the BUF diverted attention away from its anti-Semitism, so its progress amongst the working class in East London stopped.[98] Over the short term, the POA had a deleterious effect on the BUF, but like Cable Street, the damage inflicted was not terminal and certainly did not result in the comprehensive defeat of Mosley. In fact, over the longer term, by impressing on the BUF the need to become more 'respectable' it may have helped to revive the BUF. During 1938–9, Mosley experienced something of a recovery, drawing in new recruits from the middle class in areas outside East London by toning down anti-Semitism and by launching a 'Peace Campaign'.[99]

IV

The provision within the POA for imposing a ban on political processions was first used against the BUF in response to the announcement made in June 1937 that it intended a stage another march through the East End. Fearing a recurrence of disorder, the government imposed a ban on political processions in East London for six weeks. The ban was then periodically renewed until 1939 with Labour Party support. Since the limitation on political processions was intended to be used 'in moderation', the authorities accepted an alternative proposal by the BUF to avoid the East End and instead march from Kentish Town in north London to Trafalgar Square in central London on 4 July. Alteration to the route of the march meant that the responsibility for organising anti-fascist opposition did not fall on the Communist Party in East London. In any case, by this time, the Stepney Branch under the guidance of Piratin was shifting the direction of its anti-fascist work away from physical confrontation towards involvement in 'rent struggles' in fascist neighbourhoods, a move given added persuasiveness by the passage of the POA which, by prohibiting the use of threatening or insulting words and behaviour, naturally restricted anti-fascist activities.

Awake to the legal restrictions occasioned by the POA, the CPGB skilfully used the local Labour Party in St Pancras to organise opposition to Mosley's procession. A Special Branch report noted that many members of the CPGB in St Pancras had overlapping membership of the local Labour Party and that acting on instructions from CPGB leaders had been 'assiduously urging the local Labour Party officials to take the initiative in organising opposition to the fascist march on 4 July'. Subsequently, the St Pancras Labour Party decided to lead the opposition and gave immediate instructions to print 15,000 leaflets and petition sheets protesting against the proposed assembly of fascists. Two anti-fascist meetings were planned for 4 July. The first to be held at Islip Street, Kentish Town at 3.30 pm, followed by a further meeting at Trafalgar Square at 5.00 pm.[100] In the days preceding the proposed march, anti-fascists raised a petition of 3,000 signatures from local residents, which was subsequently presented to the Mayor of St Pancras following a 500-strong march to the Town Hall, organised by the local Labour Party, Co-operative Society and various trade unions. Additional pressure for a ban on the march was exerted through correspondence to the Home Secretary from various trade unions, Highgate Left Book Club and a number of anti-fascists on an individual basis.[101] These requests were denied, however, and it was at this point that Communists became 'exasperated' with local Labour Party officials, who withdrew their support for the anti-fascist mobilisation in line with established Labour Party policy.

Consequently, the CPGB was left to organise the demonstrations without the 'protection' afforded by the St Pancras Labour Party; but as Special Branch noted, the CPGB deemed the POA to be a 'serious obstacle' to effective organisation. In order not to lay itself open to prosecution (and in line with the CPGB's move to a non-confrontational position) direct appeals to rally at Trafalgar Square or St Pancras were not published in the *Daily Worker*.[102] Communist Party propaganda, therefore, 'emphasised not the ability of the masses to prevent the march, but complained bitterly that the government ought to have banned it'.[103] In order to circumvent the POA, CPGB leaders issued instructions by word of mouth to branch officials, but there were complaints that this method of communication had led to confusion over the location of assembly points. A number of leaflets were distributed by the Communist Party in St Pancras, but these were described by Special Branch as 'circumscribed' and this was also the case with a number of sticky-back labels fly-posted at various sites bearing the superscription of the London District Committee. Evidently, the POA handicapped the CPGB's organisational efforts, the effect of which was to raise concerns that the same level of support from anti-fascists as was seen prior to Cable Street was not forthcoming.

In an attempt to counter this, Communist Party volunteers were instructed to whitewash and chalk explicit instructions announcing where anti-fascists should mobilise. Curiously, some of these were (deliberately?) at odds with the leadership's policy of avoiding physical confrontation. Slogans such as 'Smash Fascism – Rally to Islip St July 4th' and 'All out July 4th – Stop Mosley – Bar the Way to Fascism' openly called for physical opposition. Presumably this was why CPGB leaders were careful to issue a statement instructing members not to be led into acts of violence so that the Communist Party could not be held liable for any subsequent violence.[104] In the event, anti-fascists generally observed official Communist Party instructions. Anti-fascist opposition was said to be 'guarded in tone' and there was 'no open incitement to violence'; none the less 27 anti-fascists were arrested and, following the fascist meeting in Trafalgar Square, a number of anti-fascists attempted to surround and assault Mosley in his car under Charing Cross Railway Bridge.[105]

Compared with 4 October 1936, the numbers mobilised on 4 July 1937 were relatively modest, and here two factors came into play. First, organisational problems inhibited turn-out. Second, the location of the procession which was mainly through central London and not through consciously anti-fascist working-class districts meant that the CPGB failed to secure wider support, especially from anti-fascist groups in the East End. According to Home Office figures, a crowd of 5,000 initially gathered in Kentish Town, but the route from Kentish Town to Trafalgar Square was said to be 'thinly lined' by anti-fascists, except where crowds of 200–300 clustered around main street crossings. In Trafalgar Square itself, 5,000 anti-fascists assembled, with another 2,000–3,000 people gathered in the surrounding area. There was much heckling and booing from anti-fascists making Mosley's speech inaudible, but because the march was not physically stopped by anti-fascists, and much to the frustration of the Communist Party, it was acclaimed by the fascist press as a great success.

The final BUF march in London to give rise to serious disorder occurred in October 1937. In September, the BUF announced its intention to hold a fifth anniversary march through the East End, but once again was prohibited under the terms of the POA. Consequently, an alternative route was proposed from Westminster in central London to Bermondsey in south-east London. Bermondsey was a Labour stronghold with a significant Catholic-Irish population employed in the docks. Although the area contained few Jews, the announcement of the proposed march sparked opposition. A local deputation headed by the Mayor of Bermondsey and the leader of the Bermondsey Trades Council, supported by the local Labour MP for Rotherhithe, the South London organiser of the CPGB and local religious leaders, called on the Home Office to request that the march be banned. The response, as in July, was that since the area contained few Jews the march did not constitute an incitement to violence. With the Home Office refusing to ban the procession, the Executive of the London Labour Party attempted to dampen down local hostility and implored all local Labour Party branches to avoid organising a counter-demonstration. A circular was issued which maintained that since fascism abroad thrived on political disorder and that fascism at home badly needed advertisement, 'the Executive advises Labour Party members and supporters to boycott the whole thing and thus reveal the small numbers and limited importance of Fascism in London'.[106] This advice was rejected by Bermondsey Trades Council which, to the obvious displeasure of the London Labour Party, called for a massive counter-demonstration, a call supported by both the Communist Party and the ILP.

Given that Mosley's march was planned to take place through a working-class area, the determination of Bermondsey Trades Council to counter the march and the embarrassment of the perceived failure of the July demonstration, the CPGB had no real alternative but to support a mass mobilisation of anti-fascist forces. These considerations would appear to explain why on this occasion the CPGB leadership opted to back militant opposition. In marked contrast to July,

Communist Party publicity was much more thorough. There were frequent articles in the *Daily Worker*, numerous meetings took place, there was extensive chalking of anti-fascist slogans and no fewer than 150,000 leaflets were distributed. But still attentive to the possibilities of prosecution under the POA, the CPGB indicated where anti-fascists should assemble without actually openly stating it. This was communicated in the *Daily Worker* on 30 September when it predicted that opposition 'would be strongest' at the junction of Long Lane and Borough High Street.[107]

Branson has argued that the scale of the mobilisation of anti-fascists at Bermondsey indicated the depth to which anti-fascist consciousness had penetrated non-Jewish sections of the working class in London.[108] Some eyewitness accounts, later recorded in the *Daily Worker*, claimed that the numbers involved even surpassed those at Cable Street. It has been suggested that as many as 50,000 anti-fascists gathered in the immediate area of Borough underground station, although this number conflicts with the Special Branch estimate of 12,000.[109] Imitating Cable Street, anti-fascists erected barricades, a move which once again precipitated serious clashes between anti-fascists and police as the police made repeated baton charges on the barricades in order to clear the route and restore order. Despite the presence of over 2,500 police, Long Lane remained steadfastly blocked by determined anti-fascists forcing Mosley's contingent of 3,400 fascists to be diverted to an alternative meeting place where they were briefly addressed by Mosley in an area secured by a police cordon. Beyond the cordon, anti-fascists gathered and interrupted Mosley's speech with shouts of 'They did not pass!' In any case, Mosley's intended meeting place had already been occupied by Sally Schwartz and Tim Walsh of the Federation of Democrats, who had 'jumped the pitch' and ingeniously entertained a large crowd by staging a local talent show.[110]

Although the anti-fascist mobilisation at Bermondsey has not attracted the same degree of interest as the 'Battle of Cable Street', it has been commended by a number of historians as another successful episode in the history of militant anti-fascism. According to Todd, for instance, such was the depth of anti-fascist opposition at Bermondsey that 'the point was made, and the Blackshirts were never again able to mount a large, provocative march through the streets of any British city'.[111] A full year after Cable Street, a significant number of anti-fascists had been mobilised at Bermondsey and this continued 'show of strength' by anti-fascist forces must have depleted the BUF's morale. Yet in May 1938, 2,000 fascists once again marched through

Bermondsey and appear to have held a successful rally attended by 50,000 people.[112] Moreover, Branson's assertion that the anti-fascist opposition at Bermondsey was an entirely local and hence non-Jewish response to fascist provocation deserves qualification. A report by Special Branch suggests significant 'outside', possibly East End, involvement. First, it estimates that 75 per cent of the 2,000 or so anti-fascists who initially assembled near Borough underground station, were Jewish. Second, of the 112 anti-fascists arrested, only about 25 had local addresses.[113] Branson's point that the significance of Bermondsey was that it had shown that 'anti-fascism was as strong among non-Jewish workers as it was among the Jews' evidently misrepresents the scale of Jewish participation in this particular anti-fascist mobilisation.[114]

V

Most chronological accounts of opposition to domestic fascism in the inter-war period end with Bermondsey. With the BUF's membership down to an estimated 5,800 by January 1938,[115] it is usually stated that after Bermondsey, the CPGB regarded the BUF as a 'spent force'.[116] In consequence, organised opposition to British fascism 'cooled' and the CPGB became increasingly preoccupied by events in Spain with its energies mainly directed towards recruiting for the International Brigades. But even if the Communist Party's interest in British fascism generally waned, anti-fascist activities continued after Bermondsey. In November 1937, anti-fascist militants in Liverpool subjected an open air meeting held by Mosley to a missile attack in which he was struck and knocked unconscious resulting in a brief stay in hospital.[117] In March 1938, the Left Book Club organised an opposition meeting to Mosley outside Portsmouth's Coliseum. It was reported in the *Daily Worker* that a hostile crowd of over 5,000 gathered outside and Mosley's car was subjected to an anti-fascist attack.[118] At Gillingham in April 1938, Mosley's visit was opposed by local Communists, who distributed leaflets calling for a 'monster demonstration against Fascism' and succeeded in mobilising 'thousands' in a display of anti-fascist hostility.[119]

Continuous opposition to fascism also occurred in areas where Mosley did not visit, such as Aberdeen.[120] Fascist activities in Scotland in the latter half of the 1930s were focused on Aberdeen principally owing to the tireless commitment and determination of an Aberdeenshire laird, Chambers-Hunter and his sister-in-law. The launch of an intensive campaign by these two BUF activists in the spring of 1936 triggered the formation of local anti-fascist group comprised in the main of CPGB and ILP members. In keeping with the policy of CPGB leaders, the group's strategy was non-violent disruption of BUF meetings, although in September 1938, an outdoor meeting by fascists in Aberdeen was subjected to an aggressive missile attack. Kibblewhite and Rigby contend that in terms of preventing fascist propaganda from being disseminated, anti-fascists in Aberdeen were 'almost totally successful. When one man who opposed fascism for almost three years was asked about the specific content of Chamber-Hunter's speeches, he replied: "Well, you see, we never heard his case ...".'[121] Favoured techniques of denying a fascist speaker a hearing in Aberdeen included shouting, whistling, singing and stamping feet, although more innovative techniques were in evidence elsewhere. In June 1937 at the Mound in Edinburgh, amongst a crowd estimated to number 10,000, anti-fascists passed a hand bell from hand to hand and threw fireworks at the speaker's van, whilst in June 1938 in Stepney, there was even a case of anti-fascists banging on baths and biscuit tins in order to drown out the voice of a fascist speaker.[122]

In turning our attention back to the East End, it should be noted that the East London Communist Party sustained its anti-fascist struggle into the late 1930s. Moreover, from June 1937 this struggle entered a new phase, led by Phil Piratin and Pat Devine, the CPGB's East End organiser.[123] Following the suspension of Joe Jacobs from the Stepney Branch – during the summer of 1938 CPGB members were instructed to hold anti-fascist meetings in the vicinity of fascist meetings rather than trying to prevent fascist speakers from being heard – emphasis shifted away from aggressive disruption of fascist meetings.[124] As an alternative to militant anti-fascism, Communists were encouraged by Piratin to become involved in grassroots community action and, in particular, housing disputes. The idea was to demonstrate clearly to fascists that the CPGB was the true defender of working-class interests and thereby break existing allegiances to the BUF. In persuading the Stepney Branch to adopt this strategy, Piratin recalls the seminal case of two BUF families threatened with eviction by a Jewish landlord at Paragon Mansions in Stepney who were 'won over' by local Communists in June 1937, leading other tenants to destroy their BUF membership cards 'voluntarily and in disgust'.[125]

Encouraged by the success of this venture, local Communists increasingly channelled their anti-fascism into the work of the Stepney Tenants' Defence League, which had been established in the autumn of 1937. This Communist-led organisation, which at its height claimed 7,500 members,[126] concentrated its efforts on winning the support of tenants in fascist neighbourhoods in Stepney, such as Duckett Street. Support for fascism in this area was eroded to such an extent that Duckett Street residents even assisted in a dispute in a neighbourhood where virtually all the local residents were Jewish.[127] In 1938, the example of Stepney was followed by Communists in neighbouring Bethnal Green. Here, Communists became involved in a successful rent strike at Quinn Square where many of the residents were pro-fascist. Reading Piratin's account, one is left with the impression that this strategy of community action effectively neutralised support for fascism in the East End. However, this isolates East End Mosleyites from developments within the BUF itself and fails to take into account the extent to which local fascists were alienated by the moderating influence of the POA on hardline anti-Semitism and the resulting launch of Mosley's appeasement campaign in March 1938 which antagonised more patriotic elements within the BUF.

Aside from the East London Communist Party, the JPC also remained active in the local struggle against fascism, that is until 1940, whereas the associated Ex-Servicemen's Movement Against Fascism had already disbanded in August 1937.[128] During 1937–8, the JPC was approached by the Board of Deputies with a view to securing a single defence organisation albeit operating under the Board's authority. This move resulted from pressure exerted on the Board by the Association of Jewish Friendly Societies, which had stressed the need for greater unity of effort within the Jewish community. Surprisingly, despite the JPC's trenchant criticism of the BoD, an 'understanding' was said to have been reached in April 1938 at a conference held between the JPC and the BoD's London Area Council (LAC) – the organisation that had taken over the Board's open air speaking campaign from the Friendly Societies in 1937. At this conference, it was agreed that one Jewish defence organisation was desirable which should function under the BoD, and that the object of this organisation should be to combat anti-Semitism.[129] Protracted negotiations followed, but the JPC refused to yield to the Board's three conditions that the JPC should be disbanded, that the JPC would have no representation on the Board's Co-ordinating Committee, and that the JPC's opposition to fascism would be dropped. Fundamental differences remained, with Jewish radicals unable to accept the Board's indifference to popular anti-fascism, although in 1939 the JPC did agree to work with the LAC for an interim period of six months.[130]

Throughout the 1930s, the Board of Deputies remained resolutely opposed to direct action against fascism and endeavoured to keep the response of the Jewish community focused on anti-defamation. In November 1936, it had set up a network of 'Vigilance Committees' throughout Britain in order to monitor local anti-Semitic activity, to oversee the press (and refute anti-Semitic letters if necessary), and to maintain a watchful eye on the activities of the Jewish community in order to prevent 'anti-social' behaviour which may have brought Jews into 'disfavour'.[131] This was combined with distribution of leaflets, which approached two million by the end of 1938, and an open air speaking campaign relaunched by the LAC. In 1938, the LAC, with its 30 members, held an impressive 788 meetings at 89 locations, but a report by a former LAC member casts doubt on the effectiveness of this campaign when he records that 'at not less than 50% and perhaps 75%' of these meetings, 'there had been practically no audience', and where there was an audience it tended to be comprised of the same people 'time and time again'. He concludes that whilst, on paper, the Board appears to have presented its case to over 150,000 people in 1938, in reality, it probably did not reach more than 10,000.[132] Yet despite a poor response, as well as the financial expense of spending some £2,000 on 10,000 people, the Board persevered with its open air speaking campaign and only brought it to a close with the outbreak of war.

Additionally, Mosley faced another source of opposition from the mid-1930s. This came from local authorities, typically Labour-controlled, which increasingly refused to allow fascists the use of halls to hold BUF meetings. Towards the end of 1938, the BUF faced almost total exclusion from large halls in Britain's main cities. In London, in the period 1936–9 the BUF encountered severe difficulties in securing indoor meeting places of any size, and Mosley attributed this to the Labour majority on London County Council.[133] The problems the BUF faced in hiring halls further isolated it from the political mainstream, forcing it to concentrate on street corner and open air meetings. These outdoor meetings were then subjected to further restrictions, such as the ban on loudspeakers which was imposed by London County Council. Evidently, the role of local authorities (and hence the Labour Party) in denying the BUF room to propagate its ideology was of significance, and towards the end of the 1930s this form of opposition probably proved more damaging to the BUF than any remaining physical opposition by anti-fascists.[134] A further block on the spread of the BUF's propaganda came in November 1937 when the Executive

Committee of the National Association of Wholesale Newsagents refused to handle copies of *Action*, the BUF's newspaper. This decision was taken without warning or explanation and was a major blow to the BUF, with the fascist press now no longer freely available at newsagents.[135]

Despite the denial of venues for fascist meetings, Mosley did manage to secure Earls Court for a major indoor event in July 1939. Special Branch reported that 11,000 people attended this meeting, although it was noticeable that there was no substantive opposition by anti-fascists.[136] A large open air rally by the BUF in central London at the end of August 1939, just three days before the outbreak of war, was also ignored by anti-fascists. By this time, militant opposition to Mosley had effectively disappeared with political interest immersed in foreign events. The case of violent opposition to fascists in Wilmslow, in November 1939, when two double-decker motorbuses carrying fascists from a meeting were stoned, now proved exceptional.[137] Indeed, the signing of the Nazi–Soviet pact in August 1939 led to an improbable transformation of CPGB policy in which anti-fascism was opportunistically discarded in order to accommodate the dictates of Soviet foreign policy. As a consequence of the Soviet Union's alliance with Nazi Germany, the CPGB underwent an about-turn and its hostility to fascism was briefly replaced by 'anti-imperialism'. This expedient new line not surprisingly provoked division within the CPGB with many of the more committed anti-fascists, especially those who had fought in Spain, leaving the party.[138]

As the CPGB endeavoured to adapt itself to the meanderings of Soviet foreign policy, the anti-fascist side of the state reasserted itself, albeit under exceptional circumstances. This came in the spring of 1940 in response to the end of the 'phoney war' and a 'fifth column' scare in which the BUF became widely perceived as a threat to national security. This scare stirred anti-fascist passions amongst the public and Mosley was physically assaulted (yet again) at a by-election in North Manchester in May 1940. More significantly, the state acted decisively against Mosley's fascists and smothered its organisation: existing Defence Regulations were amended so that fascists could be interned under defence regulation 18B and, along with internment, the BUF was proscribed and its publications banned. Altogether, some 750 BUF members were interned from a party membership estimated to now number 8,700. Identification of those interned originated from both the state's security services which had subjected the BUF to surveillance from late 1933, and from intelligence gathered by the Board of

Deputies. The Board had apparently placed a 'mole' inside the BUF, known as 'Captain X'.[139] This infiltration reflected a shifting analysis on the part of the Board, which finally declared its opposition to fascism as a result of the outbreak of war and pressure from the *Jewish Chronicle*.[140]

Although the state forced the collapse of British fascism in 1940, domestic fascism was not completely eradicated. As the threat of invasion and the fifth columnist scare abated, most internees were released and soon looked towards resuming activities albeit hampered by the continuing imprisonment of Mosley and other leading fascists. A key factor behind Mosley's prolonged imprisonment was the make-up of the wartime coalition – its Labour component in particular was strongly opposed to Mosley's fascist ideas and believed that his release would damage civilian morale. Therefore, it was not until November 1943 that the decision was made to release him. This decision was taken partly on humanitarian grounds – Mosley was allegedly ill – and partly because the government wanted to avoid Mosley becoming a martyr for British fascism. Nevertheless, the decision to release him met an outburst of popular opposition, orchestrated in the main by the Communist Party which had returned to the anti-fascist fore following the Nazi attack on the Soviet Union in June 1941.

But the CPGB's reversion to actively opposing British fascism actually pre-dated Mosley's release. In October 1942, the *Daily Worker* became preoccupied with the British National Party led by ex-BUF member Edward Godfrey. This organisation, created in August 1942, served as a focal point for ex-18B detainees based in London. According to figures provided by the Home Secretary, it only had around 100 members and was therefore numerically minuscule. But, in order to reassert its anti-fascist credentials, the Communist Party deliberately overstated the extent to which the BNP constituted a serious threat. Thus, as Douglas Hyde, the *Daily Worker's* anti-fascist correspondent, maintains in his autobiography, the CPGB's anti-fascist campaign was deliberately resumed 'for our own political ends'.[141] In early 1943, the CPGB's campaign against the British National Party culminated in a large open air meeting at Lincoln's Inn Fields in London. This meeting called on the Home Secretary, Herbert Morrison, to close down the British National Party and it subsequently disbanded in April 1943.

Then, towards the end of 1943, advance notice of Mosley's impending release reached the CPGB through a sympathiser at the Home Office and this enabled the Communist Party to raise immediate objections. The CPGB organised two large protest marches, one of which attracted a crowd numbering some 30,000 people. Hundreds of thousands of people signed mass petitions and strikes in war industries were threatened.[142] Protest was also forthcoming from the National Council of Labour, which endeavoured to dissociate itself from the action of the government. Indeed, the Labour Party split over the issue, with 51 Labour MPs voting in favour of keeping Mosley in prison. Hostility was especially marked in the East End where many rank-and-file Labourites turned to the Communist Party to register disapproval and during this time, the Stepney Branch became the strongest Communist Party branch in Britain with over 1,000 members.[143] The National Jewish Committee of the CPGB, which had been established in April 1943, used the Mosley affair to appeal directly to Jews in the East End. The role of the Communist Party in opposing Mosley's release was presented as part of a long tradition of active anti-fascist protest dating back to the 1930s. This theme was stressed in Communist Party campaign literature in the East End during the 1945 general election, undoubtedly contributing to Phil Piratin's subsequent election as MP for Mile End, a constituency in which one third of the electorate was Jewish.[144]

Aside from the Communist Party, the NCCL also continued campaigning against domestic fascism during the war years. In April 1943, the NCCL had convened a conference in London attended by some 450 delegates from 273 organisations. The aim of this conference was to organise a nationwide campaign against fascism and anti-Semitism with education presented as the key to combating fascism and anti-Semitism. The NCCL called on all democratic organisations to assist by holding meetings and discussion groups, by writing articles for journals and by pressing on authorities the need for legislation banning anti-Semitism.[145] However, the problem with the NCCL's educative strategy, as Kushner points out, was that discussion merely provided opportunity to repeat anti-Semitic charges and this tended to increase 'Jew-consciousness'. Furthermore, the underlying premise that all anti-Semitism was the result of fascist activity failed to counter anti-Semitism as a native cultural tradition.[146] Interestingly, despite casting itself as the champion of civil liberties, the NCCL also joined the Communist Party in voicing popular protest at the release of Mosley from internment. This decision was met with indignation from many of the NCCL's more liberal supporters and prompted a wave of resignations from those who insisted that Mosley should not remain in prison without a fair trial.

Although it attracted widespread support, the campaign to re-intern Mosley eventually ran out of steam. Mosley subsequently retired to the country and, as a condition of his release, disengaged from political activity for the rest of the war. But even in his continued absence, surrogate attempts were made by ex-18B internees to revive Mosleyite fascism. During 1944, these activities were centred on two organisations. The first, a registered charity known as the 18B Detainees' Aid Fund, the second, the British League of Ex-Servicemen, led by former BUF member Jeffrey Hamm. Both organisations attempted to hold meetings in Hyde Park in 1944 but found themselves opposed by hostile crowds. Towards the end of 1945, those who remained loyal to Mosley were instructed to form a network of discussion groups, book clubs and ostensibly 'non-fascist' organisations in order to prepare the ground for Mosley's come-back. The most active of these proved to be Hamm's British League of Ex-Servicemen, which returned to East London immediately after the war and sparked the beginnings of postwar anti-fascism, discussed in the chapter that follows.

Clearly, from the foregoing, opposition to domestic fascism did not end in 1938 but was sustained after Bermondsey and was carried into the war years even if the scale of activity was less than the peak of 1936–7 when the BUF's anti-Semitic campaign drew thousands of people into the displays of anti-fascist opposition. As shows of strength, the anti-fascist agitation on 4 October 1936 stands out, although other mobilisations, such as Holbeck Moor and Bermondsey, also leave an impression. In numerical terms, popular anti-fascism in 1936–7 was certainly as significant as 1934, but after 1935 it became qualitatively different. With the BUF's turn to hardline anti-Semitism, opposition to Mosley's fascists widened beyond radical-Left groups to embrace specific Jewish groups in a broad Jewish–Communist alliance. This was most evident in the East End, where it seems reasonable to speak of an anti-fascist 'movement' loosely structured on co-operation between various organisations and defined in terms of active opposition to fascism, and hence hostility to the perceived passivity of both the Labour Party and the Board of Deputies.

Although united by antagonism towards fascism, this anti-fascist alliance was not immune to its own divisions. These were apparent, especially within the Communist Party, which experienced conflict as militants increasingly turned to violent action, a strategy at odds with the leadership's yearning for closer relations with the Labour Party. The CPGB was keen to distance itself from the disreputable activities of its militants, but at the same time it wished to retain the growing local support that opposition to fascism attracted. Therefore, it was mainly through pressure from local militants that the CPGB remained at the forefront of the struggle against Mosleyite fascism. Moreover, it managed to lead this agitation, as it had done in the early 1930s, without central co-ordination. Consequently, anti-fascist activity from 1936 continued to be determined largely at the local level and this allowed community action to emerge as an alternative anti-fascist strategy in the East End. The period from 1936 also shows that anti-fascism was not the monopoly of non-governmental groups and that it did have a state dimension. The Labour Party's anti-fascist policy which looked to the state to legislate against fascism brought results through the Public Order Act even if its impact on the BUF has been overstated. None the less, by appealing to the state and enthusiastically supporting the POA, the Labour Party reinforced liberal-democratic legality and contributed to the cultural exclusion of political violence and extremism.

Compared with the early 1930s, the effectiveness of popular anti-fascism in the latter half of the 1930s is more difficult to ascertain. In the early 1930s, the BUF had been denied legitimacy by anti-fascists at Olympia, and with the loss of Rothermere's support, Mosley turned towards militant anti-Semitism. Thus, anti-fascists, as Skidelsky rather ironically puts it, 'kept Mosley in business as a fascist'.[147] Yet by adopting virulent anti-Semitism, Mosley reinforced identification with Hitler and confined himself to the realm of the disrespectable political fringe where anti-fascists helped to create public order problems which public opinion attributed to fascist provocation. This reinforced negative perceptions already held by the public that associated Mosley's fascists with lawlessness, violence and extremism. In this way, militant anti-fascists ensured that Mosley remained outside the political mainstream with his base of support contained to areas such as the East End where there was already a cultural tradition of anti-Semitism. This anti-Semitism was, therefore, as Skidelsky reflects, the price that was paid for keeping British fascism confined.[148]

Within the East End itself, it is even more difficult to arrive at a verdict on the impact of anti-fascist activities. In raising anti-fascist consciousness, one would have assumed that agitation against Mosley would have generally acted as a 'check' on the growth of the BUF, but as the example of Cable Street shows, mass action against fascism could also stimulate fascist recruitment. And yet this effect was paralleled by anti-fascism drawing in more Jewish support for the Communist Party. A situation emerged in East London during 1936–7 whereby the greater the involvement of Jews in anti-fascist protest the greater the impact of the BUF's anti-Semitic propaganda on reservoirs of potential fascist support. Given the recurring interaction between fascist provocation and anti-fascist response, ignoring fascism as the Labour Party and Board of Deputies advised clearly offered one way of breaking this cycle.[149] Another approach was community action and certainly Piratin's account suggests that this was more effective in terms of eroding support for fascism than direct forms of anti-fascist protest. But at the same time, we do well not to forget the importance of national and international developments. Between 1938 and 1939, the BUF's policy of pro-German pacifism also served to check fascism's progress amongst working-class patriots in its traditional East End fiefdoms. Finally, it is worth bearing in mind that organised anti-fascism did little to counter the attraction of Mosley's anti-war policy to more middle-class groups outside these East End strongholds amongst whom, briefly, the BUF regained ground at the end of the 1930s.

3
'Never Again!':
Anti-Fascism, 1946–66

I

The human and material cost of the Second World War alongside revelations of the Holocaust and other Nazi atrocities ensured that in the postwar world fascism was universally regarded as an evil obscenity, a doctrine of brutality, destruction, intolerance and genocide. More specifically, in Britain, anti-fascist attitudes became central to constructions of national identity, with animosity towards Nazi Germany and the heroic struggle against Hitler functioning as major sources of national loyalty and patriotic pride.[1] Significantly, this fusion of anti-fascism with nationalism reinforced perceptions, dating from the inter-war period, that fascism was essentially an alien creed inimical to British culture and traditions. Whereas the British were 'liberal', 'tolerant' and 'decent', fascists were 'foreign' and 'intolerant', 'fanatics' who were intent on the physical extermination of Jewry. From this angle, fascism was viewed as an abhorrent foreign ideology that was incapable of ever taking root in British society. The failure of Mosley in the 1930s appeared to provide further confirmation that fascism was indeed antithetical to British cultural values. Therefore, it was widely assumed that given these conditions, fascist activity in postwar Britain could be safely ignored. In short, fascism was a thoroughly shameful 'foreign import', a futile effort destined for political failure.

Not everyone, however, subscribed to popular belief that the threat of fascism in Britain ceased to exist. One contemporary challenge to the pervasive view came from Frederic Mullally, an anti-fascist journalist.[2] Although Mullally admitted that popular hostility towards fascism made a resurgence of a movement operating under a distinct fascist label improbable, he still warned against complacency. Mullally contended that the residual appeal of fascism lay in various aspects of fascist doctrine, particularly anti-Semitism and anti-socialism. Moreover, because an 'important minority' within British society was receptive to these ideological concerns and thus sympathetic to fascism 'without knowing it', the danger was 'in the emergence of a new political force preaching an out-and-out fascist doctrine with a new label'.[3] Mullally pointed to the existence of groups such as the British League of Ex-Servicemen as examples of fascist or 'crypto-fascist' activity, but his real concern was the possible re-emergence of the British Union of Fascists under a new name, attracting a middle-class clientele disillusioned by the electoral defeat of the Conservative Party and uniting around militant nationalism. The underlying message from Mullally and repeated by postwar anti-fascists ever since was that Britain did not possess intrinsic immunity to fascism. Therefore anti-fascists should be continually 'on guard' against the fascist menace and not bury their heads, to borrow Mullally's words, 'deep in the sands of complacency'.[4]

Mullally was not alone in challenging the received view that a revival of fascism could not happen in Britain. The possibility of a postwar fascist recovery was recognised even earlier by the Association of Jewish Ex-Servicemen (AJEX),[5] which had taken immediate steps to counter the reappearance of open air fascist meetings in London in the autumn of 1945. Under the guidance of Lionel Rose, a team of between 12 and 20 AJEX speakers held regular meetings at fascist pitches in Hyde Park, Bethnal Green and Dalston, where they argued against both anti-Semitism and fascism, endeavouring to draw attention to the incipient activities of former members of the British Union of Fascists, who through ostensibly 'non-fascist' organisations such as Hamm's British League of Ex-Servicemen were preparing the ground for Mosley's return. Working under the auspices of the Board of Deputies, AJEX assumed the role that it had undertaken in the 1930s. One notable difference, however, was that AJEX now openly attacked fascism. This line was endorsed by the Board of Deputies, which had, in response to the Holocaust, irrevocably discarded its pre-war policy of isolating anti-Semitism from fascism.

The place of AJEX at the very beginnings of the history of postwar anti-fascism has already been recognised by Morris Beckman who additionally notes that the first physical confrontation between fascists and anti-fascists after the war took place in November 1945 following AJEX's occupation of the fascist pitch at Hereford Street in Bethnal Green.[6] Besides heralding the return of fascist/anti-fascist violence to the old battleground of the East End, this episode also engendered disquiet within the Board of Deputies, who viewed the re-emergence of physical confrontations between fascists and Jewish anti-fascists disapprovingly. The Board had one eye on events in Palestine where the British were contending with violent Jewish oppo-sition to the Mandate and feared that militant anti-fascism would provide additional material for anti-Semites intent on stirring up anti-Jewish feeling in Britain. Moreover, because of its position within the Establishment, the Board found itself unable to condone any illegal anti-fascist activity. It therefore urged caution and impressed on AJEX the need to keep strictly within the letter of the law.

Not surprisingly, the Board's insistence on Jewish restraint gave rise to hostility and frustration from those Jewish ex-servicemen who, outraged by images of concentration camp victims, felt that maximum disruption of fascist activities through physical means was the only effective way of ensuring that fascist atrocities never happened again. There was also irritation at the Board's position on Palestine, with many Jewish ex-servicemen more concerned with stopping fascism than with events in the Middle East. The message from the Board was 'don't make waves', but as Beckman recalls, British Jewry, 'especially the ex-servicemen amongst them, were of a different metal to the community of the pre-war days. The keep-your-head-down and get-indoors-quickly mentality had gone for good'.[7] Once again, the emotive issue of fascism brought divisions to Anglo-Jewry and in a throwback to the 1930s, Jewish militants resumed their attacks on the Jewish communal leadership for its perceived failure to resist fascist provocation 'on the streets' where, by the beginning of 1946 a host of fascist grouplets were now operating, concentrated on London.

Following a spontaneous assault by four Jewish anti-fascists on a British League of Ex-Servicemen platform at Hampstead Heath in London in February 1946, a meeting was convened at Maccabi House, a Jewish community centre in West Hampstead. Here it was decided to form a radical anti-fascist organisation, independent of the Board of Deputies, which was prepared to turn its back on the Board and meet the fascists head-on. This organisation, which was in essence an offshoot of AJEX, was subsequently named the '43 Group', so-called after the number of people who attended the founding meeting. It styled itself 'non-political', that is exclusively anti-fascist with no political affiliation. Beckman, a founder member of the 43 Group, stressed that the Group had 'tunnel vision' as far as defeating fascists was concerned and accordingly there were 'no politics' inside the

Group.[8] The priority was defending the Jewish community against fascism, but a CPGB cell did operate beneath the surface which, far from threatening the dynamism of the 43 Group, actually endeavoured to provide a lead. This cell was organised by Len Rolnick, a close associate of Harry Pollitt.[9]

From its inception, the 43 Group proposed to destroy fascism by overwhelming the newly emerging fascist groups with hard physical opposition. The primary objective was to 'out-violence' the fascists and thereby deliver a knockout blow to fascism's postwar revival. Although clearly located within the militant tradition of anti-fascism, this faith in physical confrontation was not all-consuming as additional aims were also professed. For instance, the 43 Group looked to exert pressure on the government to introduce legislation making incitement to racial hatred illegal.[10] From the outset, the 43 Group declared a willingness to co-operate with all other bodies combating fascism and anti-Semitism and indeed, the 43 Group's first action was a joint operation with Communists. This involved the successful disruption of a fascist rally held at the Albert Hall in March 1946 by the British Vigilantes' Action League led by former BUF activist John Preen. After just 30 minutes the meeting was closed when anti-fascists attempted to storm the platform. The British Vigilantes' Action League failed to recover from this inauspicious episode and quickly fell into obscurity.

By the end of April 1946, the 43 Group had enlisted over 300 ex-servicemen. Not surprisingly, considering the group's roots, the new recruits were overwhelmingly Jewish.[11] As the 43 Group drew in yet more activists, attention focused on organisational development whereupon the wartime experience of ex-servicemen was used to structure the group along quasi-military lines. At the apex was a controlling committee, later to become a national executive committee, headed by a joint chairmanship of Gerry Flamberg, a former paratrooper who had served in Arnhem, and Jeffrey Bernerd. Flamberg took on responsibility for 'field operations' and led a strong-arm force of some 300 ex-servicemen, divided by area into a number of London units. Tactically, the 43 Group looked to force the closure of fascist meetings through maximum physical disruption. The key was to turn over the fascist platform; if this was not possible because of the number of stewards or police, then it was anticipated that fighting amongst the audience should be sufficient to close meetings. In turn, these field operations were co-ordinated through a headquarters established in Bayswater Road in central London which was separated into a number of departments, the largest being Security and Intelligence. This monitored fascist activity, maintained a network of 'Aryan-looking' infiltrators, and supplied information to the front-line 'commando teams'. Financially, the group was supported from within the Jewish community and could count Bud Flanagan, from the 'Crazy Gang', and Jack Sullivan, the boxing promoter, amongst its regular contributors.[12] However, there are suggestions that group funds were misappropriated. As one former activist recollects:

> We who began the movement were genuine with good intentions, but it finished up as a business, a lousy business. Though rich and influential Jews were supporting us with funds, we never got our expenses. The money that was coming into the coffers was not accounted for.[13]

According to Beckman, Jewish militants were attacking between six and ten fascist meetings a week in London by mid-1946, with two-thirds of these brought to a premature conclusion. At the same time, other group members concentrated on preventing the dissemination of fascist literature by intimidating fascist newsvendors (and in due course, raiding fascist bookshops).[14] Although Beckman claims that the 43 Group was successful in stopping the resurrection of early postwar fascism – 'Our relentless non-stop attacks, where we deliberately out-violenced them, is what really beat them'[15] – in the short term the 43 Group possibly added fuel to the fire by bringing about radicalisation in the fascist ranks. Beckman himself noted that during the autumn of 1946 fascist meetings were not being tamed; quite the contrary, they were becoming 'more overtly pro-Mosley, anti-democratic and anti-Semitic'.[16] Admittedly, if we put Beckman's observations to one side, the evidence for fascist radicalisation on account of the 43 Group's actions is rather thin. None the less, what clearly emerges is that violent disruption by the 43 Group did not put an instant end to the fascist 'street' presence. That said, the violence occasioned by the 43 Group's tactics did attract negative press publicity for British fascism. Mullally was one of the first journalists to draw attention to the activities of the British League of Ex-Servicemen, having sounded the alarm from the pages of the *Sunday Pictorial* in October 1946 in an article entitled the 'New Fascist Menace'.[17]

As the 43 Group initiated a physical response to fascism, other bodies pursued an alternative route whereby attempts were made to use institutional channels in order to try to convince the Labour government of the need to legislate against fascism. The main groups first involved in organising more formal protest were the NCCL, the Haldane Society (an organisation of Socialist Lawyers) and the Legal and Judicial Group of the Parliamentary Labour Party. The leading figure in this campaign was the left-wing lawyer D. N. Pritt MP, an active member of the NCCL and formerly associated with the Co-ordinating Committee for Anti-Fascist Activities in the 1930s. In a call to build pressure, Pritt addressed a large meeting held under the auspices of the NCCL at Kingsway Hall in London in March 1946, having already drafted a Bill in 1943 intended to outlaw fascist activities which was subsequently adopted by the Haldane Society and the Legal and Judicial Group of the Parliamentary Labour Party as the basis for legislation.[18] But despite attracting support for a ban from many trade unions and trades councils, the response of the new Labour government was that legislation against fascism was impractical because 'fascism' was too hard to define and organisations would simply alter their programme so as to fall outside the scope of definition. As in the 1930s there was also concern that such legislation threatened freedom of speech. The Labour government felt that it already possessed significant power to combat fascism through the Public Order Act and that, in any case, quite rightly, it believed that the threat of fascism was exaggerated. In April 1946, despite early indications that the new government was considering legislation to deal with fascism, a Cabinet Committee on fascism decided that new legislation was not desirable or necessary. There were attempts by both backbench Labour MPs, such as Ashley Brammall, and ordinary Labour Party members to change this policy, and over the period 1947–9, a number of Labour Party branches did call on the Home Secretary, Chuter Ede, to impose a ban on fascism. Yet this was all to no avail. For its detractors, the Labour government had gone 'soft' on fascism; for Ede, the scale of the fascist threat never warranted any additional measures. In defence of the Home Secretary, clearly fascism was now discredited and disgraced – the possibility of its attaining the support of more than the smallest minority of British society was highly improbable.

II

Intent on seeking advantage from both the volatile situation in Palestine and from austere domestic economic conditions, fascist activity increased significantly in 1947. This activity peaked in mid-1947, following the murder in Palestine of two British soldiers by Jewish terrorists at the end of July. This provided the spark for anti-Semitic rioting in Liverpool, Manchester and Glasgow.[19] Official sources confirm that these riots were not the work of organised fascists, although fascist groups certainly looked to capitalise on this outburst of anti-Semitic feeling. Fascist agitation was not directed towards those areas that witnessed the worst anti-Jewish violence, but towards London, in particular Ridley Road, Dalston, in the district of Hackney on the north-eastern surrounds of the East End. Here, the British League of Ex-Servicemen held regular outdoor meetings during 1947. Audiences grew steadily from 300 or so in April to nearly 3,000 by early October, with Ridley Road soon achieving notoriety for almost weekly 'riots' between fascists and their opponents. Other main pitches used by the British League of Ex-Servicemen in London included Hereford Street in Bethnal Green, Gore Road in Victoria Park and Rushcroft Road in Brixton. Elsewhere in London, the Union for British Freedom, led by former BUF member Victor Burgess, held regular meetings at Trebovir Road, Earl's Court and Pembridge Villas in Notting Hill. Linked to this organisation was John Webster's British Workers' Party for National Unity which was a provincial 'limb' of the Union for British Freedom based in Bristol. This held meetings at Durdham Downs, attracting audiences which at times numbered over 1,000 people.[20]

The upsurge in fascist activities in 1947 prompted the Communist Party, the first organisation to recognise the menace of fascism in the inter-war period and widely seen as its most determined opponent, to publish a pamphlet, *The Fascist Threat to Britain*, authored by the future eminent historian E. P. Thompson. The CPGB's militant tradition of fighting fascism was invoked by Thompson but in fact, this statement of policy marks the end of the gradual evolution of the CPGB's anti-fascism away from radical action. Rather than calling for 'barricades in the streets', the CPGB's anti-fascist strategy was confined entirely to an appeal for a state ban on fascism. It seems likely that the decisive action taken by the state against domestic fascism during the war had left no doubt within the CPGB leadership that a non-confrontational policy towards fascism was the most appropriate. But this cautious postwar policy should also be read in terms of the Communist Party's pre-Cold War strategy of enthusiastically supporting the Labour government and bidding for influence within the moderate labour movement. This overarching objective meant that CPGB leaders officially discouraged any anti-fascist activity likely to give the Communist Party a bad name. By demanding a state ban on fascism, the Communist Party's anti-fascist policy in 1947 was thus far removed from the CPGB's ultra-Left analysis of the early to mid-1930s when fascism had, of course, been synonymous with the capitalist state.

For anti-fascist activists on the radical Left, the recommendations of CPGB leaders must have made for depressing reading. In communications from the Communist Party's Propaganda Department, dated 7 August 1947, CPGB speakers were instructed to demand a government ban on fascist meetings, publications and organisations, imprisonment for those inciting racial hatred and perhaps most revealingly, 'police action to maintain order and democracy'.[21] Significantly, there was no call for militant direct action; if fascists came into a locality all that the 'radical' CPGB suggested was organising a local petition of protest to the Home Secretary, urging the local Borough Council, trade union or democratic political organisation to send a resolution to the prime minister, and writing personally and in groups to the local MP to press for the matter to be taken up in the House of Commons.[22] But, as in the 1930s, the official line of the CPGB was disregarded by many of its rank and file. This is clear by the involvement of local Communists in street clashes between fascists and anti-fascists recorded in the 1947 survey by Rose. This identifies communist opposition on a number of occasions at Ridley Road, Hereford Street and also at Rushcroft Road in Brixton.[23]

At first, the CPGB had deemed the forced closure of fascist meetings to be 'quite a healthy thing', but as the size of fascist meetings and associated policing increased during 1947, the Party felt that participation of militant workers in disturbances had damaged the CPGB's public standing. It was felt that involvement of Communists in street confrontations, particularly at Ridley Road, had allowed the government 'to present to the public a picture of two rival factions – Fascists and Communists – both of which were a danger to the public peace'.[24] Accordingly, CPGB leaders proceeded to distance themselves from the communist cell inside the 43 Group. Len Rolnick recalls that Pollitt asked him to resign from the Party because the 43 Group's tactics were deemed too aggressive. Pollitt did not want the Party embarrassed by public disclosure of Jewish Communists arrested as a result of street confrontations with fascists.[25]

An alternative reading of what lay behind grassroots communist involvement in fascist/anti-fascist disturbances in East London during 1947 proposes that the key motivating factor for the Communist Party was electoral interest rather than deep-rooted opposition to fascism. A journalist, writing under the pseudonym Rebecca West, maintained that the disturbances between fascists and anti-fascists in the streets of Dalston and Bethnal Green were 'highly artificial', being 'cooked up' in order to catch either Jewish or anti-Jewish votes at a possible by-election. This claim rests on the case of David Weitzman, Jewish MP for the Stoke Newington constituency who in 1947 faced prosecution for black market offences. Had Weitzman been convicted, a by-election would have resulted in his constituency, immediately north of Hackney. In the event, Weitzman was convicted but was later acquitted on appeal. No by-election was held, and according to West, local Communists eventually lost interest.[26] There may, of course, be some element of truth in this account: a militant stance against fascism would certainly attract support from those who felt betrayed by the Labour government's apparent passivity, yet this neglects the wider perspective. As in the 1930s, the CPGB realised that communist involvement in disorder would merely isolate the Communist Party from the moderate labour movement and was therefore keen to prevent violent disturbances. Moreover, West's account also fails to appreciate the prominent role of the 43 Group which had no apparent interest in fighting by-elections, though presumably it did have an interest in ensuring the victory of a non-fascist candidate.[27]

In place of militant action, the leadership of the Communist Party advocated the organisation of 'popular front' pressure on a non-party basis. The aim behind this strategy was to unite all shades of democratic opinion into a powerful anti-fascist lobby which would press for existing laws to be strengthened in order to prevent the growth of fascism. The plan was to join forces with the NCCL and encourage the NCCL to draw in the support of democratic bodies at local levels. In Hackney, for instance, the CPGB alongside the local Labour, Conservative and Liberal Parties, Hackney Trades Council, various trade unions and the North London Jewish Defence Committee, sent delegate representatives to a meeting held by the National Council for Civil Liberties at Hackney Town Hall on 19 June 1947. At this delegate meeting it was decided to form a local Area Committee of the NCCL in order to plan a campaign against fascism and anti-Semitism.[28] This committee represented some 25 organisations, and under its auspices, the CPGB circulated a petition calling for the Mayor of Hackney to convene a Town's meeting. This followed in September 1947, whereupon it was proposed that an all-party deputation be sent to the Home Secretary with a petition calling for legislation to ban fascist activities and to make incitement to racial hatred illegal. A deputation was received by the Home Secretary in November 1947 when Ede was presented with a petition signed by 8,000 people, of which at least 6,300 were Hackney residents.[29] This deputation informed the Home Secretary of escalating fascist provocation but Ede again refused to act.

Pritt argues that there were two reasons for this passive response. The first was the Labour government's anti-communism which made it 'lukewarm' to any legislation that was openly supported by the Communist Party. The Labour government was stridently anti-communist, a feature reinforced by the onset of the Cold War, but the fact that the CPGB advocated a state ban on fascism was incidental to Labour's decision not to pass legislation against fascism. Instead, the Labour government's apparent 'inertia' can readily be explained by continuity of state policy. Thus Chuter Ede was merely following Home Office guidelines set in the 1930s when the Public Order Act was deemed to have 'done the trick' in circumstances much more conducive to fascism. If existing legislation had proved sufficient in the 1930s, then there was surely no need to restrict civil liberties further when public opinion had become so resolutely opposed to fascism.[30] Secondly, Pritt identified a pro-fascist bias in the Home Office and painted a picture of Ede blindly following the advice of 'reactionary' Home Office civil servants with Ede thereby giving his blessing to police action that 'favoured' and 'protected' fascists.[31]

In a re-run of the 1930s, anti-fascists once again claimed that police showed favouritism towards the fascist side and certainly on the face of it, this appeared the case. A recently published study by Renton has calculated that between April and October 1947 the police were almost three times more likely to arrest anti-fascists as they were fascists. The police were also frequently charged with deliberately keeping fascist meetings open even when a clear majority in the audience were anti-fascist and wanted the meeting closed.[32] But two points need to be considered here. The first is that the tactics of anti-fascists were aggressive and intentionally put fascists on the defensive. The second is that under the terms of the Public Order Act the police had sole responsibility for stewarding outdoor meetings (fascists were no longer responsible for their own self-defence). This meant that it was the responsibility of the police to ensure that public meetings were protected. Given these circumstances, it is not surprising that the police arrested more anti-fascists than fascists.

With the police so apparently biased, the belief that the state was peppered with pro-fascist sympathisers was strengthened in militant circles and this underlined the need for a radical 'fighting policy'.

Thus, the Communist Party, which appeared content to restrict itself to petitions against fascism, drew criticism from other leftist organisations. One group that disagreed with the CPGB's position was the Trotskyist Revolutionary Communist Party (RCP).[33] The RCP, which at the time had around 600 members,[34] appealed to the CPGB for a militant 'united front' against the fascists but like the Labour Party's response to the CPGB in the 1930s, calls for united action were rejected. Ted Grant of the RCP complained:

> Our appeals went unheeded … Instead of rallying to Ridley Road, as the Trotskyists did, the leaders of the Communist Party discouraged their members from gathering there and thus fell into the camp of the petty bourgeois moralists and reformists who said 'ignore them'.

Grant additionally noted that the official line of the CPGB was held in contempt by many in the CPGB's rank and file:

> Despite the cowardly policy of the leadership, many rank and file members of the CP and YCL continued to rally at Ridley Road together with members of the Revolutionary Communist Party and other organisations in a united front of protest.[35]

Akin to the ultra-Left analysis of the Communist Party in the 1930s, the RCP insisted that the main task of the labour movement was to educate the workers in the class nature of fascism and that a working-class 'united front' had to be constructed if workers were to be effectively mobilised against fascism. It also advocated the formation of a Workers' Defence Corps to defend working-class meetings as well as Jewish and other minorities from fascist provocation. The parallels with the Communist Party's anti-fascist policy in the inter-war period are obvious; on closer inspection, however, it becomes clear that RCP policy was moulded more from Trotsky's writings. Not only was Trotsky an early advocate of the 'united front', but he also encouraged the formation of workers' militia in the defence of working-class organisations against fascism.[36] Curiously, even though the RCP had attacked the postwar Communist Party for its 'reformism', the RCP also demanded state action against fascism. According to Grant, this could be effective if it was 'backed by determined organised activity on the part of the workers' even if, quite correctly, historical experience 'has shown us that it is not possible to legislate fascism out of existence'.[37]

Disagreements over anti-fascist strategy went further than the CPGB/RCP divide with some groups and individuals even favouring a strategy of open debate with fascists. For instance, the Commonwealth, a predominantly middle-class left-wing group formed in 1942, staged a debate with the British Workers' Party for National Unity in Bristol in July 1947 only to have its motion, 'That there is no case for discrimination against the Jewish race', defeated.[38] The following month, Frederic Mullally challenged the British League of Ex-Servicemen to a debate at Ridley Road, but was physically assaulted by a group of fascists before being rescued by the 43 Group and spirited to safety.[39] If taken as a guide to the effectiveness of this particular policy, these incidents do provide an object lesson of how not to defeat fascists: as one fascist renegade stressed, debating with fascists merely gave them an 'air of respectability'.[40] Naturally, the idea of debating with fascists on fascist platforms was anathema to the 43 Group. As one former activist so eloquently puts it, 'We didn't ask questions. We just moved into a thing, turned over the platform, gave a few Blackshirts a beating and kicked them up the arse.'[41]

By adopting this forceful approach, the 43 Group had succeeded in establishing itself as a leading player in the anti-fascist street opposition by mid-1947. A clear indication of the 43 Group's growing status was the successful launch of its own anti-fascist monthly, *On Guard*, in July 1947. According to Beckman, this served to reinforce the identity of the group by providing an 'overall picture of what they were part of'.[42] Yet it is noticeable that the paper never conveyed the reasons for the 43 Group's policy of militant anti-fascism. This was highlighted in an editorial from the final issue of *On Guard* published in December 1949, when the paper was heavily criticised for not assuming responsibility for presenting the 43 Group's case to the Jewish community.[43]

Rather than acting as the mouthpiece for radical Jewish anti-fascism, *On Guard* assumed a moderate, non-sectarian identity which was both educative and campaigning. The function of *On Guard* was to raise anti-fascist consciousness and unite all sections of the public against the menace of fascism. On the educative side, *On Guard* sought to expose fascism at home and abroad; on the campaigning side, it looked to bring about a state ban on fascism. In its first issue, it declared that its 'ultimate aim' was the criminalisation of all fascist and pro-fascist activity, 'to ensure that those things that happened in Germany will never, can never happen here'.[44] To this end, it claimed the support of figures such as D. N. Pritt, Frederic Mullally, the Labour MP Tom Driberg,[45] the Dean of Canterbury and the left-wing actress,

Dame Sybil Thorndike. Production of the paper was the responsibility of a team grouped around Jeffrey Bernerd, it also appears to have included Douglas Hyde, news editor of the *Daily Worker*.[46] As early as its third issue, *On Guard* boasted a 'ready sale' despite the postwar shortage of newsprint and the activities of fascist antagonists who were said to be pressing newsagents and bookshops not to sell the paper. One solution to this obstruction was found in street sales, although by September 1947, *On Guard* was claiming that due to public demand newsagents were beginning to stock the paper.[47] Sales may have been in the order of 5,000 per issue, though the paper itself complained that due to a limited paper quota, demand exceeded supply 'for at least twice the permitted number of copies'.[48]

The successful launch of *On Guard* convinced the Board of Deputies that the 43 Group had assumed a lasting presence. It was becoming increasingly clear that in terms of combating fascism and anti-Semitism, the 43 Group had set itself up as a credible alternative to both the Jewish Defence Committee and AJEX. Indeed by mid-1947, Beckman calculates that the 43 Group was bringing just over two-thirds of fascist meetings to a premature conclusion.[49] But these figures have to be treated with caution. The police presence at fascist meetings grew considerably over the period April to October 1947. At Ridley Road, for instance, on 27 April only eight policemen were present at a British League of Ex-Servicemen meeting. By 7 September, this number had increased to over 300 policemen. Elsewhere, at Hereford Street in Bethnal Green, on 8 June, 20 constables and a number of senior officers were in attendance, by 17 August there were 40–50 constables plus senior officers. Given the increasing numbers of police it is doubtful whether the 43 Group could have possibly closed down so many meetings. Of the 22 fascist meetings held at Ridley Road between 27 April and 26 October 1947, disorder ensued at around 50 per cent of meetings with opposition forcing the police to bring seven meetings to an early close. At Hereford Street, Bethnal Green, of the 22 meetings held between 30 March and 26 October 1947, only two meetings were closed by police.[50] These figures suggest that Beckman's calculations are somewhat exaggerated. Revealingly, Beckman admits that no records of operations were kept by the 43 Group.[51]

Even if its effectiveness has been somewhat overstated, the 43 Group's emerging presence against a backdrop of increasing conflict between fascists and anti-fascists, especially at Ridley Road, prompted the Board of Deputies to instruct the Jewish Defence Committee to call the 43 Group to order. The Board accused the 43 Group of tactical naiveté, declaring that militant anti-fascism was counterproductive, only serving to reward fascism with unnecessary publicity and new recruits. In this way, the 43 Group was said to be hindering defence work and was thus a disservice to the Jewish community. Therefore, in an attempt to put the brakes on anti-fascist militancy, the Board tried to submerge the 43 Group into the JDC. A verbal agreement was said to have been reached between the JDC and the 43 Group as early as July 1947 where it was agreed, *inter alia*, to bring the 43 Group into the Jewish Defence Committee and provide it with a voice in the formulation of official defence policy and planning.[52] Although hostile to the anti-fascist policy of the Board, the 43 Group hoped to turn the JDC into a more activist-oriented defence body. The negotiations broke down, however, with the major sticking point being the 43 Group's insistence that it should be given a 'major voice' in defence policy.[53] Understandably, the 43 Group rejected the offer of 'merger' fearing that it would be subsumed by the JDC and that in the absence of sufficient representation, the 'reactionaries' on the Board would put an immediate end to the 43 Group's radical policy.

Although the Board of Deputies was attacked within the Jewish community for its 'appeasement' of fascism, its policy was not, as its critics alleged, a woeful case of 'do-nothingness'. The fact that the Board eschewed physical confrontation with fascists certainly should not be taken as a contemptible failure to act. By this time, the Board had developed both short-term and long-term anti-fascist strategies predicated on countering ignorance through educative work. This was the underlying rationale for the open air platforms which provided the major focus of the Board's short-term policy. AJEX held as many as 138 meetings in 1947 with anti-fascist leaflets such as *This is Your Enemy*, *Look What's Crawling Out* and *Fascism again in 1947* widely distributed. In a letter to the *Jewish Chronicle*, published on 8 August 1947, Lionel Rose maintained that AJEX had held particularly successful meetings in Hyde Park, where predominantly non-Jewish audiences had 'at times' numbered over 1,000 and at Durdham Downs in Bristol where local fascist activity by the British Workers' Party for National Unity had been exposed by an AJEX speaker to an audience numbering over 4,000.[54] Needless to say, for certain members of the 43 Group, the work of AJEX was seen as a 'complete waste of time'.[55] Critics claimed that AJEX would often hold meetings in areas where they were guaranteed a predominantly Jewish audience and were thus preaching to the converted. Unintentionally, the Achilles' heel in AJEX's approach was identified in an official JDC newsletter when it was declared 'easier' to beat the fascists on their own ground when there was an 'intelligent audience'.[56] The implication: when the audience was comprised of 'ignorant fascists' the ability of the speaker to win over the audience necessarily diminished.

As for the Board's long-term plan of campaign, this was also under-pinned by education with the Board's Central Lecture Committee assuming a key role. Its function was to counter ignorance and preju-dice by presenting factual information about Jewry and Judaism to non-Jews through a series of lectures given to various organisations, from Rotary Clubs to Women's Guilds. It also sought to impress on educational authorities the importance of teaching children mutual understanding and goodwill.[57] A further aspect to the Board's anti-fascist work, frequently overlooked by its detractors, was 'high-level' deputations to the Home Secretary. These deputations detailed fascist activities and also supplied reports from observers that police were generally misadministering the Public Order Act at fascist meetings. The main complaint, which was additionally taken up by Pritt at the instigation of the South Kensington Labour Party, was that police were frequently taking the names and addresses of anti-fascist hecklers and giving them to the chairman of the fascist meeting. This practice allowed fascists to draw up a list of opponents who could then be assaulted at a later date and thus deterred all but the most committed of hecklers. It appears that the Board may have registered some success here as clearer directives were subsequently issued to police and observers recorded a distinct improvement. The Board also campaigned against the letting of municipal halls to fascists, but this was partly frustrated by the London County Council's decision, in the interests of freedom of speech, to allow schools to be used for private fascist meetings. Evidently, although the effects of the Board's anti-fascist policy do appear patchy, it is clear from this summary that it was not 'inactive' and the Board's work did cover a wide field. Nevertheless, because it was not geared towards rousing the Jewish community into direct action, it was understandably criticised by Jewish radicals and so stood accused of 'cowardice' and 'weakness'.

III

This criticism further hardened when, towards the end of 1947, new demands were placed on those engaged in the anti-fascist opposition. Mosley's decision to stage a political comeback, announced in

November 1947, marked a turning point in the anti-fascist struggle. His return to political activity, which was given organisational shape in February 1948 when the Union Movement was formally launched, raised the stakes with anti-fascists fully expecting that Mosley's return would inject a fresh impetus into British fascism. Mosley, 'The Leader', was clearly of different stature to 'small-time' demagogues such as Hamm, Burgess and Preen, and could inspire fanatical devotion in his followers.[58] Moreover, the formation of the Union Movement brought a new unity to British fascism which now coalesced in one organisation attracting an estimated 6,000–7,000 followers.[59] And, for those who had digested Mosley's recent work, *The Alternative* (1947), it was clear that Mosley was determined not to repeat the BUF's fascist policy and may well try to distance himself outwardly from fascism. Indeed, in a bid to make the Union Movement respectable, he made repeated pledges to democracy and adopted a political programme that replaced narrow-based ultra-nationalism with a new type of 'Europeanism'.[60]

At the outset, the Union Movement directed its energies towards areas that had already been subjected to postwar fascist activity. The launching pad in 1948 was intended to be a May Day rally from Dalston in Hackney through Highbury Corner to Camden Town in north London. However, this plan was thwarted by the Home Secretary. The state continued to monitor Mosley closely and a Special Branch investigation had concluded that violence in the East End was highly probable. This had been relayed to Ede who resorted to the Public Order Act in order to impose a three-month ban on all political processions through the East End. There had also been widespread opposition to Mosley's planned march from within the borough with local Labour Party leaders and the municipal authorities requesting that Ede take measures to prevent Mosley from speaking. In the event, Mosley was still permitted to stage a meeting in Dalston, but his supporters would have to make their way individually to Highbury Corner from where they could parade to Camden Town. Some 3,000 anti-fascists gathered to oppose Mosley, with the Communist Party playing a leading part in mobilising this opposition, 'circulating thousands of leaflets and doing loud speaker work in the back streets'. The willingness of the Communist Party to organise this demonstration appears to have been dependent on a show of popular opposition, and the CPGB was later pleased to report a 'wide anti-Fascist action involving trade unionists, Labour people, Commonwealth and liberals as well as Communists'.[61]

An estimated 1,500 fascists marched to Camden Town.[62] There were

32 arrests, the majority of whom were anti-fascists, including some 14 members of the 43 Group.[63] Significantly, Beckman's account of this day concludes that it was a washout for the Union Movement. But the failure of the May Day rally resulted less from the activities of militant anti-fascists who were prevented from mounting a Cable Street-type operation by a heavy police presence, but more from other factors, namely, the appearance and oratorical 'non-performance' of Mosley who now 'resembled nothing more than a middle-aged weary civilian, puffy of cheek and eye with a drooping shoulder ... the charismatic orations that once inflamed his supporters into ecstasies of loyalty had gone.'[64] New recruits were quickly disillusioned by Mosley's un-inspired display and, predictably, his Europeanist ideas failed to strike a responsive chord from the dyed-in-the-wool nationalists who formed much of the Union Movement's early following.

Three days later, the Home Office imposed a ban on political processions in the Metropolitan area which lasted for ten months and forced the Union Movement to re-think its strategy. With the Union Movement denied the opportunity to hold formal parades in London, attempts were made to establish a Union Movement presence in various provincial centres such as Brighton, Manchester, Leeds and Newcastle, but the impact was negligible. Of these, Brighton was probably the main centre of provincial fascist activity having been deliberately targeted due to its close proximity to London where the core of the Union Movement's membership was based. The decision by the Union Movement to stage a recruitment drive in Brighton triggered the formation of a local opposition group comprised of Jewish ex-servicemen. The key figure in this local anti-fascist opposition was Major David Spector of AJEX and the JDC who, objecting to the Board's policy of non-confrontation, now gravitated towards the 43 Group. Operating alongside 43 Group activists from London, local Jewish ex-servicemen attacked a Union Movement march in Brighton in June 1948. Fierce fighting resulted with the Union Movement's keynote speaker, Jeffrey Hamm, hospitalised. The aggressive nature of the anti-fascist offensive in Brighton, masterminded by Spector, appears to have been the decisive factor in ending the local fascist presence.[65]

In Manchester, fascist activity was also countered by local Jewish ex-servicemen. In March 1948, anti-fascists from the Manchester Union of Jewish Ex-Servicemen (MUJEX) formed part of a contingent that showered a fascist loudspeaker van with bricks resulting in injuries to the van's crew.[66] MUJEX claimed the support of over 1,000 members and, although it was supported financially by the JDC, it was independent of AJEX and in fact developed close relations with the 43 Group. In May 1948, for instance, MUJEX was represented at the 43 Group's Annual General Meeting.[67] Jewish ex-servicemen in Manchester also co-operated with local Communist Party activists who, despite official policy, still aspired to break fascist meetings up 'at all costs'.[68] Similarly at Leeds, the Jewish Ex-Servicemen's Association worked closely with local Communists. This Association had some 800 members of whom 20 were CPGB members. One Communist Party member sat on the Association's Executive Committee and used this position to propose that both organisations work together in order to prevent fascist meetings from taking place in the Leeds district. On 21 April 1948, around 100 Communists plus a similar number of Jewish ex-servicemen gathered at an outdoor fascist meeting in Leeds and this show of force led local fascists to abandon their meeting.[69] The Jewish Ex-Servicemen's Association in Leeds additionally established contacts with the 43 Group and attended the 43 Group's AGM in 1948. Also present at this AGM were Jewish ex-servicemen from Tyneside where a local branch of the 43 Group was formed under the leadership of Geoff Rossman, an anti-fascist activist from the 1930s. This was said to have had a waiting list of over 200 people ready to engage in anti-fascist activity.[70]

The return of Mosley, the launch of the Union Movement and the links that the 43 Group were establishing with Jewish ex-servicemen in provincial centres such as Brighton, Newcastle, Manchester and Leeds provided militant anti-fascism with fresh momentum during 1948. The prospect of a radical Jewish anti-fascist front was now being discussed.[71] By this stage, local residents would also frequently petition the 43 Group 'to come to their district and drive the Fascists out' in areas where fascists were holding meetings.[72] These developments heightened perceptions within the Board that the JDC was being outdistanced by the 43 Group, a view additionally reinforced by the 43 Group's decision to hold joint open air meetings with the newly formed National Anti-Fascist League (NAFL). Despite its name, this was not a national organisation but essentially a small band of fascist renegades grouped around the former branch organiser of the Union Movement in Birmingham, Michael McLean.[73] Formed in July 1948, it was a non-party and non-sectarian organisation whose aim was to 'sincerely fight the bestiality of Fascism' by speaking to the general public through organised meetings. With a view to securing invitations to speak, it distributed 'underground propaganda' in left-wing organisations, the mainstream political parties and Catholic bodies (the majority of the League's members being Catholic). McLean's report on the NAFL, dated October 1948, recorded invitations to speak from a number of organisations around McLean's base in the Midlands, such as the Birmingam branch of the Peace Pledge Union, the Wallsall branch of the Co-operative Society, Leicester Catholic Action, and from the student body of Nelson Hall Teachers' College in Stafford.[74]

Although the League rejected the 'hooligan methods' of militant anti-fascism, it was prepared to work alongside the 43 Group on open air platforms. These attracted substantial crowds and probably diverted attention away from the work of AJEX.[75] Certainly the 43 Group's decision to stage outdoor meetings encroached on AJEX territory. Moreover, the Board was becoming increasingly conscious of the fact that *On Guard* was developing into an effective source of anti-fascist propaganda particularly following its disclosure that the Union Movement was planning to distribute a German language newspaper in West Germany. This story was subsequently reported in the main-stream press in September 1948, followed by further revelations in *On Guard* that Mosley planned to establish the headquarters of an international fascist organisation on Jersey in the Channel Islands. Collectively, these developments served to fuel further criticism that the Jewish Defence Committee was doing nothing to counter fascism. In particular, the JDC was incensed by the publicity the 43 Group secured with its story of the German language newspaper since the Defence Committee had obtained a copy of this newssheet through an advertisement in the Union Movement's newspaper and had already forwarded it to the authorities.

Therefore, in a bid to recover lost ground and curb anti-fascist militancy, the JDC decided to write to the Anglo-Jewish press to put the case against the 43 Group's policy, to issue its own anti-fascist newspaper and to make a renewed attempt at bringing the 43 Group into the orbit of the JDC's official defence machinery.[76] In further negotiations between the JDC and the 43 Group, it emerges that Jeffrey Bernerd was offered a post on the JDC, which he accepted provided that he was given a minimum three-year contract at £1,750 and was made responsible for the all the JDC's 'outside activity'.[77] Not surprisingly, these conditions proved unacceptable to the JDC and negotiations once again foundered. Then, in January 1949, the JDC redoubled its efforts to rein in the 43 Group's radicals. This time an appeal was made to provincial Jewish ex-servicemen's organisations publicly to oppose the 43 Group. A meeting between the JDC and MUJEX took place at the Kedessia Restaurant, New Oxford Street in London on 30 January 1949 where it was agreed that the JDC would send a formal communication to AJEX, MUJEX and the Leeds Jewish Ex-Servicemen's Association in order to arrange a conference to which the 43 Group would be invited. The idea was to use this conference in order to force the 43 Group to disband and merge with the JDC. Despite its previous association with the 43 Group, MUJEX apparently agreed to this plan.[78] Shortly afterwards, having been attacked by the *Jewish Chronicle* for its inability to restrain the 43 Group's 'youthful hotheads' in light of events at Mosley's meeting at Kensington Town Hall on 31 January 1949, the Jewish Defence Committee found itself under yet further pressure 'to do something' about the 43 Group.[79]

In the approach to Mosley's Kensington meeting, the JDC and AJEX had looked to persuade the local Conservative council to revoke its decision to allow Mosley to use the town hall to stage an event intended to give the Union Movement a new lease of life. The 43 Group, on the other hand, decided to organise a counter-demonstration on the day of the meeting. An estimated 3,000 people joined this demonstration, described by *On Guard* as the 'biggest' and 'most dramatic' since the 1930s. Inside Kensington Town Hall, Mosley's meeting was reduced to a 'fiasco' when anti-fascists exploded tear gas bombs.[80] Unsurprisingly, the actions of Jewish radicals drew immediate criticism from the Jewish communal leadership, who maintained that Mosley's meeting would not have received any publicity had it not been for the antics of anti-fascist militants. None the less, the publicity which these events attracted did reawaken opposition to Mosley within the wider community. A 200-strong Union Movement march from Ridley Road to West Green in Tottenham in March 1949 was opposed by a reported 5,000 people. At various points along the route, 43 Group activists attacked the procession but it was noticeable that Tottenham Labour Party, various trade unions and the Liberal Party also joined the protest.[81] Disorder at this march led Ede to re-impose a temporary ban on political processions and by doing so prohibited a proposed May Day procession by the Union Movement.[82]

By this time, however, support for the Union Movement had dwindled to a hard core. With the war in Palestine over and worn down by the external pressures of anti-fascist opposition, levels of fascist activity declined sharply in 1949 and by the end of the year had ground to a halt. The Union Movement had been established with high expectations; it now found itself in a state of indeterminacy. Mosley indicated his desire to withdraw from the foreground and subsequently departed to Ireland in 1951 leaving the Union Movement to 'tick over' in the hands of his most faithful lieutenants. Following earlier patterns, the decline in fascist activity had a reciprocal effect on anti-fascism. Beckman records that by the autumn of 1949, the 43 Group 'was shedding members like a tree sheds leaves in a gale'.[83] This haemorrhage of Group members also coincided with a painful course of internal conflict with the previously non-sectarian *On Guard* now giving vent to the rift between the 43 Group and the JDC. In December 1949, *On Guard* vociferously attacked the 'ultra-conservatives' of the Jewish communal leadership and astonishingly maintained that by attacking militant anti-fascism, the representatives of British Jewry were 'prepared to join in political attitudes which take them right to the door of fascism'.[84] Yet this was to be the last gasp of a dying animal. Anti-fascist militancy had derived its strength from the perceived menace of fascism but by 1950, the threat of fascism had clearly receded. No further issues of *On Guard* appeared; the Group was also suffering from precarious finances.[85] Finally, in 1950, the 43 Group assured the JDC that it was ready to disband and it came into the official defence machinery, eventually joining forces with AJEX.[86]

Were the activities of militant anti-fascists responsible for thwarting attempts to resurrect fascism in early postwar Britain? Undoubtedly, the operational capacity of various pro-Mosley bodies was curtailed. Meetings were frequently disrupted either through organised heckling or through violent opposition. Nevertheless, given the scale of policing from mid-1947 onwards, the claim made by Beckman that over the course of four years the 43 Group closed down 85 per cent of fascist meetings appears improbable.[87] It may well have been true, for instance, that what brought fascist meetings to an end at Ridley Road was not the venom of the anti-fascist opposition but the severe winter of 1947–8.[88] But perhaps the most accurate picture of the effectiveness of the 43 Group is that provided from reports received from Group spies which left no doubt that over time fascists became increasingly nervous of 43 Group activists.[89] This certainly appears to have been the case by January 1949 when the determination by fascists to continue with street activities appears to have evaporated altogether.[90] Aside from restricting operational capacities, the violent methods employed by militant anti-fascists also encouraged confrontational disorder which provided little basis for the respectability that fascism so desperately needed. Thus Jeffrey Hamm's insistence that the 'Battle of Ridley Road' had been 'fought and won' by his side[91] overlooks the fact that in terms of stemming wider support for fascism, violent street confrontations merely served to reinforce negative perceptions of fascism by inviting sensationalist headlines in the press.

Yet it would be too glib to suggest that radical anti-fascism was solely responsible for the political failure of early postwar fascism. First, this fails to acknowledge the educative work of non-militant anti-fascist groups such as AJEX, which held a total of 557 open air meetings between January 1947 and December 1950. Second, even though organised anti-fascism was divided, in all probability, what the fascists experienced 'on the ground' was something rather different. Renton makes the important point that 'What the fascist speakers experienced was a single anti-fascist opposition. One arm of the movement won the local community to the politics of anti-fascism, while the other arm attacked fascist street meetings.'[92] Third, we also have to appreciate 'outside conditions'. Fascism clearly had pariah status – marginalised not only by the democratic consensus but also by a national culture which, post-Second World War, had been implanted with anti-fascist attitudes. This pariah status was reinforced by the state, which banned processions from taking place in the East End in April 1946, in the entire Metropolitan district from May 1948 to February 1949 and from April 1949 to July 1949, before finally imposing a further three-month ban from October 1949. The state also sought to continue the press boycott of Mosley which dated from the 1930s and, with the exception of publicity surrounding the violence between fascists and anti-fascists, Mosley was generally ignored.[93] Moreover, Mosley's past associations hardly made a successful return to active politics probable. He now cut a sorry figure, his oratory was uninspired and his Europeanist political programme failed to strike a chord with the visceral ultra-nationalism of his natural constituency. Evidently, even without the presence of a militant anti-fascist opposition, a serious resurgence of fascism was very unlikely.

IV

For the most part, the 1950s in Britain were quiescent years for both fascists and anti-fascists. Indeed, in the early 1950s, fascist activity was hardly noticeable. Mosley's self-imposed exile had left the Union Movement standing still, desperate for a mobilising issue that would give it a shot in the arm. Optimism returned, however, when the anti-black 'race riots' in Nottingham and Notting Hill in August and September 1958 provided the opportunity for Mosley to stage a dramatic comeback. The Union Movement had already attempted to make use of racial populism at local elections in Brixton and the East End in the early 1950s under the slogan 'Keep Britain White', but had made little progress. In fact, from the mid-1950s more headway was registered by racial nationalist groups unconnected with Mosley, such as Colin Jordan's White Defence League and John Bean's National Labour Party. These groups, operating from a base in North Kensington, stirred up racial antagonism and helped prepare ground not only for the Notting Hill 'race riots' but also for the subsequent intervention of the rival Union Movement. Although the Union Movement was widely blamed for the Notting Hill riots, its local presence was established largely in the aftermath of events. Expecting to capitalise on local antagonism towards black immigrants, the Union Movement opened a bookshop on Kensington Park Road and a campaign against the 'coloured invasion' was quickly inaugurated. This all culminated in Mosley's decision to contest the parliamentary seat for North Kensington at the 1959 general election.

As early as 1956, attempts were made to counter the increase in fascist activity in North Kensington. In response to the activities of Mosley's rivals, the West London Anti-Fascist Youth Committee was established. Its aim was to restrict the spread of fascist and racist propaganda in the area.[94] This Committee appears to have had its origins on the Left even though North Kensington was not renowned for radical-Left activity. The area was characterised by slum dwellings, a shifting population and a large immigrant presence. Whilst this provided ideal conditions for racial agitation, it did not make for vigorous, community-based anti-fascism. Consequently, there was very little in the way of grassroots opposition to Mosley in North Kensington in the period between the Notting Hill riots and the 1959 election. The Union Movement campaigned for nearly a year in the North Kensington constituency and held a number of outdoor meetings. During the election campaign itself, Mosley held street corner meetings at four different locations every evening over the course of several weeks. The Jewish Defence Committee, having sent observers to monitor all these meetings, was able to report 'not much disorder, even on election night'.[95] The onus for campaigning against Mosley therefore fell on the JDC by default. In due course, the JDC decided to produce an anti-Mosley pamphlet for distribution in the run-up to the North Kensington election and approached all the major parties with a view to having the pamphlet sponsored. All refused, even the Liberal candidate Michael Hydleman who was the son of a former chairman of the

Jewish Defence Committee. It is not clear why although it may well have been the case that the candidates did not want to alienate local anti-immigrant electors. Still determined to put out the pamphlet, the JDC suggested publication by AJEX but in the event, no pamphlet was issued. The problem was that under electoral law, no outside body could interfere in an election campaign nor could any outside body attempt to persuade voters to vote in a particular way.[96]

Encouraged by the absence of a material challenge by anti-fascists, by sustained local activity and by Union Movement canvass returns which suggested that Mosley would poll 32 per cent of the vote, the Union Movement was confident of a major breakthrough. In fact, Mosley experienced his most humiliating electoral defeat: he polled just 8.5 per cent and lost his deposit for the first time in his political career. It was a major blow to Mosley and Union Movement activists. As Jeffrey Hamm recalls, 'Not only were all our women supporters in tears, but many of the men too wept unashamedly, shocked and stunned by this anti-climax.'[97] Rejected by the voters of North Kensington, Mosley's second comeback was brought to an ignominious ending. Even without an organised anti-fascist challenge, the sheer depth of hostility to fascism in postwar British culture ensured that despite populist appeals to anti-black racism, Mosley's political resurrection never got off the ground.

Mosley's last bid to salvage a failing political career came in 1962 when the Union Movement embarked on a period of heightened activity following a conference in Venice in March when Mosley had signed up to the formation of a 'National Party of Europe', and local elections in May when the Union Movement had polled an average of 5.5 per cent in the small number of seats it contested. In his autobiography, Mosley claims that this 'progress' led directly to a renewal of violent communist opposition at Union Movement meetings: 'When they found to their surprise we were making progress they felt that some risk must be taken to stop it: violence began again; they can turn it on and off like a hot-water tap.'[98] While Communist Party activists were possibly irked by the successful lawsuit that Mosley had brought against the Italian Communist Party,[99] it was the Venice Conference itself which, by raising the spectre of a 'Euro-based' fascism, was the source of most concern. But what Mosley conveniently forgets to mention in his autobiography is that the revival of anti-fascism in the early 1960s was additionally triggered by the first rally of Colin Jordan's National Socialist Movement (NSM) in Trafalgar Square on 1 July 1962.

Jordan had already gained notoriety on the Left and within Jewish circles as a vicious anti-Semite, having been fined in 1960 and 1961 for behaviour likely to cause a breach of the peace. Thus Jordan's decision to stage a 'Free Britain from Jewish Control' rally in Trafalgar Square was seen as deeply provocative and attracted a hostile crowd of some 2,000 people. According to Walker, such was the contempt for Jordan that 'anti-fascists were waiting for the Nazis before they even began as an organization'.[100] Feelings ran high as Jordan was shouted down and the NSM platform pelted with tomatoes, pennies and rotten eggs.[101] After just 20 minutes, the meeting was closed, with Jordan and his close associate, John Tyndall, arrested. Unfortunately for Mosley, these well-publicised clashes could not have come at a more inopportune time – he had already booked Trafalgar Square for a rally scheduled to take place just three weeks later. But this was not the end to Mosley's misfortune – Jordan's rally also gave rise to a new anti-fascist organisation. This subsequently became known as the Yellow Star Movement (YSM).

On 1 July 1962, on the steps of St Martin-in-the-Fields overlooking Trafalgar Square, the Rev. Bill Sargent, the Vicar of Holy Trinity Church, Dalston and a Hackney Labour councillor, wearing a large Yellow Star of David, had stood in lone protest against Jordan's National Socialists. Harry Green, an active member of AJEX, chanced upon him and then joined him along with some 40 others.[102] As the two principal demonstrators, Sargent and Green agreed to maintain contact and subsequently planned to protest against Mosley's scheduled meeting at Trafalgar Square on 22 July 1962. In the approach to this meeting, Sargent led a deputation to the Home Office bearing a petition calling for the Conservative Home Secretary, Henry Brooke, to impose a ban on Mosley's rally. This was supported by the CPGB, which also called on the Conservative government to 'Ban the Square to Fascism'.[103] Further calls were made by trade union leaders and South Paddington Labour Party.[104] However, despite the protest, Mosley was allowed to stage the rally as he had held some seven meetings in Trafalgar Square since 1959 without serious incident. At a meeting which heard a report from Sargent's deputation, a further peaceful counter-demonstration on the steps of St Martin-in-the-Fields was therefore proposed.[105] On the day of Mosley's rally, a few hundred supporters initially gathered on the steps wearing Yellow Stars in sympathy with the Jews murdered by Nazis. In due course, as the crowds in Trafalgar Square grew to some 10,000 people, Sargent was joined by more than 1,000 supporters who were handed Yellow Stars.[106]

Within Trafalgar Square itself, however, there was serious disorder. Such was the determination to stop Mosley's rally that a police cordon around the platform was broken and violent confrontations resulted. Fearing further disorder, the meeting was closed even before Mosley had arrived. There were over 50 arrests. The Union Movement insisted that Communists were responsible for the violence, having 'assembled in large force from all over the country for the purpose of smashing the meeting' and pointed to court convictions for people 'imported' from Glasgow and Coventry as evidence of a highly organised operation. For the Union Movement, this was calculated aggression, coming after a botched attempt by the CPGB to disrupt an indoor meeting held by Mosley at Birmingham Town Hall in March 1962 where Communists had been ejected with 'little difficulty'.[107] The Union Movement also claimed that 'all who wore the Yellow Star did not demonstrate peacefully' at Trafalgar Square and alleged that two female members of the Union Movement had been viciously assaulted by a group of Jews wearing Rev. Sargent's Yellow Star.[108]

Sargent, of course, could not contenance violence and indeed what struck him most was the need for an anti-fascist organisation capable of curbing fascist activities without recourse to violence. This was the case especially as disturbances quickly followed at Union Movement meetings at Manchester on 29 July, Ridley Road on 31 July and Bethnal Green on 2 September. At all three meetings, Mosley was assaulted.[109] Therefore, when the Yellow Star Movement was launched towards the end of July 1962, it rejected 'punch-up politics' in favour of peaceful persuasion. The favoured tactic, used in the 1930s as well as by AJEX and the Communist Party in the 1940s, involved 'jumping the pitch', i.e. occupying fascist speaking-sites in order to deny fascists an opportunity to hold meetings. The police operated on a principle of 'first come, first served' which meant that the speaker who arrived at a pitch first could claim it for as long as (s)he wanted provided no serious disorder occurred. Perhaps the most impressive example of this tactic in operation was an 'all-day speakers' marathon', which the Yellow Star Movement organised to prevent a fascist meeting from being held in Dalston on 2 September 1962. Anti-fascists camped out overnight on two sites and persuaded no fewer than 136 speakers to become involved, including local MPs, councillors and clergymen.[110] Additionally, the Yellow Star Movement inaugurated a national petition against incitement to racial hatred which aimed to gather 500,000 signatures. It was assisted in this project by the Board of Deputies and AJEX, who became co-sponsors. By the end of November 1962, when the petition was presented to parliament, 440,000 signatures had been collected.[111] Nevertheless, parliament refused to bend to pressure – many MPs still insisted that legislation against racial hatred would infringe freedom of speech. It was not until 1965, in the form of the Race Relations Act, that legislation against racial hatred was finally passed. However, this probably had little to do with combating fascism. Of more concern was the potential that the race issue had for sparking intra-party divisions. This explains the bipartisan consensus on race which emerged in the 1960s and combined anti-discriminatory legislation with strict immigration control in order to take race out of mainstream political debate and so end potentially explosive intra-party conflict.[112]

In organisational terms, the Yellow Star Movement remained informal. It appears that Sargent wanted the Movement to remain 'loose' so that it could be activated in periods when fascist activity was on the increase and then revert to a dormant state when fascist activity subsided.[113] There were no 'members' as such, only supporters. Harry Green claimed that the Yellow Star Movement had 8,000 supporters. Geoffrey Ashe, a former supporter, suggests a figure of 6,000 was 'perhaps exaggerated, but not absurdly so'.[114] Most support came from AJEX and the broad Left, with significant overlap between the YSM and the Campaign for Nuclear Disarmament. Particularly worrying for Sargent, however, was a Jewish faction of militant anti-fascists that he found unable to restrain. These donned the Yellow Star and passed themselves off as YSM supporters, but turned increasingly to violence.[115] This faction, known as the '62 Group' or '62 Committee', modelled itself on the 43 Group and likewise sought to oppose fascism through combative force. Understandably, given the nature of its activities, the leadership of the 62 Group remained highly secretive, though many were 43 Group veterans. One such figure was Harold Bidney, at the time a manager of the Limbo Club in London's Soho who was later singled out by John Tyndall as the 62 Group's 'activities organiser, paymaster and recruiting sergeant'.[116] Only very recently has it emerged that the chair of the 62 Group was Baron Moss, a Jewish businessman, who had once worked at the *Daily Worker* as its publicity director.[117]

Under the influence of this faction and various leftist elements, the Yellow Star Movement began to adopt a more forceful line, though on occasions it still pursued peaceful action. In early 1963, for instance, it organised an anti-fascist jazz and folk concert, and also held a peaceful picket of a Mosleyite rally at Kensington Town Hall.[118] However, since the YSM was managed through an 'advisory panel' (to ensure broad representation) and was subject to review, the composition of the panel was volatile and progressively drifted to a more radical position from September 1962 onwards. Harry Green had more sympathy for militant anti-fascism than Sargent, who, uncomfortable with the YSM's growing reputation for violence, now began to associate with the moderates in the London Anti-Fascist Committee. This body, which had also been set up in 1962, had Fred Tonge, a London County Councillor, as its secretary and was sponsored by, amongst others, Fenner Brockway (now a Labour MP) and Jeremy Thorpe MP (future leader of the Liberal Party). The primary role of the London Anti-Fascist Committee was to press for legislation against race hatred. It also formed a number of grassroots anti-fascist committees, the most significant of which was the North and East London Anti-Fascist Committee, which appears to have appropriated the original anti-fascist policy of the Yellow Star Movement.[119]

V

With the National Socialist Movement paralysed by the imprisonment of Colin Jordan and John Tyndall for paramilitary activities,[120] the Union Movement encountered most of the ensuing anti-fascist opposition. Shrewdly, the Union Movement responded to the recurrence of violent opposition by holding 'snap' meetings without advance publicity. Adopting this method, Mosley was able to hold orderly meetings in September 1962 at Earls Court, Bethnal Green, Highbury and Dalston. A meeting held at North Kensington on 18 September was advertised in advance but there was still no disorder. Consequently, the Union Movement became convinced that it had beaten the opposition and had exposed the 'myth' that Mosley was responsible for violence: 'Once we started snap meetings their much vaunted "intelligence" system failed. No Yellow Star – no violence.' Triumphantly, in October 1962, the Union Movement declared: 'We are on top again – bigger, stronger, and with wider public sympathy than before.'[121] But clearly the Union Movement had not counted on a switch in tactics by anti-fascists. The 62 Group responded to 'snap' meetings using two methods. The first was to launch physical attacks on individual members of the Union Movement, such as Robert Row, editor of the Union Movement's paper, and David Wheeler, its West London speaker.[122] The second method, used in Ridley Road in particular, was to organise a 'fast call-out scheme' whereby stall-holders and shop owners would immediately inform 62 Group members when fascists arrived intending to hold a meeting, thereby enabling 62 Group members to be mobilised within a short space of time. Once mobilised, according to one former 62 Group activist, the *modus operandi* in these situations was either quiet infiltration of the audience and 'then do them' or meet a quarter of a mile away and then, with enough numbers, form 'a running wedge straight in, and do them'.[123]

With anti-fascist militants refusing to drop the cause, the victory over its antagonists that the Union Movement had announced in October 1962 proved premature. In 1963, no longer able to speak at open air meetings, the Union Movement conceded defeat. The anti-fascist opposition had, says Lewis, 'swept Mosley from the streets for the last time'.[124] In Walker's opinion, anti-fascist groups had been much more effective than in the 1930s and stopped Mosley; although this was no major achievement as the Union Movement, with a mere 1,000 supporters lacked either the ability or the resolve to withstand sustained opposition.[125] Evidently, anti-fascist militancy is at its most effective when the adversary is small and deficient in commitment and resources, but an equally important factor in the Union Movement's final demise was the decision by municipal authorities to deny it premises for indoor meetings. Here, the JDC appears to have played a key role by making various representations to local authorities. By July 1963 Mosley had been restricted to only a handful of premises.[126] Without space (both outdoor and indoor) to propagate its ideology, the Union Movement retreated into the political backwaters. After briefly resurfacing to contest the 1966 general election as a candidate for Shoreditch and Finsbury, in which he polled a nugatory 4.6 per cent of the vote, Mosley finally retired from active politics and the Union Movement sank without trace.

On the anti-fascist side, of the organisations created in 1962, the Yellow Star Movement had effectively collapsed by mid-1963. With the retreat of the Union Movement, the original stimulus disappeared. By May 1963, the YSM was struggling financially so much so that supporters could no longer even be contacted by mail. Moreover, the YSM's reputation for violence had discredited it in certain quarters, notably the JDC, which had distanced itself from the Yellow Star Movement in December 1962.[127] The end came in August 1963 with the hospitalisation of Olga Levertoff, the YSM's secretary.[128] Elsewhere, the London Anti-Fascist Committee and the associated North and East London Anti-Fascist Committee continued to exist nominally before eventually, towards the end of the 1960s, the resources of the London Anti-Fascist Committee were placed at the disposal of the NCCL.[129] The 62 Group, on the other hand, remained operative. However, with the withdrawal of the Union Movement from conventional political activity, the efforts of the 62 Group were concentrated on small-scale clandestine operations, principally assaults on individual members of fascist groups and raids on fascist property.

Over the period 1962–5, John Tyndall claimed that Jewish militants from the 62 Group had been responsible for, *inter alia*, a raid on the Union Movement's headquarters, numerous assaults on members of John Bean's British National Party (the successor to the National Labour Party), various attacks on members of the National Socialist Movement, assaults on members of his own Greater Britain Movement (launched in 1964 following a split with Jordan), and breaking and entering the flat of the 'historian' David Irving, who was suspected of pro-Nazi sympathies.[130] An internal Greater Britain Movement document also records a raid by Jewish militants on its headquarters in Norwood in south London following the failure to break up a GBM meeting in Dalston in October 1965.[131] These activities probably inflamed anti-Semitic passions and precipitated a wave of 'revenge' attacks on Jewish synagogues and property in the period November 1964 to October 1966.[132] Indeed, in early 1966, a number of NSM members were convicted for a series of arson attacks on synagogues in various parts of London. But even if these 'revenge' attacks did benefit the anti-fascist cause by providing tangible proof of the extremist and violent nature of British fascism, to suggest that these counter-measures were intentionally provoked by the 62 Group would involve taking a very cynical view of the 62 Group's motives.

Faced with reporting an escalating number of anti-Semitic attacks, the *Jewish Chronicle* expressed a lack of confidence in the Jewish Defence Committee and thereby initiated a new round of the 'defence debate'.[133] The *Jewish Chronicle's* criticism of the Board's defence policy was then taken up by the so-called 'Jewish Aid Committee of Britain' (JACOB), a body that helped finance the 62 Group. Returning to well-trodden ground, JACOB criticised the Board's 'weak' and 'passive' attitude. It asserted that the Board of Deputies had allowed the arson attacks to occur through a defence policy that was 'frighteningly inadequate', the result of an 'ageing' and 'timid' leadership, complacency, lack of information and a 'hush it all up' attitude in which Jews were instructed to avoid all publicity. A clear distinction was drawn between this 'official' policy and 'unofficial' policy 'taken by an increasing number of young Jewish citizens who feel that they have learned other lessons from the experience of the past and who want a more positive anti-fascist policy, a policy of "direct action" ...'[134] According to JACOB, these young Jews had been 'brushed aside' disdainfully by John Dight, the Chairman of the JDC, without consultation with any other members of the Defence Committee.[135] JACOB demanded the election of a 'new virile young' leadership to the JDC in order to pursue an alternative defence policy. This had to be more forceful, with a 'strong hand', and should consist of the following elements: legislation to ban racist organisations (the recent passage of the Race Relations Act was deemed insufficient), the establishment of an information service to collect and analyse intelligence, the formation of an Anti-Defamation Centre based on the model of the B'nai Brith Anti-Defamation League in the United States (to expose fascist and racist activities as well as reply to Jewish defamation), and, community protection (where synagogues and youth clubs would provide courses in self-defence).[136]

Clearly angered by JACOB's attack and anxious to deny it any cred-ibility with the Board, the JDC circulated a counter-statement to all members of the Board of Deputies entitled 'Defence with Responsibility'. In this, the JDC denied that official defence policy was a 'passive', 'hole in the corner' type. It claimed its approach was to expose fascists and deprive them of support; though careful to draw a distinction between appropriate publicity and 'undue publicity':

> ... it does not believe that it is in the best interests of the Jewish Community, or the wider public for that matter, to have front-page stories about these minuscule fascist bodies in the TIMES, the DAILY TELEGRAPH, DAILY EXPRESS, DAILY MAIL, DAILY MIRROR, GUARDIAN, the SUN and SKETCH, six days a week, every week.[137]

Quoting from Colin Cross, author of *The Fascists in Britain* (1961), the JDC argued that violence against fascists resulted in unnecessary publicity and produces a 'boomerang effect' where opportunities for putting fascism's case are limited, but fascist activities are brought 'to the attention of a much wider public than they would otherwise command'.[138] Yet for JACOB, the notion that publicity builds fascism was too simplistic, failing to take into account other factors, such as quality of leadership of fascist organisations, ability to exploit certain situations, and so on. Absent from both analyses, however, was serious consideration of types of publicity because clearly, contrary to what the fascists themselves often thought, not all publicity is good publicity. Negative association with violence and extremism is unlikely to make for a 'respectable' party with wide political legitimacy, especially in Britain where the consensus on liberal values remains deeply entrenched. Typically, fascist groups portrayed this violence as the responsibility of 'Communists' in order to represent their own violence and ideology as a legitimate response, but this tactic was rendered ineffective by both the liberal consensus and the CPGB's political insignificance. Moreover, those attracted to fascist groups through media reports of violence may increase the fascist street presence, but this presence will almost certainly be comprised of 'young toughs', who are attracted to violence and carry greater potential for extremist action.

Conclusively, the scale of the divide between the JDC and JACOB revealed itself in their respective assessments of the strength of contemporary fascist organisations. Although the JDC insisted that there was no room for complacency, its analysis of fascist performance at the 1966 general election seemed to confirm that the voting strength for fascist parties such as the Union Movement was negligible. JACOB agreed that Mosley, 'the old man of British Fascism looks like ending his days as a political "has-been"'; but made the point that groups like the British National Party and Tyndall's Greater Britain Movement were making headway by 'cashing in' on the immigration issue.[139] JACOB warned that this could not be ignored by the Jewish community because although the fascists were concentrating on the 'colour question', they will eventually 'turn their hate on the Jews'.[140] Predictably, JACOB's call for a 'new dynamic in defence' went unheeded by the leaders of Anglo-Jewry, and the historic breach between militant anti-fascism and the Board of Deputies remained. Of course, with hindsight, the Board should have been more receptive to the views of JACOB as the following year several fascist and racial populist organisations, including the Greater Britain Movement and the British National Party, came together and consolidated the 'dangerous nucleus' that JACOB had already identified. The result was a new organisation – the National Front.

Bringing this chapter to a close, it is clear that when set side by side, the scale of popular involvement in anti-fascist activity in the period 1946–66 fell far short of the mass opposition to Mosley of the 1930s. As a reactive phenomenon, the relative scale of anti-fascist activity is naturally determined by the measure of the fascist threat. In the wake of the Second World War, with anti-fascism firmly embedded in national culture, the threat of home-grown fascism was minimised. Therefore, anti-fascist activism contracted to a core of Jewish ex-servicemen understandably sensitised and radicalised by the Nazi genocide; its most radical elements motivated more by a revengeful desire to give fascists 'what was coming to them' than a considered assessment of the potential for fascist growth. During 1947–8, and then again during 1962–3, anti-fascist opposition extended beyond this core to incorporate left-wing, liberal and, as in the case of Hackney in 1947, even Conservative elements. None the less, we should not lose sight of the fact that both in the late 1940s and early 1960s, the scale of anti-fascism (and fascism) was localised. Notwithstanding isolated activity in provincial areas, the centre of fascist/anti-fascist activity in Britain was London. Therefore, we do well not to exaggerate the wider importance of fascist and anti-fascist activity in this period.

As in the 1930s, organised anti-fascism was a house divided against itself with differences once again apparent over the question of the desirability of violent resistance, so graphically illustrated in relations between the 43 Group and the Jewish Defence Committee. Militant opposition undoubtedly lessened the opportunity for postwar fascism to revive by disrupting its activities, by limiting its public space and by denying it respectability. In this regard, radical anti-fascism was clearly of consequence (even if its impact is typically overstated). Moreover, non-violent anti-fascist groups also contributed to the political failure of postwar fascism, although the educative work of bodies such as AJEX was arguably of less significance and those bodies (such as the Communist Party) that called for a state ban on fascism in the mid- to late 1940s were to be disappointed. None the less, even though there was no specific anti-fascist legislation, the state eventually introduced anti-racist legislation in the form of the Race Relations Act in 1965 and through this piece of legislation, the state did secure convictions of leading fascists, including Colin Jordan. Throughout this period, the state also continued to keep an eye on Mosley's activities, it put the Public Order Act to use to prohibit fascist processions in the late 1940s, and on the grounds of disruption to holiday-makers, also refused permission for three fascist meetings to take place in Trafalgar Square in August 1962.[141] We should recognise as well the contribution of local authorities in denying public halls to fascist organisations and recall that in the early 1960s in particular, Mosley was denied room to disseminate his ideology in indoor as well as outdoor arenas.

Having said all that, the role of anti-fascism should always be placed in context: the scope for fascist growth was so limited in Britain during this period that even without the existence of an organised anti-fascist oposition, fascism would have struggled to find popular appeal. What anti-fascism therefore achieved between 1946 and 1966 was further marginalisation of various manifestations of an ideology already contained by a continuing liberal-democratic consensus and a British national identity infused with patriotic hostility towards Nazi Germany. Only through adapting to this forbidding environment, by drawing a veil of anti-immigrant populism over its fascist ideology and by unifying various splinters into a coherent whole, could the extreme Right possibly hope to effect a major electoral breakthrough. This point was recognised by the National Front, which from the very beginning, set its sights on becoming an 'acceptable' challenge to the mainstream political parties. As the National Front's first chairman, A. K. Chesterton, a former Director of Publicity and Propaganda for the BUF and erstwhile leader of the postwar League of Empire Loyalists[142] understood, this meant ensuring that '*we* do not give *ourselves* a bad public image'.[143] Accordingly, the National Front's fascism became hidden behind the 'respectability' of racial populism and so during the 1970s, when the politicisation of the immigration issue created the opening for its racial politics, the National Front assumed a greater presence than any of its postwar predecessors. And, as we shall see in the next chapter, anti-fascists consequently found themselves facing their most serious challenge since Oswald Mosley's British Union of Fascists.

4

'The National Front is a Nazi Front!': Opposition to the National Front, 1967–79

In all probability, the moment that opposition to the National Front (NF) is mentioned, it is the Anti-Nazi League (ANL) which springs to mind. This organisation, formed in late 1977, grew rapidly to become the Front's most memorable opponent. In its first year, it recruited some 40,000–50,000 members, distributed over five million leaflets and sold around one million anti-Front badges and stickers. Such was the level of its popular support, the Anti-Nazi League was widely regarded as the largest extra-parliamentary movement since the Campaign for Nuclear Disarmament in the early 1960s.[1] By mobilising mass opposition to the National Front, and by smearing the Front with the lethal Nazi label, the Anti-Nazi League has been judged an unqualified success. Many claim that the ANL was largely responsible for the electoral demise of the National Front at the end of the 1970s and have urged others, such as opponents of the Front National in France, to follow its example.[2] But in point of fact, support for the National Front may have already peaked by the time the Anti-Nazi League was launched. Moreover, the concentration on the activities of the Anti-Nazi League has meant that the work of other anti-fascist groups that either pre-dated or paralleled the ANL has been largely ignored. This narrow focus has also precluded wider consideration of other sources of anti-fascism. It may well have been the case, for instance, that hostility from the mainstream media impeded the National Front more than the activities of opposition groups. Certainly this was the view of the National Front, who after the 1979 general election identified the media and not the ANL as its 'number one enemy'.[3]

At the very start, given that anti-fascist activities had narrowed to a militant hard core, the National Front largely escaped a baptism of fire. Even though groups of anti-fascists demonstrated outside the Front's first annual conference in October 1967, opposition to the NF in the late 1960s was mainly restricted to a small band of militant anti-fascists who followed the pattern of covert activity previously undertaken against the NF's immediate predecessors. Walker records a number of incidents in London in 1969, for example, when the office of the Croydon organiser of the National Front was raided, when a lorry was backed into the NF's headquarters in Tulse Hill and when the annual conference of the NF at Caxton Hall, Westminster was sabotaged by two men who smashed up electrical equipment with axes.[4] But for the most part, the formation of the National Front elicited little response from potential antagonists on the Left. Two reasons possibly account for this lack of interest. First, whilst the National Front claimed 10,000 members in April 1968 and by May 1969 had branches in London, Leeds, Liverpool, Sheffield, Manchester, Bradford, Wolverhampton and Glasgow,[5] it was still relatively unknown as a political party outside militant Jewish circles and had yet to make a serious intervention in the electoral arena. Second, the radical Left was more concerned about the racial populism of Enoch Powell than the National Front. The scale of working-class support for Powell following his 'rivers of blood' speech in April 1968, when thousands of workers had staged demonstrations of support, had overwhelmed the Left. The International Socialists (IS) (later to become the Socialist Workers' Party) had tried to respond by proposing a single organisation to meet the 'Urgent Challenge of Fascism' that Powellism was said to represent. But with other radical-Left groups suspicious of IS's motives and given the inherent difficulties of challenging ingrained racist attitudes in the workplace, this proposal came to nothing and Powellism, which lacked any organisational form, was left to run its course.[6]

In 1969, in a specific bid to raise awareness of the National Front on the Left, an Anti-Fascist Research Group was formed by a handful of undergraduates in London. Briefly acting as an 'information service' on contemporary British fascism, this group published a series of *Anti-Fascist Bulletins* which were then circulated to various left-wing groups, trade unions, immigrant associations and Jewish organisations. The publications of the Anti-Fascist Research Group remained anonymous and its authors were never identified.[7] Readers of the *Bulletin* were encouraged to undertake practical anti-fascist work at grass-roots level and seek maximum co-operation between all local organisations that professed to be 'anti-fascist'. They were also urged to distribute anti-fascist and anti-racist literature in their districts, read the local press and reply to racist features and letters, and also to expose fascist groups and their front organisations to the widest possible audience.[8] The *Bulletin* additionally reported anti-fascist activity which by 1971 was evolving on an *ad hoc* basis in response to announced NF activities and in much the same way as anti-fascist activity had developed in the early 1930s, it was localised, disparate and lacked central co-ordination.[9]

The *Bulletin* reported, for example, that as early as March 1971 anti-fascists in Hertfordshire had established a North Hertfordshire Campaign for Racial Equality in order to organise a counter-demonstration to a National Front march through Hitchin. Some 2,000 people had assembled to oppose the Front with anti-fascist objectors throwing smoke-bombs and rotten fruit. In June 1971, an alliance of local anti-fascists in the Bristol area had distributed anti-NF leaflets along the route of a National Front march before heckling NF members as they made their way into a meeting.[10] Elsewhere, *Spearhead*, the NF's monthly, reported that a local 'Human Rights Group' had been formed in Huddersfield which had circulated an anti-NF leaflet calling for opposition to proposals by the National Front to open a regional headquarters.[11] Yet notwithstanding these cases of isolated opposition, awareness of the National Front remained low. Clearly anti-fascist consciousness was not at levels required for an opposition movement of any real significance to form and this situation was made worse by a marked failure of the radical left-wing press to report fascist activities. Ignorance of the NF was brought home to the Anti-Fascist Research Group in October 1971, when some 20–30 members of the National Front successfully infiltrated an anti-Common Market demonstration in London that had been supported by trade unions, members of the Labour Party and several branches of the Communist Party. A number of NF activists were said to have freely sold anti-EEC literature, anti-immigrant literature as well as copies of *Spearhead*. In its subsequent press release, the Anti-Fascist Research Group was evidently not best pleased with 'a TOTAL FAILURE to oppose the National Front, even though first real signs of resentment at their presence would certainly have warned them off ...'[12]

In 1972, some five years before the founding of the Anti-Nazi League, an attempt was made to call together a national anti-fascist organisation in response to moves by the National Front to extend its influence in the workplace. The support that the working class had given Powell in 1968 had impressed on the National Front that racism could be a potentially powerful force in the trade unions provided that trade unions could be wrenched from the Left. Consequently, in 1972, *Spearhead* called on its readers to prepare for a major propaganda and recruitment drive amongst the trade unions. In reply to this, a group calling itself 'Trades Unionists Against Fascism' produced a one-off report to draw attention to the NF's plan, which was then distributed to trade union executive officers, branches, trades councils and district committees. This report did not foresee a 'vast upsurge of fascism in 1973, overwhelming the labour movement', but did point to 'a worrying growth in fascistic organisation, a real potential problem for trade unionists and socialists in Britain'.[13] Having recognised that local *ad hoc* alliances against fascism tend to disintegrate when fascist activity subsides, it therefore recommended that a permanent anti-fascist organisation be established on a national basis. What weighed against the recommendations of Trade Unionists Against Fascism, however, was the National Front's decision to put its trade union campaign on the back-burner until 1974. With the Front giving priority to a series of 'Stop the Asian Invasion' demonstrations during the Ugandan Asians crisis, this particular cause for concern passed and hence a national anti-fascist organisation in the workplace failed to materialise.

Yet the Conservative government's decision to accept thousands of Asians expelled from Uganda by Idi Amin stimulated a period of rapid membership growth for the National Front. It has been suggested that membership of the Front increased by 50 per cent between October 1972 and July 1973 and may have even reached 17,500.[14] This growth combined with 16.2 per cent of the vote at a parliamentary by-election in West Bromwich in May 1973 and a set of encouraging results in local elections, where the NF polled an average of 19.9 per cent in Blackburn and 13 per cent at Leicester, served to invite greater attention from the Left. It was, however, the Front's decision to enter the national political arena and field over 50 candidates at the February 1974 general election and thus establish a broader geographical presence than any of its postwar predecessors, that finally aroused more substantive opposition. With the Communist Party, the chief grouping on the far Left with some 25,000 members, seemingly preoccupied with trade union work and winning over the Labour Left, it was the more militant groups that first began to vocalise opposition to the National Front. Towards the end of 1973, the International Socialists (with around 3,000 members) issued a pamphlet in which a commitment to oppose the National Front physically was declared. At the February 1974 parliamentary election, the International Marxist

Group (IMG) (less than 1,000 members) also declared itself to be in favour of physical opposition and advocated a 'no platform' policy for fascists.[15] This policy was further supported by the National Union of Students, a body within which the IMG exerted considerable influence. On the mainstream Left, concerned at the NF's electoral performance and the Front's renewed interest in extending its influence within the trade unions, the Transport and General Workers' Union called on the TUC and Labour Party to expose the National Front as a fascist organisation.[16] And at the local level, more *ad hoc* anti-fascist committees emerged, in Manchester, Coventry and Kent.[17]

Moreover, the fact that the NF intended to field over 50 candidates at the February 1974 general election, and thereby qualify for five minutes of TV and radio broadcasting time, also compelled the Board of Deputies to make known its opposition to the National Front. The Board wanted to publicise the Nazi backgrounds of the National Front leadership and so produced an anti-NF leaflet which pulled no punches in 'Exposing the Hatemongers'. A photograph of John Tyndall, the National Front's chairman, in full Nazi uniform at the 1962 National Socialist Movement camp was reproduced and hundreds of thousands of leaflets were apparently distributed by candidates of all three main political parties in those constituencies in which the Front stood both at the February general election and at the October general election.[18] Clearly displeased at this 'smear campaign', the National Front leadership complained to the authorities that the leaflet constituted a breach of electoral law. In the event, the Board escaped prosecution, but local distributors were successfully prosecuted only to be acquitted on appeal because the leaflet did not explicitly state 'Don't vote NF'.[19]

Dramatically, the mounting opposition to the Front converged on Red Lion Square in London in June 1974 where an anti-fascist demonstration resulted in serious disorder and the tragic death of an anti-Front protester, the first fatality at a demonstration in Britain since 1919. This anti-Front mobilisation had been called by Liberation (formerly known as the Movement for Colonial Freedom), an anti-imperialist and anti-racist alliance figure-headed by Lord (Fenner) Brockway[20] and comprised of individuals from the Labour Left, such as Sydney Bidwell, Labour MP for Southall, and Communist Party members such as Kay Beauchamp (Liberation's London Secretary) and Tony Gilbert.[21] On hearing of the NF's plans to hold a meeting at Conway Hall to mark the end of a march through central London on 15 June, Steven Hart, General Secretary of Liberation, booked a small hall adjacent to the NF's intended meeting place inside Conway Hall. The idea was to organise a counter-demonstration to the National Front inside the hall itself as well as in the surrounding area of Red Lion Square. Following discussions with police, it was agreed that Liberation would hold a peaceful open air meeting in Red Lion Square whilst a small contingent of anti-fascists would be allowed into Conway Hall to hold an indoor meeting, but would enter through a side entrance, thereby avoiding any contact with the National Front. In order to maximise the show of opposition at the open air meeting, Liberation proceeded to invite a number of radical-Left groups to participate, most notably the International Marxist Group and the International Socialists. Unbeknown to Liberation, however, was the determination of the IMG to organise a mass picket at the main entrance of the hall thereby denying the NF access.

On 15 June 1974, around 1,500 anti-fascists marched to Red Lion Square. Located to the rear of the march was a group of some 400–500 IMG supporters and a smaller number of International Socialists. As the anti-fascist procession reached Red Lion Square, the IMG and IS contingents broke away and made directly for the police cordon around the main entrance of Conway Hall whereupon violent clashes between police and militant anti-fascists ensued. It was in these confrontations, which lasted for less than 15 minutes, that Kevin Gately, a student from Warwick University was fatally injured. Following the restoration of order within the Square, a second confrontation later took place on the southern periphery of the Square at Vernon Place where a large group of anti-fascist demonstrators attempted to block the NF's procession. A variety of missiles and two smoke-bombs were thrown from the anti-fascist side before police cleared the demonstrators onto the pavements and dispersed the crowd. In all, one person died, 46 policemen and at least 12 demonstrators were injured, 51 people arrested and the whole police operation had cost an estimated £15,000.[22]

In the view of Walker, the anti-fascist agitation at Red Lion Square backfired, turning the National Front into a household name and it was the NF who 'emerged as the innocent victims of political violence, the Left who emerged as the instigators ...'[23] Consistent with Walker's reading of events, Clutterbuck insists that:

> The result was precisely what the NF would have wished – publicity for the purpose of *their* demonstrations, discrediting of their detractors, increasing applications for membership and a substantially

increased vote both at the next general election and at subsequent by-elections.[24]

Yet Taylor has succeeded in casting serious doubt on Clutterbuck's claim that Red Lion Square boosted the NF's performance at the October 1974 general election. Although the Front polled relatively well in a number of constituencies in London, such as Newham North East, Wood Green, Tottenham and Hackney South and Shoreditch, where it received a higher percentage of the vote than in February, in the 44 seats contested both in February and October, the NF's share of the vote remained more or less static. Moreover, its overall average fell marginally from 3.3 per cent in February to 3.1 per cent in October. By the same token, since the decrease in the NF's overall share of the vote was insignificant, Taylor dismisses the opposing view that the Red Lion Square events hampered the electoral performance of the National Front. With some justification, Taylor therefore concludes that no side could claim a victory as Red Lion Square 'neither helped nor hindered the NF in October 1974'.[25]

However, events at Red Lion Square did bring about further anti-fascist activity with one spin-off being that more anti-fascist committees were formed at the local level. At Oxford, for instance, a newly created anti-fascist committee took on the NF during the October general election campaign with two meetings organised by the Front's candidate, Ian Anderson, successfully disrupted.[26] Another consequence was that the volume of anti-NF literature increased. Of particular note was the publication of a pamphlet by *Searchlight*, entitled 'A Well-Oiled Nazi Machine', which was an exposé of the National Front and other extreme-Right organisations.[27] *Searchlight* had been irregularly published in the 1960s as a newspaper edited by two Labour MPs, first Reginald Freeson and then Joan Lestor;[28] though this pamphlet was a collaborative effort between Maurice Ludmer, a former CPGB member and anti-racist activist, and Gerry Gable, *Searchlight's* original research director.[29] Along with literature distributed by the Board of Deputies, 'A Well-Oiled Nazi Machine' was said to have been one of the first public documents to have revealed the Nazi pedigrees of the Front leadership, and quickly sold out. This indicated the necessity for such a publication amongst anti-fascist circles and as a result, Ludmer and Gable relaunched *Searchlight* in magazine format in February 1975.[30]

Besides encouraging the emergence of additional local anti-fascist committees and circulation of anti-Front literature, at least two large, albeit peaceful, demonstrations against the National Front took place following Red Lion Square with both involving significant numbers of people. At Leicester, in August 1974, an estimated 6,000 anti-fascists gathered to oppose a 1,500-strong National Front procession. This particular anti-fascist mobilisation had broad support, ranging from the local Labour Party, trade unions and Liberal Party, through to the Indian Workers' Association and Communist Party.[31] And in London, in September 1974, the route of a National Front march through Hyde Park was occupied by a crowd of 7,000 anti-fascists forcing the police to re-route the NF march.[32] Evidently, despite adverse publicity that the Red Lion Square disorder had generated for the Left, more anti-fascists than fascists could be mobilised at street level – clearly a dispiriting state of affairs for the National Front.

Yet what proved more damaging to National Front morale was a hostile TV programme screened in September 1974 to an audience of over eight million viewers. In this programme, John O'Brien, who had been replaced by Tyndall as chairman of the NF in 1972, alleged that Tyndall and Martin Webster (the Front's National Activities Organiser and erstwhile member of the NSM) had close connections with national socialists in West Germany.[33] The programme stirred up a hornet's nest inside the Front, aggravated hidden tensions between 'moderates' and 'extremists' and shattered National Front unity.[34] Tyndall was promptly ousted from the chairmanship of the National Front and replaced by the more 'moderate' former Conservative, John Kingsley-Read. Thereafter, a lengthy period of internal wrangling between various factions ensued with the result that a rival offshoot was formed in November 1975 in the shape of the National Party led by Kingsley-Read.[35] Tyndall resumed leadership of the Front, although at significant cost: the NF haemorrhaged 2,000–3,000 members to the National Party and lost considerable ground. Thus as early as 1974, adverse media treatment negatively impacted on the Front and this underlines the point that opposition to the NF involved more than simply displays of street hostility.

In 1975, notwithstanding the fact that the National Front was immersed in internal altercations, the Front did try to get an anti-EEC campaign under way. But even this was stifled by anti-fascist opposition. First, more than 120 Labour-controlled local councils refused to allow municipal halls to be used by the NF, which indicated growing opposition from the Labour Party albeit at a local level. Second, anti-fascists continued to mobilise in numbers against the Front. In March 1975, in Islington in north London, 6,000 anti-fascists opposed an NF demonstration which had been called by the Front to protest against a local council ban.[36] In May 1975, 600 anti-fascists formed a mass picket in front of the entrance to Oxford Town Hall where the NF had booked a meeting. Anti-fascists then proceeded to charge the police cordon, but were driven back by police and NF stewards in riotous scenes that lasted for 90 minutes. That same month, 70 anti-fascists were arrested after trying to stop a Front meeting in Glasgow – the Front was able to hold its meeting, but only 12 people were brave enough to attend.[37] Finally, in October 1975, an estimated 1,000 people demonstrated outside the NF's AGM at Chelsea Town Hall where a mass picket was organised by the International Socialists and the International Marxist Group.[38] Hence, at the beginning of 1976, anti-fascists could look back over the period since Red Lion Square with relative satisfaction. National Front morale had been undermined through continued shows of force and anti-fascists had also ensured that the NF's anti-EEC campaign had not got off the ground. Coming second best, the National Front now looked destined for an early return to the political margins. Yet the Front refused to admit defeat and, during 1976, it unexpectedly bounced back.

II

It is commonly accepted that the unrestrained press sensationalism that accompanied the arrival of Malawi Asians to Britain in May 1976 led directly to the National Front's revival. As Walker so aptly puts it, 'It was the story of the Ugandan Asians all over again ...'[39] Inflammatory press reports of 'four-star hotel' Malawian Asians enjoying luxury at the taxpayers' expense, over-inflation of the numbers of Malawi Asians that were expected to enter the country and publicity surrounding NF demonstrations at various airports, meant that the National Front experienced both a sudden influx of around 3,000 new members[40] and some disturbing electoral successes. In local elections in May 1976, the National Front fielded 48 candidates in Leicester and polled 43,733 votes in all, some 18.5 per cent of the vote. In Bradford, 21 candidates stood, capturing 9,399 votes, some 10 per cent of the vote. Shortly afterwards, in July 1976, at a by-election in Deptford in south London, the combined vote for the National Front and the National Party reached an alarming 44 per cent.[41] These results startled anti-fascists with the consequence that locally based anti-fascist committees 'mushroomed to meet the threat'.[42] Significantly, these attracted support not only from the radical Left, but also from the mainstream labour movement. Indeed, in sharp contrast to the 1930s, the involvement of grassroots Labour Party members in these local anti-fascist groups was actively encouraged by Labour leaders who had become increasingly concerned about the success of the extreme right in working-class areas, having identified 21 seats that could possibly fall to the Conservative Party in the event of NF intervention. And, running parallel to the mobilisation of these anti-fascist committees (AFCs) were religious groups which began to oppose fascism. One of the first to declare its opposition to the NF was All Faiths For One Race, which published a number of anti-Front leaflets specifically targeted at Christians.[43]

Previously, the response of Labour leaders to the National Front had been to disregard it. Now, at its annual conference in 1976, the Labour Party called on all its branches to assist in the development of the network of locally based anti-fascist and anti-racist committees, and implored all Labour councils to deny the National Front and National Party use of council premises.[44] Before 1976, local trade unions, moderate trades councils and Labour Party branches had tended to avoid participation in local anti-fascist committees (there were, of course, exceptions) because either they were nervous of addressing the issue of racism which was deeply implanted within the working class and/or they did not wish to be associated with radical-Left groups which were inclined to violent opposition. Following the electoral successes of the Front, however, the Labour Party and TUC grasped the nettle and towards the end of the year launched a joint campaign against racism and the National Front. Yet for Taylor, this campaign produced modest results: there was distribution of literature and a march in London which drew close to 30,000 people, but otherwise nothing significant.[45]

The formation (or in some cases re-formation) of local anti-fascist committees over the course of 1976–7 did not follow a set pattern. In Harringey, Lambeth and Southwark, for instance, AFCs emerged from radical-Left connected or sustained trades councils, whilst in other areas (for example, Lewisham) the Race Equality Councils and the Labour Party were chief instigators.[46] Typically, the work of AFCs in the localities involved leafleting, fly-posting, preventing NF paper sales, raising awareness of the NF in trade unions, holding public meetings, petitioning local councils or police to ban NF meetings or marches, and organising pickets or counter-demonstrations. But as in the 1930s, co-ordination of anti-fascist activity at the national level was absent. Attempts were made to impose some central co-ordination in the autumn of 1976 when the Northern Committee, comprised of a network of AFCs from the North-West, Yorkshire and the north Midlands, called a meeting along with *Searchlight*, to establish a National Co-ordinating Committee of Anti-Fascist Committees. This set itself the task of producing joint anti-fascist propaganda, exchanging information and producing a co-ordinating bulletin for each local anti-fascist committee. However, the work of the 'National Committee' remained geographically restricted to the North and Midlands and so anti-fascists in London were left to steer their own course.[47]

In fact, it was not until May 1977 that 23 anti-fascist committees in London came together to form their own All London Anti-Racist Anti-Fascist Co-ordinating Committee (ARAFCC) which adopted *CARF*, the paper of the Kingston Campaign against Racism and Fascism, as its bi-monthly.[48] All London co-ordination had started with preparations for a counter-demonstration against the National Front's St George's Day march through Wood Green, North London, on 23 April 1977. Anti-fascists in Harringey had managed to assemble an impressive alliance of local branches of the Labour Party, anti-racist groups, trade unionists, as well as the Indian Workers' Association, the International Marxist Group, the Socialist Workers' Party (SWP), Communists, local West Indians, Cypriots and even Conservative councillors into a 3,000-strong protest. There was, however, some disagreement over tactics, with minority elements on the anti-fascist side, led by the Socialist Workers' Party, urging physical confrontation.[49] Thus, whilst moderate anti-fascists addressed a meeting at one end of Duckett's Common at Wood Green, the SWP assembled away from this meeting and proceeded to subject the NF column to a series of ambushes and a barrage of smoke-bombs, bricks, stones, bottles, eggs and rotten fruit. In the most serious case of fascist/anti-fascist disorder in London since Red Lion Square, 81 people were arrested, of whom 74 were anti-fascists. None the less, despite the number of arrests, militant anti-fascists held that the Wood Green mobilisation had produced a favourable result, demoralising the Front by reducing the NF marchers to 'an ill-organised and bedraggled queue'.[50]

The anti-fascist solidarity that emerged from the Wood Green demonstration ran through the 1977 Greater London Council (GLC) elections the following month.[51] At these elections, the Front captured 119,063 votes in the 91 seats it contested. Although this averaged out at a relatively insignificant 5 per cent, the National Front polled impressively in East London where it won over 15 per cent of the vote in five seats in Hackney and Tower Hamlets, and in a number of other boroughs where it captured between 5 and 15 per cent of the vote. Perhaps most sensationally, the NF had beaten the Liberals to third place in 33 seats and now claimed to be the country's third most popular political party, a claim given credence by highly impressionistic reports that equated the GLC elections with levels of party support at general elections. Later analyses confirmed that the NF vote at the GLC elections was not evidence of growing support, but residual support distorted by the effects of differential turnout.[52] Nevertheless, the NF's apparent electoral success injected new urgency into the anti-fascist opposition and with the NF seemingly set for a major electoral breakthrough, anti-fascists stiffened their resolve. This was particularly true of the Socialist Workers' Party, which became even more determined to use physical force to 'clear the Nazis off the streets'.[53]

On 13 August 1977, the SWP gave further practical demonstration of what its intentions were at Lewisham in south London. Here, an 'anti-muggers' march had been called by the Front in an area where young blacks suspected of mugging offences had recently been targeted by police in a series of early morning raids. Not surprisingly, the Front's march excited much indignation and was clearly intended to fan the flames of racial tension. The AFC in Lewisham was the All Lewisham Campaign against Racism and Fascism (ALCARAF) which was a broad-based alliance formed in January 1977 and affiliated to the All London Co-ordinating Committee. Understandably, given ALCARAF's wide composition, which included representatives from the mainstream political parties, radical-Left groups, churches, trade unions, the local council, black organisations and women's groups, difficulties were encountered in agreeing on how ALCARAF should best respond to the Front's provocation. Consequently, the initiative passed to the Socialist Workers' Party which was intent on coming to blows with the National Front, to stop it from marching and thereby inflict an embarrassing defeat on the Front's leaders who had promised that Lewisham would be its biggest demonstration to date.[54]

Despite its initial hesitancy, ALCARAF was able to win broad support for a peaceful demonstration through Lewisham on the morning of 13 August, but ALCARAF scheduled it to take place at a different time and location from the Front's march. The SWP, on the other hand, called for a separate demonstration at Clifton Rise, which was the NF's intended assembly point, and scheduled it for just before the NF was set to arrive. The All London Co-ordinating Committee then stepped in between ALCARAF and the SWP and informed their chief stewards of respective plans. There was little attempt to restrain the SWP, not least because SWP members were active in many local AFCs, and besides, within the AFCs themselves there was undoubtedly radical elements that were favourable to militant anti-fascism.[55] Thus, despite intervention by the All London Co-ordinating Committee, two separate demonstrations were still planned – hardly an indication of successful co-ordination. In the meantime, repeated appeals were made for the National Front's march to be banned by three local MPs, the local Labour council, the TUC, ALCARAF, church leaders, 1,500 Christians, Lewisham Community Relations Council and the majority of the national and all the local press. Yet on the grounds of freedom of speech, Merlyn Rees, the Labour Home Secretary, refused to ban the march, even though this was clearly a suitable case for treatment under the Public Order Act. Rees was reported as saying, 'Even if we despise, disagree with, and hate the people involved, there is a right to demonstrate.'[56] But there was clearly an expectation of serious disorder with one quarter of the Metropolitan police subsequently called in to Lewisham with riot shields issued for the very first time.

The ALCARAF march, led by the Roger Godsiff, Labour Mayor of Lewisham, Mike Power, a member of the CPGB National Executive, Mervyn Stockwood, the Bishop of Southwark, and Martin Savitt, Chairman of the Jewish Defence Committee, attracted 4,000 antifascists and passed off without serious incident. What attracted most notice was a leaflet handed out by the CPGB calling on people not to attend the SWP march in the afternoon. This was a riposte to the SWP which had attempted to hijack the radical anti-fascist tradition from the CPGB by earlier distributing 'They shall not pass' leaflets in the borough. Whilst it may be true that, as a national body, the Communist Party had done little to counter the National Front and had surrendered militant anti-fascism to the IS/SWP and IMG, Communist Party members were often key figures in local anti-fascist committees.[57] Analogous to the policy pursued in the mid- to late 1940s, the Communist Party's line was that the way to oppose fascism was by building a broad front amongst a range of organisations so widening opposition to include the 'big battalions' of the labour movement. Within the AFCs, CPGB members looked to gain the confidence of moderate Labourites in the struggle against fascism and then win them over to Communism. In a repetition of well-versed arguments, the CPGB maintained that physical confrontation blocked the development of mass opposition to fascism as 'only street fighters are likely to apply', thereby isolating anti-fascists from the rest of the labour movement.[58] Interpreting Cable Street as a community-wide anti-fascist action, it therefore insisted that: 'The line of historic continuity between the great victory [at Cable Street] and the struggle against fascism today runs through the approach argued for by Communists in the Alcaraf, and not through the tactics of the SWP.'[59]

In fact, the Socialist Workers' Party had appealed to the Political Committee of the CPGB in June 1977 for 'united left action' against fascism but had been cold-shouldered.[60] The SWP then proceeded to hit back at the CPGB's 'reformism' and derided the AFCs as 'class collaborationist anti-racialist committees stuffed full of reformist trade union bureaucrats, jolly liberal clergymen and other such riff-raff'. Accordingly, the SWP advised that 'we should not ignore these bodies, but we have to recognise very clearly that they cannot and will not lead the physical struggle against fascism'.[61]

Whilst the first anti-fascist demonstration at Lewisham was peaceful, the second, involving 3,000–5,000 anti-fascists, unsurprisingly resulted in violent disorder. Contingents led by the SWP, which had resolved to 'stop the Nazi Front',[62] broke through the police cordon shielding the NF march and succeeded in splitting the march in two, whereupon police intervened and diverted the Front marchers, numbering some 500–600, into back-streets and then on to a small meeting addressed by John Tyndall. In response to attempts by the police to disperse the counter-demonstration, the SWP attacked the police in Lewisham High Street where the main 'battle' took place. While the numbers of anti-fascists present at the 'Battle of Lewisham' fades into insignificance when compared to the numbers at Cable Street, more than twice the number of anti-fascists (214) were arrested. It has been suggested that Lewisham marked a new stage in the escalation of the anti-fascist struggle by attracting significant numbers of local black people to militant anti-fascism.[63] Yet this has perhaps been exaggerated. Although ethnic origin is not clear, of those arrested at Lewisham, only 47 came from the local area.[64]

Predictably, the SWP claimed to have effected a major victory over the National Front at Lewisham, where 'the Nazi Front got the hammering of their lives'.[65] For one anti-fascist, such was the scale of the Front's defeat that 'if I was a National Front member I'd be hitting the bottle by now'.[66] The fact that the number of Front marchers had fallen from the 1,000 or so at Wood Green to 500–600 at Lewisham was taken as evidence that violent opposition was working: 'we know for a fact that many NF members are bloody angry with the leadership for putting them at risk'.[67] And, despite negative press publicity which had equated the 'Red Fascists' of the SWP with the National Front, and had in some cases (e.g. *Daily Mail, Daily Express*) proclaimed the SWP to be 'nastier' than the Front,[68] confrontational tactics were repeated at the Ladywood by-election in Birmingham on 15 August 1977, when anti-fascists clashed with police outside a Front election meeting in Handsworth.

In his defence of violence, Alex Callinicos of the SWP argued that failure to stop the Front from marching would empower Front leaders to build aggressive self-confidence amongst supporters and allow fear and intimidation to be spread amongst black and Asian people. Front recruits would then become 'hardened' Nazis and would soon turn on the working class itself.[69] Violence against the National Front would prevent this: it would shatter the illusion of fascist strength, break faith in the NF's leaders and cut down levels of support. Yet matching the short-term impact of Cable Street on BUF membership, it appears that the NF may have recruited 50 new members a day immediately following events at Lewisham and Ladywood.[70] There is also evidence to suggest that the Front picked up the support of around one in ten of the white electorate in Ladywood during the last few days of the campaign, possibly as a reaction to disorder by the extreme Left at Lewisham five days earlier and during the Ladywood campaign itself. This disorder may well have frightened a small minority of white electors who were then polarised to the Right. In the event, the Front polled 5.7 per cent of the vote and finished ahead of the Liberals.[71] Certainly the SWP's claim that the National Front's 'bubble burst at Lewisham'[72] can be questioned, and in terms of NF recruitment, as at Cable Street, physical confrontation appears to have had the opposite effect to what militant anti-fascists had originally anticipated.

Even if Lewisham did provide a boost to the Front, it proved very ephemeral. One consequence of the rise of militant anti-fascism was that the police became more inclined to ban marches under the Public Order Act. Thereafter the state increasingly denied the Front opportunities to hold processions as once again it fulfilled its historic role and sought to contain extremist disorder. At Manchester in October 1977, a NF march was banned, leading to the extraordinary sight of Martin Webster staging a lone protest in defence of free speech protected by 1,000 police. A two-month ban on demonstrations in London then followed in February 1978 in order to cover two by-elections contested by the Front. Indeed, by May 1978, the National Front had become convinced that the police had adopted a new anti-NF policy with Martin Webster claiming that the attitude of the police had changed from 'impartiality and fairness to a policy of bullying and intimidation'.[73] But perhaps the most widely known consequence of Lewisham was that the Socialist Workers' Party initiated the formation of the Anti-Nazi League. It had become obvious to the SWP that many people outside the SWP were keen to oppose the National Front but wanted little to do with the SWP itself. The SWP was ill at ease with the media's 'Red Fascists' smear and realised that its tactics were alienating it from more moderate opposition groups.[74] Therefore, the Socialist Workers' Party was anxious to develop a specific anti-fascist organisation that would not only draw in the widest possible range of opposition to the National Front, but would also counteract hostile reporting of the Socialist Workers' Party. As one anti-fascist explained:

> The problem with using violence is that it gets you bad publicity. You could argue that if people end up with an attitude of 'a plague on both your houses', you have still won because people aren't supporting the fascists – even if they don't support you either. But most anti-fascists would probably want to get approval for their cause, and this means being careful about what you do when the press is about.[75]

III

Widgery records that the idea of an anti-Nazi united front was first mooted a fortnight before Lewisham in the back garden of the home of Jim Nichols, the SWP's National Secretary;[76] though it was presumably the after-effects of Lewisham that led Paul Holborrow, a leading SWP activist, to take on the plan with such zeal. Holborrow succeeded in enlisting support from figures on the Labour Left, in particular Peter Hain, a prominent anti-apartheid campaigner, and Ernie Roberts, a former anti-nuclear campaigner, who was the prospective Labour candidate for Hackney North. In early November, the Anti-Nazi League was formerly launched at a meeting held at the House of Commons and, by the end of 1977, had secured the support of the majority of Tribune group of Labour Left MPs, known anti-fascists such as Maurice Ludmer (editor of *Searchlight*), Lord Brockway and Sid Bidnell, as well as prominent trade union leaders. Most noticeably, it also boasted sponsors from outside politics. These, as Taylor has already noted, were clearly intended to act as so-called 'opinion leaders' and provided much of the ANL's early publicity.[77] This group included actors (Alfie Bass, Warren Mitchell, Prunella Scales, Miriam

Karlin), comedians (Dave Allen, Derek Griffiths), authors (Iris Murdoch, Melvyn Bragg) and even football managers (Jack Charlton, Brian Clough).[78] A national steering committee was subsequently elected; the three executive positions of Organiser, Press Officer and Treasurer taken by Holborrow, Hain and Roberts respectively; the other committee members included Maurice Ludmer (thus guaranteeing *Searchlight's* input), a group of four Labour Left MPs including future Labour Party leader Neil Kinnock, Nigel Harris (a leading figure in the SWP) and the actress Miriam Karlin. Of these, Holborrow was the only full-time salaried official, with the Rowntree Trust pledging £600 every quarter until the next general election. Financial support was also forthcoming from an undisclosed Jewish businessman.[79]

With a view to becoming an all-embracing 'broad front' accommodating all those opposed to the growth of the British Nazism, the Anti-Nazi League stressed the need to forgo political differences and unite against the National Front on a national basis. In this sense, the launch of the Anti-Nazi League was a defining moment in the history of British anti-fascism as even at the height of Mosley's popularity in the 1930s there had been no national body solely dedicated to the anti-fascist struggle. In its founding statement, the League's stated objective was 'to organise on the widest possible scale against the propaganda and activities of the Nazis in Britain today'; more specifically, it put itself forth as a propaganda organisation that would counter the National Front at the forthcoming general election:

In these months before the General Election the Nazis will seize every opportunity to spread their propaganda. During the Election itself, National Front candidates will be entitled to equal TV and radio time to the major parties. The British electorate will be exposed to Nazi propaganda on an unprecedented scale.... Millions of leaflets and posters will have to be distributed. To have the necessary impact, this demands a campaign on a national and massive scale.[80]

This campaign began in earnest at a NF-contested parliamentary by-election at Bournemouth East at the end of November 1977 when an Anti-Nazi League team put up posters stating 'Never Again: Stop the Nazi National Front' and distributed an estimated 25,000 fact sheets exposing the 'real views' of the National Front.[81] The Front's poor showing of 3.8 per cent of the vote encouraged further local interventions by the ANL, although, understandably, initial forays into local electoral arenas raised concerns amongst the existing network of grass-roots anti-fascist groups that the ANL 'might swamp local activity and initiative'. None the less, the All London Co-ordinating Committee welcomed the launch of the Anti-Nazi League and advised that since the ANL was 'specifically geared towards fighting fascism at elections and will most probably dissolve after the next general election', the work of local AFCs would 'complement rather than compete with the aims of the Anti-Nazi League' and so local AFCs should make full use of ANL propaganda.[82] Indeed, at least over the short term, collaboration between the ANL and local AFCs followed. In April 1978, at a by-election in Brixton, the local AFC, known as the All Lambeth Anti-Racist Movement, worked closely alongside the Anti-Nazi League to organise a large public meeting and produced 30,000 joint leaflets.[83]

Such was the general level of concern over the Front's apparent progress, that as well as the Anti-Nazi League, various other anti-NF initiatives appeared towards the end of 1977. Joan Lestor, Labour MP and former editor of the original *Searchlight,* was the key figure behind the Joint Committee Against Racialism which was launched in December 1977. This, as Taylor identifies, was an 'alternative to the ANL for moderates'.[84] It attracted wide support from the Labour Party, Liberal Party, the Board of Deputies, the British Council of Churches, various immigrant organisations, the National Union of Students and, despite the protestations of Margaret Thatcher, the National Union of Conservative Associations. Unsurprisingly, with such broad representation, difficulties were encountered in agreeing to policies, and consequently, activity appears to have largely centred on distribution of anti-racist literature. Moreover, a national campaign against the National Front was also launched by the British Council of Churches, which essentially involved a declaration against racism signed by the Archbishop of Canterbury, which was then circulated to congregations for signature.[85]

More significant, however, was the Labour Party's decision to devote a TV broadcast in December 1977 to a 'hard-hitting' attack on the Front. This directly linked the NF to Hitler, Mussolini and the concentration camps – so critical that the BBC had to censor parts of it.[86] This broadcast, the cornerstone of a renewed joint campaign by the Labour Party and TUC against the National Front, was initiated by the Party's Press and Publicity Committee. It was devised by a non-party member, Ian Morrison, and resulted from Labour Party concerns over the 'inroads' that the NF was supposedly making into the Labour's working-class vote.[87] By using the mainstream media as the vehicle for anti-fascism in such a dramatic way, the Labour Party's broadcast had considerable impact. The simple 'NF = Nazis' message was driven into millions of homes, with the popular press further encouraging wide acceptance of this message by responding in complimentary terms. The *Daily Mirror's* editorial congratulated the broadcast which 'tore into the National Front head-on, the only way it will ever be routed',[88] and the *Sun* agreed that 'The Front ARE about the nastiest bunch of characters on the British political scene. Their so-called policies are a load of sickening rubbish.'[89]

Indeed, by early 1978, such was the depth of Labour Party disquiet about the Front's potential to become a vehicle for working-class protest, that the Anti-Nazi League had now gathered the support of over 50 Labour MPs, with many grassroots Labour Party activists also becoming ANL members. As Messina has noted, high-profile Labour politicians would often address ANL rallies, including Tony Benn who was then a Cabinet Minister. However, the Labour Party stopped short of official endorsement.[90] Naturally, it was cautious about aligning itself with an organisation linked to the SWP, which the Labour Party had already denounced following events at Lewisham in August 1977. Nevertheless, the Labour Party leadership was prepared to turn a blind eye to participation of its members alongside radical-Left groups in the Anti-Nazi League because with possibly close to 50,000 members by the summer of 1978, the ANL clearly had the potential to erode popular support for the Front in marginal constituencies. The Anti-Nazi League was thus politically advantageous for the Labour Party at a time when Labour's electoral prospects were bleak. As one anti-fascist publication put it, 'it was a chance to counteract NF electoral gains in Labour strongholds' so 'Labour saw the ANL primarily as an electoral machine for fighting the NF at the ballot box ...'[91]

However, notwithstanding growing Labour Party involvement, the Socialist Workers' Party still remained the Anti-Nazi League's leading player. Other radical-Left groups, such as the IMG and CPGB, did rally to the cause, with the latter having ditched its hostility to the SWP in the interests of popular anti-fascist unity; but with the ANL's structure based heavily on existing SWP networks, the Socialist Workers' Party supplied the Anti-Nazi League with its organisational backbone. Most local ANL branches were run by SWP activists and therefore, as well as having Holborrow installed in the ANL's top position, the SWP also dominated the ANL's local base. According to the National Front, SWP activists controlled ANL branches at Sheffield, Hull, Harrogate, Huddersfield, Rotherham, Bradford, Pontefract, Wakefield, Cardiff,

Manchester, South-East London, North Devon, Swansea, Pontypridd, Leeds and Newcastle.[92] Naturally, the rapid growth of the ANL also provided the SWP with recruitment opportunities. *Socialist Worker*, the SWP's weekly, reported on 27 May 1978 that owing to its lead in the struggle against the Front, people were joining the SWP at a rate of 150 a month. In one revealing issue, it was declared 'crucial that members of the SWP and supporters of our paper visit every member of the Anti-Nazi League in their locality to ask them to take out a subscription to *Socialist Worker*'.[93] Undoubtedly, the SWP recruited well through the Anti-Nazi League, with SWP membership rising to around 5,000 by the end of the 1970s.[94]

The linchpin of Anti-Nazi League activity was the dissemination of anti-fascist propaganda. As this chapter noted earlier, over five million leaflets were distributed within the League's first year; possibly as many as nine million leaflets were distributed in all. Initially, anti-fascist literature was put out during local campaigning at elections, but its dissemination widened considerably, commensurate with the scope of ANL activity which, during 1978, extended to the staging of mass rallies and the organisation of various workplace ANL groups (such as teachers, civil servants, railworkers, firemen, busmen, factory workers, and so on). Repeatedly, ANL propaganda branded the National Front a 'front for Nazis' and was unrelenting in its exposure of the Nazi credentials of the National Front's leaders. In this respect, the contribution of *Searchlight* proved vital. *Searchlight* supplied photographs of NF leaders Tyndall and Webster in Nazi regalia and provided revealing quotations from both Tyndall and Webster, who had both been members of the National Socialist Movement in their youth.[95] The fact that the leaders of the National Front had such irrefutable Nazi pasts was certainly advantageous for anti-fascists – as far as posing 'respectable' was concerned, Tyndall and Webster were hardly an exemplary choice. Not only did anti-fascist revelations raise awareness amongst the wider public of the Front's 'hidden agenda', anti-fascist propaganda also encouraged defections by NF sympathisers who had originally joined the Front because it was the only party speaking out against immigration but were horrified to discover a virulently anti-Semitic brand of fascism at the core. It has been suggested that around 12,000 people joined and then left the National Front in the 1970s[96] and unquestionably the Anti-Nazi League contributed to this rapid turnover of members by helping expose the Front's fascist ideology.

Additionally, as Gilroy has observed, the Anti-Nazi League also manipulated the residual anti-fascism of postwar British nationalism in order to betray the National Front as 'sham patriots' who were insid-iously importing an 'alien' and 'unpatriotic' ideology. Here Gilroy is worth quoting at length:

> This inauthentic patriotism was exposed and contrasted with the genuine nationalist spirit which had been created in Britain's finest hour – the 'anti-fascist' 1939–45 war. The neo-fascists wore the uniform of Nazism beneath their garb of outward respectability.... The League leaflets were illustrated with the imagery of the war – concentration camps and Nazi troops and were captioned with the slogan 'Never Again'.... Above all, the popular memory of the anti-fascist war was employed by the ANL to alert people to the dangers of neo-fascism in their midst. Pictures of the NF leaders wearing Nazi uniforms were produced as the final proof that their Britishness was in doubt.[97]

But critics of the Anti-Nazi League on the far Left were quick to point out that by arguing that the NF was 'unpatriotic', the ANL merely re-inforced patriotism. In this way, the ANL supported the British 'imperialist state', covered up the 'racist' immigration controls of the Labour government and thereby contained racism within a bourgeois democratic framework. Therefore, according to Maxine Williams of the Revolutionary Communist Group,[98] the ANL assumed a reac-tionary role where it eroded popular support for the NF merely 'to prevent support for racism from upsetting the bourgeois democratic apple cart ...'[99]

One does not necessarily have to agree with this radical analysis, however, to acknowledge that League propaganda paid little attention to the popular racism in which support for the National Front was located. This was quite deliberate because the ANL rightly assumed that British public opinion would find the designation 'NF = Nazis' much more offensive than simply objecting to the Front's 'racism'. The ANL thus looked to reactivate patriotism generated by the Second World War rather than address the roots of fascism in popular ideolo-gies of racism. The latter option was obviously far more problematic, especially when mainstream politicians like Thatcher legitimised racist attitudes, declaring on national television in a *World in Action* inter-view in January 1978, that she felt 'really rather afraid that this country might be rather swamped by people with a different culture'.[100] By side-stepping racism, the ANL's propaganda was more responsive to the sensitivities of public opinion, but this should not detract us from the weaknesses of this type of anti-fascist propaganda: first, by reducing the NF to a Nazi conspiracy, the issue of racism is disregarded (it even comes close to being anti-German) and second, what happens when the extreme Right, as Gilroy notes, 'shrug(s) off accusations of Nazism' and starts presenting itself 'credibly as nothing more than concerned British patriots'?[101]

While the Anti-Nazi League remained confident that appeals to anti-fascist patriotism would inhibit support for the NF amongst older cohorts, it believed that the National Front's decision to target youngsters necessitated new departures. At a press conference in January 1978, the Young National Front announced that it had produced a leaflet aimed at schoolchildren entitled 'How to Spot a Red Teacher' and was intending to distribute 250,000 copies. Equally disconcerting for anti-fascists were the results of two surveys in March 1978 which had found that one in seven young people were willing to support the National Front. Faced with this, the ANL responded in two ways. The first was the formation of an ANL sub-section known as 'Schoolkids Against the Nazis' organised by Chris Timbry, a member of the SWP. The second, more innovative response, was the decision to join forces with Rock Against Racism (RAR). This had been formed in August 1976 by a group of SWP activists in a bid to counteract the apparently racist comments of rock stars Eric Clapton and David Bowie. It had emerged on the back of the 'punk rock' youth movement and already by December 1977, had organised over 200 concerts, sold 12,000 badges and produced four issues of a magazine, *Temporary Hoarding*, courtesy of SWP resources.[102]

In the spring of 1978, the Anti-Nazi League approached RAR with the idea of staging a march and rock concert in London in order to appeal directly to young people. It was decided that a rally would be held in Trafalgar Square followed by a march to Victoria Park where the rock concert would take place in what would be termed a 'Carnival Against Racism'. On 30 April 1978, in the largest anti-fascist demonstration since the 1930s, an estimated 50,000 anti-fascists marched from Trafalgar Square to Victoria Park with effigies of Adolf Hitler and John Tyndall also on display. In Victoria Park itself, the crowd swelled to 80,000. This event was followed by a series of provincial carnivals with 35,000 people in Manchester, 8,000 in Edinburgh, 5,000 in Southampton, 5,000 in Cardiff, 2,000 in Harwich and 2,000 in Bradford. The sequence of rallies was then brought to a close with Carnival Two, held at Brockwell Park, Brixton in September, which attracted an impressive 100,000 people.[103] The scale of these events also contributed greatly to ANL funds, with the *Daily Telegraph* reporting on 26 April 1979 that the ANL had raised £175,000 from private and trade union donations during 1978.

Given the scale of popular participation in these events, it is hard to escape the conclusion that the ANL's alliance with Rock Against Racism connected with thousands of people, especially youthful sectors of society, and did much to neutralise the Front's appeal amongst these specific target groups. Arguably, it was here that the Anti-Nazi League was at its most effective, using a very contemporary medium of popular culture as a 'bridge' to carry anti-fascism to Britain's youth. Indeed, the scale of popular involvement in these anti-fascist events, in numbers not witnessed since the 1930s, led some commentators to suggest that the Anti-Nazi League had become the largest mass movement since both the Campaign for Nuclear Disarmament and the Vietnam Solidarity Campaign. In fact, by fusing with a cultural movement, the rise of the ANL was far more rapid, with this type of anti-fascist activity marking a radical new departure from more traditional forms of anti-fascist mobilisation.[104] Moreover, by embracing young people in such numbers, organised anti-fascism also succeeded in extending itself beyond its traditional base in the labour movement and Jewish community to unprecedented degrees.

All the same, the Anti-Nazi League continued to attract criticism from other radical-Left groups. According to the Workers' Revolutionary Party (WRP), an organisation of not more than 3,000 members,[105] since the working class was growing in strength – both trade union membership and militancy were on the increase – the Anti-Nazi League had exaggerated the threat from the National Front. Second, from a Trotskyist 'united front' perspective, the WRP argued that the ANL was a 'popular front' essentially comprised of 'middle-of-the-roaders' and 'centrists' who were mainly interested in the suppression of socialism and the defence of capitalist democracy. Preoccupied by theory, the Workers' Revolutionary Party refused to join the Anti-Nazi League and the same isolationist stance was taken by the Trotskyist Militant Tendency,[106] which also criticised the ANL for its failure to mobilise around an overall socialist programme.

A less doctrinaire criticism came from the Hackney Committee Against Racialism, a local AFC in East London. The Hackney Committee was appalled by the failure of the Anti-Nazi League to mobilise against a National Front march on May Day, just 24 hours after the first ANL carnival in April 1978. The Front's march from Portland Place in the West End to Cornet Square, Hoxton in East London went totally unopposed by anti-fascists. The Hackney Committee had pressed the Anti-Nazi League to mobilise opposition from the platform at the Carnival but ANL organisers insisted that they had become aware of the Front's intentions too late to organise mass opposition to the NF march. For those anti-fascists associated with the Hackney Committee, this failing indicated a shift in priorities whereby the Anti-Nazi League was diverting anti-fascist protest off the streets and into the parks, so avoiding direct confrontation with the National Front. It was noted, for instance, that despite the rapid growth of the Anti-Nazi League, the numbers of people mobilised against fascist meetings in London had dropped significantly, falling from 2,500 at the Ilford by-election in February 1978, to 1,000 at Brixton in April 1978 and finally to zero on May Day.[107] Anxious to retain the support of moderates and influential sponsors, the Anti-Nazi League was reluctant to put a radical 'no platform' policy into practice. One former anti-fascist activist recalls: 'Sure, the ANL in *some* areas created 'squads' to take on the fascists on the streets. But that wasn't the general picture. After the Battle of Lewisham the SWP were often the keenest to direct people away from militant confrontation.'[108] Indeed, the ANL's position became all too clear in September 1978 when the NF announced its intention to march through East London on the same day as the second ANL carnival was scheduled to take place in Brixton. Even though the local Hackney and Tower Hamlets Defence Committee[109] had called on the ANL to re-direct large numbers to the East End to protest against the NF, the ANL failed to respond with any sizeable numbers.[110]

A further gripe amongst anti-fascists was that the advent of the Anti-Nazi League also helped put an end to attempts to create a unified national structure by the existing network of 100 or so local anti-fascist committees. The swift growth of the ANL served to weaken local campaigns by drawing away SWP activists into an alternative organisation. That said, the failure of the National Anti-Racist, Anti-Fascist Conference in June 1978 also played its part in sinking proposals for a national organisation. This conference, which was organised by the 'National Committee' and the London Committee, flopped, falling prey to divisive ideological bickering between rival sects, with some groups reportedly pushing for 50 per cent of the conference agenda to be devoted to sexism.[111] Worse still, there was also disagreement between those that favoured a national steering committee elected from the conference and those wanting the national leadership to be based on existing AFCs. Predictably, the collapse of the conference alienated more moderate elements who could not fail to have been impressed by the ANL's well-organised national conference held the following month. This attracted 810 delegates compared to the National Anti-Racist, Anti-Fascist Conference which drew a relatively modest 152 delegates.[112]

Rather than compete with the Anti-Nazi League, the All London Co-ordinating Committee disbanded in September 1978, though a radical-Left collective did emerge from the London Committee which continued to publish *CARF*. In *CARF*'s analysis, the Anti-Nazi League had lost sight of the racism of white people which 'provides the breed-ing ground for groups like the National Front', and accordingly rebranded itself as a 'paper which speaks to white people on the ques-tion of racism'.[113] *CARF* endeavoured to redirect efforts towards local anti-racist campaigns and, through locally based struggles, hoped to build a grassroots anti-racist movement. In this regard, the plight of the Bengali community in the East End of London absorbed most attention following a series of racially motivated killings and racist disturbances between April and June 1978. For *CARF*, these events were part of a wider onslaught against the black community not only from fascists, but also from politicians, press, police, judges and the law. Faced with this onslaught, *CARF*'s response was to make the case for black and Asian self-defence. This did not mean racially motivated revenge-attacks on whites, but 'patrolling of areas by members of the community to allow its children to return unmolested from school, its workers to reach home unharmed, its youth to walk the streets without fear, its houses and businesses to withstand vandalism'.[114] It was to this end that *CARF* directed local groups, but with more moder-ate elements having withdrawn from the original network, sales of *CARF* fell. Consequently, at the end of 1979, *CARF* was incorporated into *Searchlight*, which had by this time established itself as Britain's leading anti-fascist magazine.

Searchlight had originally started life in 1975 with the objective of 'winning the argument' that the National Front was a Nazi conspiracy and records that 'At the time, the fashionable opinion was that the NF was no more than a particularly virulent anti-immigration pressure group, unpleasant, yes, but certainly not nazi in the classic sense …'[115] In order to prove its point, *Searchlight* put a three-part plan into action. First, it repeatedly revealed the Nazi pasts of the Front leader-ship. Second, it exposed the NF as a violent organisation by listing the criminal convictions of NF leaders and revealing connections between the NF and the loyalist paramilitaries in Northern Ireland. Third, it publicised links between the Front and neo-Nazi organisations at home (for example, the League of St George) and also abroad. In 'turning the searchlight on the extremists', *Searchlight* was assisted by 'moles' placed inside the extreme Right, one of the earliest being Dave Roberts, a former member of the CPGB and a leading figure in a small group known as 'Anti-Fascist Democratic Action'.[116]

This group began publishing *Forewarned Against Fascism* in March 1978 'with just £20 and a typewriter',[117] and claimed a circulation rising from 300 per issue to 2,500 by mid-1978.[118] *Forewarned* wanted to spark debate on the true nature and causes of fascism which, it said, resulted from landowners resorting to fascism in a conflict with capitalist industrialists. Whilst there is little evidence to suggest that this idiosyncratic analysis gained any wider currency amongst the anti-fascist movement, on a more practical level, its 'isolate a Nazi strategy', which published names and address of fascists probably proved a useful resource for those militant anti-fascists intent on subjecting fascist adversaries to individual attention.[119] In *Forewarned's* report on *Searchlight*, published in 1978, it emerges that *Searchlight* underwent a difficult period in early 1976 when under the editorship of Ken Sprague, sales fell to around 500 a month. However, once Maurice Ludmer returned as editor in May 1976 sales picked up and quickly rose to 2,500 a month – largely a consequence of the NF's electoral revival and media interest following *Searchlight's* exposure of the activities of Column 88, an alleged neo-Nazi paramilitary cell.[120]

By this time, as well as exposing the Nazi backgrounds of Front leaders, *Searchlight* had also began to expose their Nazi 'foregrounds' by drawing attention to current articles in *Spearhead* which revealed how strongly attached the Front's leadership was to authoritarianism, anti-Semitism and Holocaust revisionism.[121] Through the relative quality of its analysis, sales of *Searchlight* grew to perhaps 5,000 a month by 1978.[122] *Searchlight* now assumed a pivotal role in anti-fascist circles. It not only provided up-to-date information to activists but also materials for distribution in propaganda. Indeed, the work of *Searchlight* in this regard cannot be overemphasised: as one anti-fascist recalls, 'Nearly all the facts that packed our Anti-Nazi League leaflets and other material originated with Maurice [Ludmer]. His work literally passed through millions of hands.'[123]

IV

Armed with materials supplied by *Searchlight*, Husbands believes the Anti-Nazi League spread the 'NF = Nazis' message 'more widely and successfully than almost any other medium could have done',[124] a view supported elsewhere, notably in a study by Wilkinson.[125] Clearly the Anti-Nazi League deserves credit for 'hammering out' the anti-Nazi message but it is important to remember that the Anti-Nazi League was not the only medium for anti-fascism, a point largely unrecognised by most commentators. Of crucial importance in this respect was undoubtedly the mainstream media, yet research into the ways in which the National Front has been reported in Britain has been slender. Most focus, especially by Troyna, has concerned the national news media and in particular the national press. According to Troyna, it was the national press, by firmly exposing the Front's 'Nazi side', that had a 'most profound effect on public consciousness, and succeeded in discouraging further support for the party'.[126] But of course adverse reporting was repeated in other areas of the media as well. In addition to the 'hard-hitting' TV programmes already mentioned, the Front experienced more hostile treatment in July 1978 when Granada TV's *World in Action* programme investigated cases of racial violence in Leeds and linked them to NF members. To make matters worse for the Front, the NF was largely excluded from TV and radio and thus had little right to reply – Ludovic Kennedy's interview of Martin Webster for the BBC TV programme *Tonight* screened in December 1977 being a notable exception.

In the case of national press coverage, reports of disorder at Red Lion Square had already negatively associated the NF with violence, lawlessness and extremism ('Violence in the Streets', the *Sun*, 17 June 1974; 'Storm over Battle in Red Lion Square, *Daily Express*, 17 June 1974). This association was reinforced in 1977 following the clashes at Wood Green, Lewisham and Ladywood ('Thug Law', *Daily Express*, 15 August 1977; 'Hate Mob Runs Riot in Brum', *Daily Mirror*, 16 August 1977). Although it brought much sought after publicity for the Front, these violent episodes were typically portrayed as clashes between opposing groups of 'extremists' and with the exception of those minority elements attracted to street violence, this type of publicity only served to deny the Front political legitimacy. Moreover, this reporting was increasingly coupled with exposure of the National Front as a 'Nazi front' (e.g. 'I see the NF Hate Machine at Work', *Daily Mirror*, 4 July 1976; 'The Secret Crimes of Fuhrer Tyndall', *News of the World*, 11 December 1977). Indeed, such was the spread of negative press coverage that Troyna's survey conducted over the winter of 1978–9 found that over 65 per cent believed that their daily paper was anti-NF. Noticeably, there were repeated references to articles and leaders which focused on the Front's alleged fascist agenda.[127] And, although no such survey has been carried out for the provincial press, Eatwell makes the further point that even the ordinarily apolitical local press 'often took up the anti-fascist attack'.[128] This is clearly important as the combined circulation of local weeklies, bi-weeklies, provincial morning and evening papers far surpassed the circulation of the national press in the 1970s.

Significantly, the pattern of reporting the Front, especially at the local level, became noticeably more critical from 1977 onwards. This was a consequence of media workers becoming conscious of the fact that the press had helped whip up popular racism in 1976 and had therefore been mainly responsible for the NF's resurgence. Thus in the approach to the GLC elections in 1977, the Campaign Against Racism in the Media (CARM),[129] pressed journalists to adopt a hostile line when reporting statements and activities of fascists and racists. It also called on journalists to boycott letters/phone-ins from National Front/National Party candidates and supporters, pressed local candidates to endorse the view that the media should not be used for the expression of racist views and policies, and recommended industrial action where coverage was racist.[130] Moreover, the National Union of Journalists (NUJ) issued a series of guidelines, which recommended that the media should not be used as a platform for racist propaganda and that the National Front should only be reported in critical terms.

On occasions, however, the urge to speak out against the Front could give rise to conflict within local papers. For instance, on the *East Ender* (based in Newham), three journalists were reportedly 'harangued' and one of them physically assaulted by another reporter follow disagreements over anti-fascist policy.[131] On the *Hackney Gazette*, NUJ members went on strike for three days during the GLC elections following the decision of the management to publish an issue of the paper which carried a National Front advertisement. Presumably this was why, as Juliet Alexander, a former reporter for the *Hackney Gazette*, recalls, 'As far as the NF was concerned, we were a "Nigger-loving Commie rag", which is what they sprayed on the building.'[132]

Three of the most prominent examples of anti-fascism in the local press appeared in 1977 in the *Hornsey Journal*, the *South East London and Kentish Mercury* and the *East Ender*. The *Hornsey Journal* responded to the Front march in Wood Green with a graphically illustrated front page that drew an explicit analogy between the NF and Hitler's Nazis. The headline read 'Forty years on: the evil march ... of fascism fouls our streets' between which were captioned four pictures. The first in the top left-hand corner showed Hitler at a Nazi rally dated 1937, in the top right-hand corner a picture of Jews in a railway carriage truck dated 1940, in the bottom right-hand corner, a picture of a Front rally dated 1977 and in the bottom left-hand corner a blank photograph with a question mark dated 1980. The implication of the message was clear. Below these pictures it read:

Their objectives are no different from those of Hitler. The target may be blacks instead of just Jews. The military-style tactics may be less overt. But the cancerous symptons [*sic*] of Nazy-style [*sic*] nationalism are just as obvious, potent and inhuman.[133]

Shortly afterwards, at the GLC elections, the *South East London and Kentish Mercury* ran an anti-fascist election day plea under the headline 'YOU'D BETTER BELIEVE US … The National Front and National Party are making an offer you MUST refuse'. A picture of both Tyndall and Kingsley-Read with the former in paramilitary *Spearhead* uniform appeared alongside the following:

FOR THE first time every voter in SE London has a chance to tell the National Front and National Party: CLEAR OFF! Every one of you can go to the GLC polling stations and tell their candidates … NO! NO! 100,000 TIMES NO!… Vote Labour. Vote Tory. Vote Liberal. Vote Communist. Vote Fellowship Party. Even vote for the GLC Abolitionist Party! Vote for the Sunshine Club of Sydenham if you can find them. Put your cross against anyone else on the voting form. But for your sake. Our sake. Your children's and their future's sake … DON'T VOTE National Front or National Party.[134]

The *East Ender*, having adopted a 'neutral' stance at the GLC elections in May, published a racy exposé of the NF in August 1977 under the sensational front page headline 'EXPOSED: THE NAZI MENACE IN THE EAST END' aloft a photograph of two Nazi-saluting Front followers. This exposé was based on revelations by a National Front defector, John Considine, who declared that the Front was 'Something very evil masquerading as a party'. The front page read:

THE new Nazis are stalking the streets of London. Thirty years after the politics of hate were crushed in Europe, fascism is again raising its head. A new breed of violent fascists is making a mark in the East End. They celebrate Hitler's birthday, they honour the swastika and read 'Mein Kampf'. They peddle violence and preach hatred against black people and Jews. It was this grim picture which opened the eyes of National Front member John Considine. He was sickened by the ideas, the hate and the violence.[135]

By the late 1970s, local press opposition to the National Front was commonplace.[136] Even the *Leicester Mercury*, which had been previously criticised for running stories with racist sentiments, finally answered its critics and came out against the NF: 'To give the National Front the chance of power to implement its cruel policies would be a rejection of humanity' (*Leicester Mercury*, 29 April 1977).

Evidently, with the local press joining the national media in its opposition to the Front, the mainstream British media became the Front's most telling antagonist. Towards the end of the 1970s, not only was the Front largely excluded from the media, it had also been associated with violence, exposed as a fascist organisation to millions of television viewers and had been correspondingly identified as a Nazi-type organisation in both the national and local press. For some anti-fascists, however, the media had not gone far enough and there were calls for broadcasters to take the unprecedented step of refusing the National Front party political broadcasts. To this end, CARM joined forces with the Anti-Nazi League and launched a 'No Plugs for the Nazi Thugs' campaign in August 1978. This was a response to the Front's decision to stand over 300 candidates at the 1979 general election and was intended to apply pressure on the broadcasting networks to deny the NF a party political broadcast. As it turned out, this campaign rebounded on CARM and the ANL: there was an unfavourable reaction in the press and also from broadcasting chiefs who insisted that the National Front, as a legally formed political party, could not be denied a broadcast simply because the ANL disapproves of its policies.[137] Yet in practice, despite the fact that Front was fighting a far greater number of seats, it was granted the same broadcasting time in 1979 as in 1974. Moreover, in terms of more general reporting, the Front received less media coverage in 1979 than at both elections in 1974, and even 'reached the stage of farce when we were granted radio interviews by American and Canadian networks which exceeded in length and scope anything granted by the national broadcasting services in Britain!'[138]

V

Following the GLC elections in 1977, it had been widely feared that the National Front was on the verge of an electoral breakthrough; the Front's performance at elections in 1978 suggested otherwise. In its previous strongholds outside London, levels of National Front support decreased sharply and only in London, in the East End, did the Front retain significant support. None the less, the Front still harboured pretentions to serious electoral credibility and accordingly mobilised all its resources to field a record 303 candidates at the 1979 general election. The Front's strategy was to try to reach as many people as possible and so was forced to stretch its campaigning efforts across multiple constituencies. It did not plan on mass canvassing, but instead relied on meetings and free broadcasting time to generate publicity. And since the terms of the Representation of the People Act (1949) made it incumbent on local councils to make council property available for all candidates contesting an election, the National Front managed to secure a number of premises for election meetings. Meetings were therefore scheduled to take place in April 1979 at Battersea, Islington, Southall and Newham in London and elsewhere at Plymouth, Binas Powys in South Wales, Lewes, West Bromwich, Bristol, Rochdale and Bradford. The Front also planned to hold election rallies at Crawley, New Brighton on Merseyside and Glasgow, with a final national election rally booked for Caxton Hall, London on 1 May. In addition, a national march to an election meeting was planned for 21 April in Leicester.

If during election periods any candidate had the right to hire council premises; the decision to allow the NF council premises was entirely at the discretion of the council at all other times. Consequently, towards the end of the 1970s, the National Front had been increasingly refused the hire of halls outside election periods and thus faced exactly the same problem as Mosley had previously encountered in the 1930s and early 1960s. According to Tyndall, Labour-controlled local authorities would refuse on the basis that halls should not be made available to racists, a policy further endorsed by the Labour Party's National Executive Committee in September 1978,[139] whereas Conservative-controlled councils usually insisted on prohibitively large insurance premiums to cover possible damages.[140] In fact, there were even cases of anti-fascist local authorities refusing the National Front candidate council premises during election periods. Typically, this refusal was on the grounds that the council was not satisfied that the meeting would be made public and, under this pretext, the Front had been denied the use of school premises during a by-election in Manchester in June 1978, and had been refused a school hall in Brent in north London in April 1979.[141]

Despite the electoral advance of the Front having clearly floundered by 1978, the fact that the Front was contesting so many seats at the 1979 general election was understandably viewed with concern. The Board of Deputies predicted that if the Front's overall vote was less than 2 per cent 'the leadership, both national and on a local level, will not only be demoralised but generally discredited'. It thus set itself the task of updating anti-NF leaflets and making them available to the three main political parties through contacts established at the local level between constituency agents and the Board's local committees and AJEX branches. In addition, the Defence Department would collate information about NF candidates, provide information about these candidates to the news media and would also make special information packs available exposing the true nature of the Front. Moreover, National Front meetings and marches would be monitored and ethnic minority groups approached to ensure the highest possible voter turnout.[142] Meanwhile, the Anti-Nazi League would mobilise opposition to National Front marches and rallies as well as organise opposition to the Front's election meetings. In particular, it would try to ensure that these meetings adhered to the Representation of the People Act and were bona fide public meetings. The Anti-Nazi League anticipated that once inside a hall, its activists could then disrupt the meeting by heckling speakers and on at least two occasions during the 1979 general election campaign, this tactic proved effective: at Plymouth, where anti-fascists managed to gain access to the hall and forced the meeting to be abandoned, and at West Bromwich when police cleared the hall following attempts by National Front stewards to evict hecklers forcefully.

It was fortunate for the Anti-Nazi League that the National Front had pinned its hopes on a relatively small number of election meetings, marches and rallies, because following the series of carnivals in the summer of 1978, the ANL had stagnated. A variety of reasons account for why activity had died down over the winter of 1978–9. First, moderate ANL supporters were becoming unhappy at SWP domination and the lack of internal democracy. The belief that the SWP was using the ANL as a recruitment front was gaining credence, leading a number of organisations to withdraw and high-profile sponsors to resign. This may have resulted in part from the National Front's distribution of an apparently well-researched booklet *Lifting the Lid off the Anti-Nazi League* which had been specifically sent to ANL sponsors, though the booklet did stretch the truth when it declared the Anti-Nazi League to be the creation of the Board of Deputies (and hence part of the Jewish conspiracy).[143] In reality, the Board's relations with the ANL remained somewhat fraught, not least because of the SWP's anti-Zionism. Many grassroots ANL activists were also alienated by the SWP's decision to 'workerise' the Anti-Nazi League by trying to move it into the factories. This was part of a wider strategy aimed at gaining the SWP a foothold in the trade unions, as the SWP's leading figure Tony Cliff made clear in *Socialist Worker*; 'The more the ANL is rooted in the workplace, the more the inter-connection between *all* aspects of struggle will be clear to everyone.'[144] There is also a suggestion that it was deliberate policy by the Labour Party to 'keep the ANL on ice' until the general election and consequently, as one radical-Left group records, 'many ANL supporters were allowed to drift away and did not return in May 1979'.[145] Consequently, the ANL found it difficult to mobilise numbers for the 1979 general election, with one NF activist observing that the ANL's campaign 'was a total failure, especially the mass leaflet-ting campaign which failed to materialise at all'.[146]

Yet the Anti-Nazi League still made its presence felt, particularly at Leicester and Southall. Since both were areas of high immigrant density, the ANL was especially determined to stand up to the Front's incursions into these localities. At Leicester, where the Front had planned a St George's Day march to an election meeting, the Labour, Liberal and Conservative candidates, local churches, the Anti-Nazi League and Asian organisations had all called on the authorities to ban the march. But in the interests of free speech, Leicestershire Chief Constable, Alan Goodson, refused to bow to pressure and drafted in some 5,000 police from no fewer than 21 police forces. On 21 April 1979, an estimated 2,000 anti-fascists mobilised to oppose no more than 1,000 Front supporters. Following attempts by the ANL to waylay the Front, there were confrontations between counter-demonstrators and police, with television pictures later showing police dogs chasing anti-fascists onto Leicester University campus. The reported numbers arrested ranged from 40 to 82 but these numbers were insignificant when compared with the mass arrests just two days later at Southall, in the London borough of Ealing.[147]

Although the Conservative-controlled council in Ealing did have a policy of not letting halls to the Front, it felt obligated under the terms of the Representation of the People Act to make Southall Town Hall available for National Front use provided that a third of seats inside the hall were reserved for members of the general public. In early April, the local community had become aware of the NF's plans and the Southall Indian Workers' Association had subsequently called a meeting to discuss ways in which the Front's meeting could be opposed. Aside from the IWA and Ealing Community Relations Council, the local branch of the Anti-Nazi League also attended. The IWA proposed that there should be closing down of businesses in Southall on 23 April from 1 pm onwards as a sign of protest, but that the NF meeting at the Town Hall should be ignored. The ANL, on the other hand, proposed a demonstration outside the Town Hall. Eventually, the meeting agreed that there should be a mass, peaceful sit-in on roads around the Town Hall and that those arrested should not resist police arrest. The meeting also set up a Co-ordinating Committee which proceeded to distribute some 25,000 leaflets and 1,000 window posters around the borough stressing that the protest was to be peaceful.

But not all publicity emphasised the intended peaceful nature of the protest. The ANL's leaflet, for instance, issued in both English and Punjabi, called on people to 'Stop the Nazi meeting'. This slogan was repeated in *Socialist Worker*, with the SWP also calling on all its followers in London and the surrounding area to mobilise for the Southall demonstration. On 18 April, representatives from the Co-ordinating Committee met Merlyn Rees, the Home Secretary, who was visiting Ealing as part of Labour's election campaign. Rees maintained that, legally, he was not in a position to ban a public election meeting but undeterred, on 22 April, a 'March for Unity and Peace' was organised when between 3,000 and 5,000 anti-fascists marched in peaceful protest to Ealing Borough Town Hall in a final, albeit unsuccessful bid to have the Front's meeting cancelled. This march was, however, subjected to 'snatch arrests' by police, which served to sour relations between the police and local community before the main demonstration scheduled to take place at 5 pm the following day.

In the early afternoon of 23 April, anti-Front demonstrators began to assemble outside Southall Town Hall. The first group to attempt to congregate was the Southall Youth Movement which was intent on picketing the Town Hall in order to ensure that no NF supporters could gain access to the hall before the main demonstration. As the number of protesters grew, the police guarding the Town Hall, numbering around 3,000, decided to clear the crowd from the crossroads outside the Town Hall. By 4 pm, the police had established a cordon which split the demonstrators into distinct groups thereby preventing the possibility of a peaceful sit-down protest. Serious disturbances between police and demonstrators then followed at various locations. Missiles were thrown at police from the anti-fascist side, including flares, smoke-bombs and a petrol bomb, which was hurled at a police coach. The police also contributed to disorder, first by making peaceful protest impossible, and then by attempting to disperse the crowd using aggressive tactics, such as 'snatch squads', charging with riot shields, truncheons and horses, and even driving vans into the crowd. It was therefore not surprising that a fatality occurred: at around 7.45 pm, Blair Peach, a member of both the SWP and the ANL was killed.

Suspecting that Blair Peach had died following a blow to the head, anti-fascists accused the police and, in particular, officers from the Special Patrol Group.[148] On 28 April, 10,000 people marched to mourn the death of Blair Peach and in June, 8,000 people attended an all-night vigil prior to his burial. Yet despite the weight of evidence implicating the police, the government refused an official inquiry, no police officer was ever prosecuted and at Blair Peach's inquest, the verdict passed was 'death by misadventure'.[149] For many on the radical Left, the actions of the police at Southall represented a crucial moment in the anti-fascist struggle, with the state now replacing the NF as the main adversary. The police unquestionably used excessive force at Southall with the scale of arrests of over 700 (342 charged) even surpassing the numbers arrested at Lewisham. With few exceptions (for example, the *Daily Mirror*), the media reacted to events by blaming 'extremist outsiders' (that is, the ANL and SWP) who were said to have come into Southall determined on violent confrontation with police.

There are clearly a number of problems with this reading of events. First, Southall had its own local ANL branch which did agree to plan for peaceful protest. Second, although a number of ANL members did come into Southall from other parts of London, such as Blair Peach, a New Zealander who lived in East London, and ANL activists were also present from Oxford and Kingston, the majority of the demonstrators were Asians from the local community who were clearly angered by Front activity on their doorsteps. Third, according to figures in *CARF*, 95 per cent of those arrested came from the local area.[150] It therefore seems reasonable to conclude that outside involvement was minimal and that overall responsibility for the violence must rest with the National Front whose incursion into Southall set the local community at odds with the police after the police had denied the Asian community the opportunity to hold a peaceful demonstration.

If Front leaders hoped that the publicity resulting from Southall would boost the NF's electoral prospects, they were sorely disappointed. The National Front secured a derisory 1.3 per cent of the vote at the 1979 general election. This represented a fall of 2.8 per cent in relation to the previous general election in October 1974 with an extra 213 candidates having yielded only an additional 76,220 votes. Even in its recognised strongholds, its share of the vote fell. In fact, for all its claims to be the country's third most popular party, the Front failed to poll more than any Liberal candidate in any constituency and only in Hove, in Sussex, did the Front manage to poll more in 1979 than in 1974, but this was an increase of only 0.2 per cent.

Electorally, the National Front had clearly come to grief and at last, for all but the most dedicated and vigilant anti-fascists, it could finally be written off. The Front's election defeat was overwhelming and, as the Board of Deputies predicted, dissenting elements quickly called the leadership to account thus setting off a damaging period of internal warfare resulting in the formation of a number of rival offshoots.[151] In truth, the National Front should have seen this coming because even though it had tried to present a respectable face, it could not offset anti-fascist censure because no matter how many times it condemned National Socialism, trimmed its policies, reasserted its 'commitment' to democratic politics, its leadership (Tyndall and Webster) was far too transparent. How far the National Front's identification with Nazism had penetrated society is clear from a survey conducted by NOP Market Research in February 1978 which found that 64 per cent of its sample 'strongly agreed' or 'tended to agree' that the 'National Front has a Nazi side to it'.[152] It is obvious, therefore, that anti-fascism, emanating from a variety of sources, especially the media as well as anti-fascist groups, had successfully pinned the Nazi label on the NF. This discouraged potential support for the Front by equating the NF with a pernicious ideology, by reactivating patriotism and thereupon divesting the National Front of any remaining political respectability.

But as we have seen, anti-fascist propaganda did not address racism. Indeed, those with very determined views on the race issue might still have supported the Front in spite of its 'Nazi' label had it not been for the Conservative Party which was able to attract these voters through Margaret Thatcher's calculated exploitation of the race issue in 1978. So whilst anti-fascism spread the perception that the National Front was fascist and this was clearly a major factor in its widespread rejection, it does not fully account for the Front's demise. On this point, Griffin has recently argued that the revolutionary threat of fascism is so marginalised in mature liberal democracies that 'it was not the election of the Conservative Party in 1979 that forestalled a National Front takeover of Britain, any more than it was the Anti-Nazi League that clipped its wings'.[153] Yet what Griffin's argument fails to acknowledge is that the National Front operated on two levels where revolutionary nationalism was hidden behind the outward respectability of racial populism. The key to the National Front's limited success was not revolutionary ideology but the 'soft sell', presenting itself as a democratic political party with reasonable policies. It was only when anti-fascism had exposed this outward appearance as a cover for Nazism and Margaret Thatcher had simultaneously drawn the racist constituency towards the Conservative Party, that the ground was finally cut from under its feet.

With tens of thousands of people involved in displays of opposition to the National Front, the level of popular participation in anti-fascist activity in the 1970s was clearly significant. Rough comparisons with the 1930s suggest popular involvement on a similar scale. And it was noticeable that anti-fascism developed in like manner through locally based responses on an *ad hoc* basis which took the form of broad front committees. In the early 1970s, numbers involved in the initial phase of anti-fascist mobilisation were not inconsiderable but certainly fell short of the heights attained by the Anti-Nazi League in the late 1970s. Particularly from 1976 onwards, participation increased as anti-fascist committees multiplied across the country in order to counter the National Front's revival. Yet what transformed organised anti-fascism into a mass movement was not the growing network of local anti-fascist groups but the launch of the Anti-Nazi League and in particular, its fusion with Rock Against Racism. This changed the face of traditional anti-fascist activity by merging political agitation with a particularly vibrant form of popular youth culture and so carried anti-fascism beyond its traditional bases in the labour movement directly to Britain's youth. At the same time, also in a new departure, black and Asian communities increasingly mobilised against the Front. At Lewisham, this may have been overstated, but ethnic minority groups did organise against Front activity in their districts, most notably at Southall.

Undoubtedly, the extent of anti-fascist unity in the 1970s was impressive. This, despite tactical disagreements, particularly over the question of whether countering the National Front primarily meant countering Nazism or the roots of NF support in popular racism. Yet the cynic will have noted from this chapter that even though the ANL did achieve much in the way of anti-fascist solidarity, it was essentially a marriage of convenience between the SWP and the Labour Party. In this sense, radical-Left critics were right when the ANL was proclaimed not a genuine 'united front' but a 'behind closed-doors alliance of the Socialist Workers' Party and some MPs'.[154] Whilst the SWP 'disappeared' within the Anti-Nazi League and then used it as a vehicle to convert non-affiliated individuals, the Labour Party saw the ANL as a tool for eroding the NF's working-class support in marginal constituencies. Thus, unlike the 1930s, when the Labour Party had little to gain from collaboration with the extreme Left in anti-fascist activity, in the 1970s, electoral exigencies dictated co-operation with groups that under 'normal' circumstances the Labour Party would have kept at a distance. So not surprisingly, once it had become clear that the National Front had been beaten, Labour quickly abandoned ship. And, despite the fact that the ANL had probably put a stop to the SWP's decline, with the arrival of Thatcher's right-wing adminstration, the attentions of the Socialist Workers' Party leadership and its grassroots turned elsewhere. Now, in Margaret Thatcher, the SWP had a far weightier adversary.

5
Fighting Fascism in the 1980s and 1990s

At the beginning of the 1980s, with the National Front having fallen on hard times, the urgency that had rallied mass opposition to the NF between 1977 and 1979 disappeared. But not only had the threat of fascism abated, political space for anti-fascism had also been cut by the arrival of Margaret Thatcher whose austere, right-wing policies raised more pressing issues for the Left. In consequence, in the early 1980s anti-fascism lost momentum and petered out. Although a few local Anti-Nazi League groups continued to exist, the ANL wound down and dwindled to vanishing point.[1] There were efforts to reinvigorate it during 1980-1 when the activities of the NF's main rival, the British Movement, generated concerns about the rising popularity of the Nazi cult amongst working-class youth, but these efforts came to nothing and the ANL failed to establish a permanent presence.[2] The size of the Anti-Nazi League picket at the founding press conference of the British National Party (BNP) in April 1982, when fewer than ten activists stood outside in the rain, confirmed that it had come to the end of its run. Already in October 1981, *Searchlight* had described a situation where there was 'no anti-racist, anti-fascist movement to speak of' and had called for the formation of a new, nationally co-ordinated organisation dedicated to the fight against fascism and racism.[3] To this end, a meeting was convened in May 1981 to mark the first anniversary of the death of the Maurice Ludmer at which it was hoped that new initiatives to sustain the anti-fascist struggle might emerge. Yet with only 60 people in attendance in a hall that could seat 1,200, it was all too clear that the scale of the fascist threat had diminished to such an extent that the formation of a mass anti-fascist movement in the near future was an unlikely prospect.

Of the local Anti-Nazi League groups still functioning after the 1979 general election, one of the most active was the branch based in Islington which objected to NF activity at Chapel Street market where the Front had established regular paper sales during 1981. Despite vicious intimidation, where on one occasion, ANL members were apparently attacked by a large group of 'brick-wielding' fascists,[4] the local ANL continued to leaflet the market and collected a petition signed by over 800 shoppers opposing NF violence and sale of fascist literature. Of more significance, however, was the regular presence of Patrick Harrington, a young NF local branch organiser. In April 1983, an article entitled 'Who Polices the Nazis?', which carried a photograph of Harrington selling literature at Chapel Street market, appeared in *Fuse*, the student magazine at the Polytechnic of North London (PNL). Following the publication of this article, students to whom Harrington had attempted to sell *National Front News* identified him as a first-year undergraduate at the polytechnic and after verification from *Searchlight*, Harrington became known to the student body as an NF activist. Following a brief campaign by students objecting to his attendance at the polytechnic, Harrington promptly disappeared, only to return to the polytechnic in February 1984 to brazen it out. In doing so, a wave of anti-fascist protest was initiated resulting in a series of events, aptly described by one polytechnic lecturer as a 'comic opera',[5] involving mass student pickets, confrontations between riot police and students, High Court action, the presence of a High Court tipstaff in classes ruling what could and could not be discussed, the threat of 14 lecturers being jailed and, unsurprisingly, calls from the right-wing press to close the polytechnic down. In an amusing analogy, a *Times* editorial suggested that the script – an unfortunate student being 'victimised' for his right-wing views – had been written a decade earlier by Malcolm Bradbury in his novel, *The History Man*.[6]

The comic analogies aside, why did the presence of a lone individual cause such mayhem? In the first place, Harrington was more than just a passive member of the National Front, he was a leading activist – the treasurer of Kensington/Chelsea NF, a student and Young National Front organiser, assistant editor of *National Front News*, and an officer in the NF's Publicity Department. Moreover, there were allegations that he was a former editor of *South London News*, a publication which had featured hitlists of anti-fascists alongside details of how to send opponents faeces in the post as well as advice on how to tape razor blades to envelopes. Harrington had also been suspected of organising attacks on anti-fascists in Islington in 1981 and allegedly advocated the use of firebombing in a conversation recorded on tape by an ANL member. Moreover, it was widely held that Harrington was not a bona fide student. His attendance record at classes during his first year had been poor and he had not even registered for a library card. Add to this the multi-ethnic composition of the student body at the Polytechnic of North London and its reputation as the most left-wing college in the country, where on average there had been demonstrations or disruptions four times a year over the previous 14 years;[7] then had Harrington deliberately conspired to enrol at PNL to cause trouble and so attract publicity for the Front, he clearly could not have chosen a more appropriate place to 'study'.

Whether a conspiracy or not, Harrington's reappearance in February 1984 was certain to cause disquiet. Initially, a small group of philosophy students began to mount pickets in March 1984 objecting to Harrington's attendance at lectures. Gradually, organised by the Socialist Workers' Student Society, these pickets grew and culminated in a mass picket on 1 May 1984 when hundreds of students, joined by polytechnic trade unionists and a number of outsiders, gathered to prevent Harrington from gaining entry to the Polytechnic's Kentish Town site. By this time, however, Harrington had initiated legal action in the High Court and had obtained an injunction restraining, in both a personal and representative capacity, Steve Phillip (a black sociology student and member of the Socialist Workers' Student Society) from interfering with his contractual right to attend lectures. The mass picket against Harrington on 1 May was therefore in breach of this injunction. Having baited the trap, the NF photographed students participating in the picket and then applied to have those students identified and imprisoned. On 21 May, Judge Mars-Jones ordered 14 lecturers to disclose the identities of anti-fascist students photographed on the demonstration, but after staff were granted leave of appeal, the order was eventually discharged on technical irregularities.[8] Meanwhile, the Polytechnic Directorate attempted to defuse the situation by offering Harrington private tuition. This Harrington refused and, with considerable police protection, was able to carry on attending lectures in the company of the High Court tipstaff despite ongoing protest, which on 22 May saw several hundred students demonstrate outside the Kentish Town site of the polytechnic, whilst inside some 300 students lined the corridors in 'silent protest' and occupied all the seats in the library.[9]

Interrupted only by the summer vacation, the disruption at the polytechnic continued into the new academic term. At an emergency general meeting of the students' union in October 1984 a decision was taken to defy the High Court order and resume mass picketing. This drew immediate criticism from the National Union of Students, which called on students not to take any illegal action. The NUS then withdrew its support and instructed all affiliated student unions to follow suit, at which point splits started to emerge in the 'Harrington Out' campaign with many students having concluded that further protests would result in pointless confrontation and would likely lead to the closure of the polytechnic.[10] Then, in a bizarre twist, the Director of the Polytechnic, Dr David MacDowall, announced his resignation. In an open letter circulated to staff and students, MacDowall admitted, ironically, that by discouraging students from protesting, by threatening disciplinary action and by naming students for NF lawyers, he had acted 'in a totally fascistic manner'. In his parting shot, MacDowall even wished 'all the picketing students the best of luck in their campaign'.[11] Yet despite the resignation of MacDowall, which called further attention to the polytechnic's maladministration, and despite the reservations of a growing number of students, there was no immediate end to the protests. Consequently, in November 1984, Harrington once again resorted to legal action and made a committal application against two polytechnic students who had broken the injunction. At a subsequent hearing, the two students, Steven Tisane and John Leatham, were imprisoned for refusing to give an undertaking that they would stop trying to prevent Harrington from attending the polytechnic.[12]

In the end, it was January 1985 before the new director, Dr John Beishon, was able to broker a deal whereby Harrington would be taught in isolation in a small polytechnic house away from the main sites, whilst in return, the student body agreed to call off the pickets.[13] Although there were complaints of a 'sell-out', most students welcomed the deal as a '90 per cent victory' and after ten months of disruption, some semblance of peace finally returned to the polytechnic.[14] But there were suggestions that this 'victory' came at too great a cost, with the media reporting Harrington and not his objectors as the injured party. As one commentator said, the media portrayal of Harrington was that of a victimised individual 'modestly and courageously claiming his right to education' with anti-fascist students having 'handed, on a plate, more publicity to the Front than it has had for years'.[15] Certainly, Harrington's position within the Front's elite was strengthened – he even won a National Front bravery award – and the Front did obtain considerable publicity. However, Harrington's 'heroic' deeds failed to rescue the National Front from further decline, with membership having contracted continuously from 10,000 at the time of the 1979 general election to just below 1,000 by January 1985.[16]

Inadvertently, the major consequence of the 'Harrington Out' campaign was the damage it inflicted on the already beleaguered reputation of the polytechnic. Leading the calls for the polytechnic's closure was Baroness Cox, who in quite hysterical terms, warned in the *Daily Mail* that the Polytechnic of North London was producing 'graduates in the art of anarchy' and was 'a malignant cell in the body of higher education, spreading its pernicious influence into the wider society'.[17] Yet even if the 'Harrington Out' campaign scored an 'own goal' in this respect, the episode does retain significance in the wider history of British anti-fascism. It was the first example of students at a higher education institution coming together to oppose a leading member of a fascist organisation whose presence, they feared, would lead to racial attacks on the multi-ethnic student body. This points to the uniqueness of this case and underlines the very diversity of the British anti-fascist experience. But in another sense, it merely follows in the line of other historical examples of community-based responses to fascism. The difference on this occasion, however, was that the community was the student body and although other episodes of student opposition to a fascist presence on campus have arisen since, the scale of disruption at the Polytechnic of North London has never been repeated.[18]

II

As students at the Polytechnic of North London initiated their anti-fascist protest, a timely warning of the potential dangers of right-wing extremism was served by Channel Four when, in March 1984, it screened *The Other Face of Terror*. This was a 75-minute television documentary in which Ray Hill,[19] a *Searchlight* informant, revealed how he had sabotaged a fascist plot to plant a massive bomb at the Notting Hill Carnival in 1981. In this programme, Hill alleged that Tony Malski, the leader of an obscure neo-Nazi grouplet known as the National Socialist Action Party, had planned to start a race war by detonating a bomb supplied by French fascists at Europe's largest black street carnival. In order to thwart the plan, Hill leaked the story to the *Daily Mirror*, which carried it on its front-page a few days before the Notting Hill Carnival was due to take place. According to Hill, this alarmed Malski who swiftly dropped the plan and so the plot was foiled. But this was not the limit to Hill's sharp practice as it also emerged that whilst working undercover for *Searchlight*, he had successfully infiltrated the British Democratic Party (BDP), a National Front splinter group led by Anthony Reed-Herbert, a solicitor based in Leicester. For a moment, the BDP offered the possibility of becoming a serious rival to the NF, yet in a story that originated with Ray Hill, Reed-Herbert's involvement in a gun-running operation was exposed in a *World in Action* programme in July 1981 and this, by forcing Reed-Herbert into self-imposed exile in Ireland, led to the collapse of the British Democratic Party. Moreover, Hill claims to have triggered the disintegration of the British Movement, the successor to Colin Jordan's National Socialist Movement, first by establishing a leading presence within that organisation and second, by engineering a split whereby he delivered half its membership to Tyndall's British National Party in 1982. Hill then ensured that the newly launched BNP faltered by putting a stop to an alliance between Tyndall and Joe Pearce's faction of the National Front.[20]

Through his anti-fascist work, Ray Hill believes that 'major successes were chalked up'[21] and there is no denying that he put himself at considerable risk for the anti-fascist cause. Clearly, if there had been a plot to bomb the Notting Hill Carnival then by saving many lives, Hill's tip-off to the press was of major significance. Yet there are doubts as to whether such a plot actually existed as no prosecution was ever brought. One commentator has even speculated that the plot was deliberately fabricated by *Searchlight*.[22] As for the damage inflicted to both the British Democratic Party and the British Movement, it is worth bearing in mind that the former may have had potential for growth but it was still a tiny grouping; the latter, more significant with perhaps 2,000 members, was also very much part of the political fringe. Moreover, the British Movement was oblivious to the need for political respectability and so unlike the National Front, made no attempt to hide its neo-Nazism. Despite possessing potential for expansion amongst disaffected skinhead youth, the British Movement's prospects for wider growth were therefore miserable. Indeed, in his auto-biographical account, Hill records that a television team from *TV Eye* had already revealed the British Movement's neo-Nazism to the nation 'and the images of *sieg-heil-ing* skinheaded hooligans stamping through west London which were beamed to the general public ... did little to enhance BM's pretensions to being the government of the future'.[23] Also, the launch of Tyndall's British National Party was hardly memorable and with or without Pearce's faction of the National Front, the British National Party posed little threat. Thus the reality was that the activities of Ray Hill had no real bearing on the relative electoral position of British fascism in the early 1980s. Yet perhaps this misses the point. In the wake of the collapse of the National Front, elements on the fascist Right did look to re-establish a presence, not necessarily by fighting elections but by fomenting racial violence, whether covertly (possibly through bombings) or overtly through the street activities of skinhead organisations like the British Movement. By exposing these developments Hill reinforced fascism's illegitimacy and by encouraging organisational friction, Hill further dislocated an extreme Right that was already at odds with itself following the National Front's resounding electoral defeat in 1979.

One result of the electoral collapse of the National Front and the subsequent fall in general fascist activity was that a successor to the Anti-Nazi League did not finally emerge until July 1985 when, at a conference held at Conway Hall, London, attended by some 300 activists, Anti-Fascist Action (AFA) was launched. But even then, this new organisation was brought into being at a time when electoral support for fascist groups in Britain was negligible. At the 1983 general election, the National Front had polled a derisory 1.1 per cent of the vote from 58 seats contested, whilst Tyndall's BNP, its main rival, had captured an unremarkable 1.3 per cent for its 53 candidates.[24] Given that anti-fascism is quintessentially a reactive phenomenon, why was the formation of AFA deemed necessary when electoral support for organisations like the National Front had so obviously declined? To put it succinctly, the 'nature of the beast' had changed. First, a radical faction had emerged in the National Front known as the 'political soldiers' who openly advocated political violence; the fear was that the NF was intent on 'pushing racist violence beyond intolerable limits'.[25] Second, black and Asian communities in the inner cities were now being subjected to a rising level of racist attacks. The Anti-Nazi League was found guilty of having abandoned these communities and was charged with allowing fascists space to 'regroup in the inner cities in a campaign of unmitigated violence on black families'.[26] Third, the NF's interest in so-called 'destabilisation politics' had widened to include grassroots activity ostensibly directed towards left-wing constituencies, such as organising support groups for striking miners, infiltration of animal rights organisations and protesting at the presence of American nuclear bases in Britain. As Unmesh Desai, a member of AFA's national secretariat, said, 'AFA was also formed to awaken these organisations and the labour movement in general to the new fascist threat.'[27] Yet what struck a jarring note in particular was the relative ease with which a group of some 70 National Front skinheads had physically attacked two bands on stage at the GLC's 'Jobs for a Change' festival held in central London in June 1984. By exposing the weakness of the Left to fascist aggression, this attack had apparently 'brought matters to a head'.[28]

In its founding statement, Anti-Fascist Action promised to oppose fascism and racism both physically and ideologically, whilst also recognising the rights of black and Asian communities to self-defence against fascist and racist attacks. The new organisation was to be 'non-sectarian', a broad alliance of left-wing groups, both 'liberal' and 'militant', with each affiliated group having one vote on a national committee. With British fascism now electorally marginalised, AFA could never aspire to reach the dizzy heights of mass popularity that the Anti-Nazi League had enjoyed in the 1970s, yet backed by *Searchlight,* support was drawn from the National Union of Students, a number of Labour Party branches, teachers' groups and black and Asian community organisations.[29] This was in spite of AFA's commitment to physically oppose fascism, a principle guaranteed by the presence of radical-Left groups such as Red Action,[30] Workers' Power,[31] and Class War.[32] At the start, AFA's energies were directed towards opposing the National Front's traditional Remembrance Sunday march past the Cenotaph in London's Whitehall. In November 1985, around 100 anti-fascists occupied the assembly point at Victoria which, aside from causing the NF some embarrassment, obtained favourable anti-fascist publicity. The *London Standard* fiercely attacked the National Front for its hypocrisy in parading at the Cenotaph when 'the traditions which the NF so stridently uphold are not peace but war: the stirring up of racial conflict, the nazi obsession with purity of race at whatever the cost in suffering of those outside the pale'.[33] Yet for all the negative publicity that this attracted for the Front, the NF's march was still repeated the following year. This time, in a more substantial show of force and changing tactics, 2,000 anti-fascists marched to Whitehall before proceeding to a rally in south London. The aim was to reclaim Remembrance Sunday from the NF and a small contingent, which included Blair Peach's widow, laid wreaths at the Cenotaph to honour those who had died fighting fascism in the Second World War as well as present-day victims of fascism. On this occasion, however, not all media comment was so approving, with the *Daily Mail* criticising anti-fascists for supposedly manipulating Remembrance Sunday for their own ends.[34]

By the end of 1986, a number of local AFA groups had emerged outside London, especially amongst students who were often its most active members. It was reported in *Searchlight* that AFA had established about 30 student groups, with the largest based in the Manchester area and at Essex University.[35] In step with this organisational growth, the work of AFA became many-sided: it disseminated anti-fascist propaganda, monitored and exposed fascist activity, organised public meetings, networked within the labour movement and liaised with black and Asian community groups. However, it became most noted for militant anti-fascism. Its radical wing was led by Red Action, a hardline pro-IRA group, which counted among its founders, former members of the Socialist Workers' Party expelled in 1982 for supporting physical confrontation against fascists.[36] Predictably, Red Action claims that one of the major successes of AFA in the period 1985–9 was the 'smashing' of an NF march through Bury St Edmunds in 1986, which it maintains led directly to the National Front's fragmentation into two rival camps, with the 'political soldier' wing abandoning the tactic of marches whereas the Flag Group remained modelled on the old-style NF.[37] In reality, the cause of this National Front split was far more complicated with ideological differences and personal rivalries the key factors.[38] Radical anti-fascists claimed further victories in the period 1985–9, such as physical disruption to a National Front Flag Group election meeting in Greenwich in 1987[39] and to a Flag Group march in Stockport in 1986, when at one point anti-fascists apparently overturned a car containing NF supporters and then subjected its unfortunate occupants to a smoke-bomb attack.[40] However, not every group within AFA's national structure was so determined on militant direct action and unable to reconcile differences in one single organisation, by 1988 Anti-Fascist Action had devolved to independent regional organisations.

In the north, a northern anti-fascist network was established comprised of a variety of local groups, such as Bradford Anti-Racist Anti-Fascist Action, which in alliance with local Trades Councils and Bradford Labour Party, prevented the British National Party from staging a rally near the War Memorial in Eccleshall in September 1989 by holding a wreath-laying ceremony to the victims of fascism and racism.[41] On Tyneside, fascist activity was opposed by the Tyne and Wear Anti-Fascist Association (TWAFA), a group that dates from 1983, formed when local anti-fascists reacted to news that the BNP intended to hold a march through Newcastle. The Tyne and Wear Anti-Fascist Association is significant because it was the first anti-fascist group to receive local council funding, which probably accounts for its relative longevity (still active in the 1990s) and also appears to have been the first anti-fascist group to have successfully confronted the sale of fascist literature at football grounds.[42] This type of fascist activity dates back to the 1950s when Colin Jordan's White Defence League had sold literature outside Queens Park Rangers and West Ham United,[43] though it is more commonly associated with the National Front. The NF had started to target London football clubs in the late 1970s – so giving birth to ANL sub-groups such as the 'Gunners Against the Nazis' at Arsenal – and had achieved notoriety in the 1980s for selling racist literature at many football grounds across the country. One of its prize sites was St James' Park, Newcastle, where the NF had established a foothold amongst a large body of Newcastle United supporters. Taking exception, TWAFA responded by holding regular pickets outside the ground whilst at the same time distributing anti-fascist materials, such as stickers and leaflets. Faced with rising numbers of anti-fascist objectors, the NF presence lessened and by 1989 had gone altogether. Indeed, such was the success of TWAFA's campaign, its example was followed by other local anti-fascist groups, such as Leeds Anti-Fascist Action, which along with the local Trades Council had, by early 1990, eliminated the NF presence at Leeds United.

In the south, Anti-Fascist Action became concentrated in the London region where in 1989 a number of successes were recorded against the neo-Nazi 'Blood and Honour' organisation. The focal point for hardcore skinhead subculture, Blood and Honour's chief was Ian Stuart Donaldson whose band, *Skrewdriver*, had attracted a sizeable international following. This subculture, which emerged around an abrasive type of rock music, had originally been encouraged by the National Front as a riposte to Rock Against Racism. Detached from the mainstream music business, it became an important source of income for the National Front – so much so that by mid-1987, the NF's 'political soldiers' faction were diverting a not inconsiderable sum earned through concerts, merchandise, record and tape sales away from Donaldson directly into National Front coffers. This led Donaldson into an acrimonious split with the NF and he subsequently created the Blood and Honour network. In early 1989, Anti-Fascist Action launched a campaign against the sale of Blood and Honour and associated neo-Nazi merchandise in two shops in London's West End. This campaign won the support of the Labour MP Jeremy Corbyn, as well as representatives from Westminster Council and *Searchlight*. After some five months of campaigning, which included a number of demonstrations, petitions, appearances on TV and radio, AFA succeeded in forcing the closure of one of the shops whilst the other withdrew neo-Nazi material. In addition, AFA frustrated a plan by Blood and Honour to stage a large rally in London in May 1989 by first managing to cancel a booking at Camden Town Hall which Blood and Honour had reserved under a false name, and then by mobilising 500 anti-fascists to occupy Blood and Honour's re-direction point in Hyde Park where the 500 or so neo-Nazis expected to discover the location of the rearranged venue. According to AFA, this campaign led to the 'virtual collapse' of Blood and Honour in London as Ian Stuart Donaldson made a brisk retreat to Derbyshire.[44]

Yet these apparent successes were overshadowed by internal disagreements within London AFA, which became especially heated in the approach to the NF's Remembrance Sunday march in November 1989. The militant wing insisted that the AFA Cenotaph march should not be repeated because marches in 1987 and 1988 had seen numbers of participants fall, had generated no useful publicity and had failed to stop fascists from marching. The only positive aspect to these marches, AFA's militants argued, was the mobilisation of AFA 'defence squads' which after the march would defend the anti-apartheid picket outside the South African embassy in Trafalgar Square from attack by fascists. Thus in the event, around 500 AFA militants decided against marching to the Cenotaph but occupied the fascists' assembly point at Victoria instead. In doing so, anti-fascists delayed their opponent's march for over an hour and clearly rattled the fascist contingent as there was no subsequent attack on the anti-apartheid picket. However, this 'victory' came at a price. Unity within London AFA collapsed when between 150 and 300 moderate anti-fascists, comprising elements from Islington Anti-Racist, Anti-Fascist Action and representatives from a variety of organisations such as the TUC, the NUS and the Union of Jewish Students, marched to the Cenotaph, led by Gerry Gable, editor of *Searchlight* and Glyn Ford, a leading Labour Party MEP.[45]

Significantly, those who argued for a more radical line cut loose and Anti-Fascist Action was relaunched as the militant wing of the anti-fascist movement. What this involved has been graphically described by Jim Kane, an AFA activist:

Militant anti-fascism has a single goal – to forcefully disrupt the fascists from going about their business. Our aim is to prevent them selling their papers, distributing their leaflets, putting up their stickers and posters. Our intention is to make it impossible for them to stand candidates in elections, and where they do manage to stand, disrupt their campaigns at every stage. Ultimately, our aim is to crush them completely, to wipe them off the face of the earth.[46]

In terms of the radical anti-fascist tradition, it is important to note that Anti-Fascist Action was not a carbon-copy of the 43 or 62 Groups. Besides the fact that it was non-Jewish and had no interest in Jewish community defence, AFA was driven by an overarching political objective – to clear fascists out of working-class areas and fill the resulting vacuum with a radical-Left alternative. This political line was promoted through an uncompromising magazine, *Fighting Talk*, advertised in *Searchlight* along with a regular list of AFA contact addresses. By putting AFA in touch with a wider audience, *Searchlight*, whose circulation may well have now been in the region of 7,000 copies,[47] lent its support despite marked differences of approach, particularly over the question of whether anti-fascists should appeal to the state in the struggle against fascism. Whilst *Searchlight* was prepared to call for 'legal' anti-fascism, AFA's position left no room for compromise: 'If you seriously oppose the fascists in a way which is effective, you are operating against the state. This is a fact of life.'[48] Beyond *Searchlight's* readership, an even wider audience was reached in May 1992 when AFA's case was broadcast to the nation in a documentary entitled 'Fighting Talk' shown on BBC 2's *Open Space* programme. Unsurprisingly, not everyone was convinced by AFA's case and the BBC was swiftly attacked by the *Daily Mail* (19 May 1992) for giving a national platform to 'a group which looks suspiciously like left wing fascists eager for a street war with right wing fascists'.[49]

In reality, AFA's position was more carefully thought out. According to AFA's class-based analysis, support for fascism was said to come from the disillusioned white working class betrayed by a mediocre Labour Party that had ditched socialism. So without a credible alternative, the working class had no choice but to turn to popular racism by default: 'In the absence of class, race. In the absence of socialism, nationalism.'[50] Thus, the underlying objective behind the relaunched AFA was 'to create the climate whereby progressive left and anarchist groups can bring their ideas and programs to those targeted by the fascist gangs both as victims of their abuse and as victims of their recruitment'.[51] However, the precise nature of this alternative was never made explicit, though behind the scenes, this 'progressive alternative' was presumably the libertarian communism of Red Action, AFA's dominant faction. None the less, Anti-Fascist Action always insisted that 'AFA is not, and must never be a front for any one organisation.'[52] It declared itself a non-sectarian, broad-based organisation and accordingly, in October 1991, expelled the tiny Revolutionary International League on the grounds that this grouplet was intent on hijacking AFA and converting it into a political party.[53]

By 1990, Anti-Fascist Action's chief adversary had become Tyndall's British National Party, which had now succeeded in displacing the National Front as the leading organisation on Britain's far right.[54] During 1990, the BNP ventured into East London and through its 'Rights for Whites' campaign witnessed an encouraging improvement in its local electoral scores, especially in the district of Tower Hamlets. Where previously, the BNP would poll 1–2 per cent of the vote, it now began to poll 8–10 per cent. Standing four candidates in local elections in Tower Hamlets in May 1990, the BNP polled more than Conservative Party candidates and at one local election in the St Peters Ward in August 1990, the BNP polled 12.8 per cent of the vote. Ominously, given the ethnic composition of the area, 50 per cent white and 50 per cent Asian, the BNP had received votes from around one in four of the white electorate.[55] What was particularly depressing for militant anti-fascists was that these votes were recorded despite an energetic counter-campaign by Anti-Fascist Action. In May 1990, AFA had distributed thousands of leaflets on white housing estates in Tower Hamlets which had followed the tried-and-tested formula: a photograph of John Tyndall in neo-Nazi regalia with voters urged 'Don't vote Fascist! Don't vote BNP!'. Furthermore, a BNP election meeting at Weaver's Field School in Bethnal Green in April had been disrupted by AFA militants whilst in a park next to the school, a public demonstration against the BNP had been held by a variety of organisations, including the local Labour Party and Socialist Workers' Party.[56] Later in the year, AFA once again disrupted an election meeting at Weaver's Field School, occupied the BNP's regular paper sale at Brick Lane and in order to build a locally based opposition, held a public meeting at Whitechapel after having earlier distributed thousands of leaflets defining AFA's militant strategy.[57]

Alive to the possibility of the BNP taking root in East London, this anti-fascist groundwork was followed up in the new year with yet further local activity. AFA held another demonstration against the paper sale at Brick Lane in March 1991 and afterwards successfully besieged a local public house favoured by BNP activists. In September 1991, an anti-fascist Unity carnival at Hackney Downs Park was organised which drew more than 10,000 people, in October 1991, 300 anti-fascists staged a mass picket of the paper sale in Brick Lane and then in November, a national march against racist attacks was held in Tower Hamlets which was attended by 3,500 anti-fascists. Writing in September 1991, AFA believed that through its application, the British National Party had been denied a foothold in Tower Hamlets and was hopeful that 'the fascists' slow retreat in London' could be turned 'into a national rout'.[58] In the spring of 1992, AFA remained confident that it had 'recorded an impressive number of successes, particularly in East London'.[59] As it turned out, however, AFA had got it entirely wrong. Despite opposing the BNP's 'Rights for Whites' campaign from the very beginning, anti-fascist militants had not removed BNP influence from the area. In truth, quite the reverse happened: in September 1992, a BNP candidate polled 20 per cent of the vote in a local election in Millwall, and it was in Millwall the following year that the British National Party won its first ever council seat. All the more surprising given that from late 1991, a succession of new players emerged in the anti-fascist arena, including a re-established Anti-Nazi League.

III

The first anti-fascist group to (re)appear was the Campaign against Racism and Fascism. This broke with *Searchlight* in October 1990 and relaunched itself as an independent bi-monthly magazine with financial help from the London Alliance against Racism and Fascism, formed in 1989 from local anti-racist organisations in Hackney, Greenwich, Southall and Newham.[60] *CARF* explained that the reason for the break with its host publication was fundamental differences of approach, 'to the extent of riding rough-shod over our views, and our claims to space and autonomy'.[61] *CARF* maintained that *Searchlight* had discontinued the analysis pioneered by Maurice Ludmer which established that fascism could only be countered effectively if fought alongside popular racism. In *CARF's* view, anti-black racism was being discounted by *Searchlight* with the anti-fascist/anti-racist struggle now subsumed to the fight against anti-Semitism. Instead of recognising that contemporary fascism's breeding ground was anti-black racism and not Europe's anti-Semitic past, *Searchlight* was repeating the same mistake as the Anti-Nazi League in the 1970s when fascism had been situated 'historically, ideologically linked to anti-Semitism and the holocaust'.[62] In going its separate way, *CARF* aspired to 'develop a more vigorous and responsive anti-racist forum to co-ordinate and service the various anti-racist initiatives that are taking place up and down the country'.[63] Essentially it saw itself as a co-ordinating body that would collate and exchange information about local anti-racist campaigns and would in addition, draw attention to the plight of black people, migrants and refugees in Britain and in Europe generally, as well as exposing new forms of 'state racism' associated with the emergence of 'Fortress Europe'. Thus, the primary function of *CARF* was 'to service and inform' grassroots anti-racists. Although it wanted to build unity between locally based campaigns, *CARF* was not a national anti-racist, anti-fascist movement as such and was in fact produced on a 'shoe-string' budget by a very small team of politically non-aligned volunteers based in London.

As to building a national anti-racist movement, a well-sponsored organisation such as the Anti-Racist Alliance (ARA), founded in November 1991, therefore offered more promise. Indeed, within the first seven months of its existence, the Anti-Racist Alliance could boast the support of 70 MPs, including prominent Labour MPs such as Ken Livingstone, Diane Abbott and Peter Shore, as well as the backing of 24 national trade unions; it also won support from, amongst others, the NUS, Liberty (formerly the NCCL) and the Anti-Apartheid Movement. Yet to begin with, the origins and objectives of this organisation were something of a mystery and even the usually well-informed *Searchlight* confessed in January 1992 that 'Nobody knows who the steering committee is or what its aims and objectives are.'[64] It soon emerged, however, that the ARA was led by Marc Wadsworth, a black television presenter who had interviewed Patrick Harrington for Thames Television's six o'clock news in 1984,[65] and that the ARA had been set up by black political activists instrumental in creating the Labour Party's black sections in the 1980s. These activists were clustered around the Black Liaison Group which represented some 50 organisations, including the Society of Black Lawyers, the National Convention of Black Teachers and the Association of Black Journalists. Although formally independent of any political party, the Anti-Racist Alliance was therefore very close to the Labour Party and trade unions and so well positioned to secure substantial backing from within the labour movement.

Ostensibly a response to rising levels of racist attacks, the Anti-Racist Alliance defined itself in opposition to racism. But since it also wanted to stop fascist groups from getting the foothold in Britain that extreme-Right parties had already established in other European countries, the Anti-Racist Alliance also expressed a will to counter fascism. What made the ARA unlike all other predecessors, however, was its belief that the 'most crucial alliance which needs to be created to stop the extreme right' is 'that between Black and minority communities'.[66] Thus the ARA's historical significance lies in the fact that it was the first organisation to advocate as a 'non-negotiable' principle, 'Black' (that is black and Asian) self-organisation and leadership of the anti-racist struggle.[67] Yet beyond this, there was little analysis of either the causes of racism or fascism. There was certainly no 'class analysis'; the ARA's anti-fascism was instead expressed in simple moralistic terms as a case of 'good versus evil'. Tactically, the Anti-Racist Alliance positioned itself on the moderate wing of the anti-fascist movement and looked to integrate itself within mainstream structures of state and society. Thus, it did not support physical confrontation against fascists but advocated a legal policy of pressure group tactics whereby members were encouraged to lobby to influence state legislation. ARA members were invited to write to the press and to politicians, to draw up petitions, to send delegations to MPs, MEPs, European Commissioners and to stage protest demonstrations.[68] During its first year, the Anti-Racist Alliance pressed for a Racial Harassment Bill to be introduced, organised opposition to the Asylum Bill, held demonstrations of support for Rolan Adams, murdered in south London in a racist attack, and campaigned for the closure of the BNP's national headquarters at Welling in Kent. As for its organisational structure, the ARA created a network of local groups and borrowed from the original Anti-Nazi League model by establishing specialist sections, such as Lawyers Against Racism, Youth ARA, Lesbian and Gay ARA, and Student ARA. It also staged an 'ARAfest' music festival modelled on the ANL/RAR carnivals which attracted some 25,000 people to Brockwell Park in south London on 1 August 1992.[69] Clearly the Anti-Racist Alliance convinced many of its viability and was confident that it could secure a long-term future within the mainstream of British political life as a broad coalition capable of extending itself to most of Britain's anti-racists.

However, the Anti-Racist Alliance soon found immediate detractors. *Searchlight* was quick to identify Lee Jasper, ARA's vice-chair, as a black nationalist who had invited Louis Farrakhan, the US black separatist and anti-Semite to Britain only two weeks after the Anti-Racist Alliance was launched.[70] This charge was fiercely denied by both Wadsworth and Jasper and, in separate letters to the *New Statesman and Society*, Wadsworth maintained that the ARA was unequivocally opposed to anti-Semitism whilst Jasper replied that *Searchlight's* claim was 'complete and utter rubbish' and was a cynical attempt by the white Left to undermine black organisation.[71] Elsewhere, even though there was a 50–50 black–white representation amongst the ARA's executive officers, Anti-Fascist Action attacked the ARA's policy of 'black' leadership, which it said excluded white activists and so reduced the potential for mass anti-fascist opposition. AFA refused to accept the ARA line that only victims of racist attacks could define the anti-fascist struggle as all sections of the working class were held to be potential victims of fascism. Moreover, the principle of 'Black' organisation was said to have little support within black and Asian communities, and organisations such as the Society of Black Lawyers were deemed by AFA to be 'careerist'. Hence, by implication, the leadership of the ARA was middle class, interested only in self-advancement and would, in the long run, demonstrate a gross lack of commitment. AFA also claimed that the Anti-Racist Alliance had made 'no tangible difference' to the everyday struggle against racism and fascism. Despite the ARA holding a demonstration and mounting some 14 pickets of the local Tory council, the BNP's headquarters in Bexley, Welling was still open in middle of 1992. Moreover, for all the assistance the ARA gave to publicising the Rolan Adams case, racism remained prevalent at Thamesmead where Rolan Adams had been stabbed to death in February 1991. On the local housing estate, the Wildflower public house still operated a colour bar.[72]

The ARA also faced hard competition for Labour Party and trade union support from a revived Anti-Nazi League whose successful record in the 1970s gave it a hold on the Left. In January 1992, at a House of Commons press conference, in the same mixture as before, founder members Paul Holborrow, Peter Hain and Ernie Roberts came together once again to set the Anti-Nazi League in motion. As in 1977, this move was initiated by the Socialist Workers' Party which had apparently contacted *Searchlight* on 12 December 1991 to inform it that the SWP intended to re-establish the ANL.[73] At the statement made on the relaunch, it was explained that the ANL was being brought back because of the 'significant advances' made by 'Nazis' in Europe and that whilst fascists in Britain were still much weaker than their continental counterparts, 'Nazi' organisations like the British National Party were beginning to 'regroup' and 'are making a concerted bid to gain a fresh toehold in political life in Britain'.[74] Yet for all the ANL's cachet, its relaunch met a mixed response with *Searchlight*, the Anti-Racist Alliance and Anti-Fascist Action all quick to question the SWP's motives. The prime suspicion was that the SWP had opportunistically re-established the ANL as a ploy to recruit new members, a charge given some credibility by *Searchlight* which disclosed that the ANL was falsely claiming that the BNP was to stand 50 candidates at the 1992 general election in order to exaggerate the threat from the BNP and so reap greater support for the Anti-Nazi League. With this in mind, the ANL was also said to have tricked the media into believing that the BNP was to meet French Front National leader, Jean-Marie Le Pen, on a recent visit to London.[75]

Naturally, the accusation that the ANL was a 'front' for the Socialist Workers' Party was denied by Holborrow,[76] but in the final pages of an SWP booklet, *Killing the Nazi Menace*, published at the time of the ANL's relaunch, Chris Bambery makes the SWP's overriding position very clear:

> As socialists we will stand alongside anyone who wants to fight the Nazis. But we know that fascism springs from capitalism. It is spawned in the sewers of a rotten system ... if we are to once and for all rid this world of fascism and racism we need to rid it of a rotten system – a capitalist system which breeds war, famine and recession.[77]

In the end, we are left with no doubt as to the SWP's ultimate objective. But if capitalism was to be destroyed, as Bambery concedes, then a revolutionary alternative had to be built – a task incumbent on the Socialist Workers' Party. Bambery detected 'a sea of bitterness' in the recession-hit Britain of the early 1990s where 'The Tories are hated. But Labour offers no answers'.[78] Accordingly, instead of being 'just another group' on its 'extreme margins',[79] the SWP had to join forces with the working class and then, 'If socialists give a lead we can turn that anger against the government, against police harassment and this rotten system.'[80] Thus the purpose of the ANL, like that of AFA, was not merely to stop Nazis from having a 'free hand' to divert working-class anger into racism, but likewise, the political task the SWP set itself was to unite black and white and then redirect working-class anger against the capitalist system. However, in contrast to AFA's publications, this was never said outright in ANL literature. As in the 1970s, the message was reserved for party members where in the SWP's journal, *Socialist Review* for instance, Bambery openly draws on the historical experience of the CPGB in the 1930s to demonstrate that a successful fight against fascism could draw non-party sympathisers into the wider socialist struggle.[81] Clearly, if such intentions were openly expressed in ANL literature, they would risk alienating large numbers of people and the fear was that as a result, the Anti-Nazi

League would end up like AFA-type 'squads', 'more and more conspiratorial, more and more isolated and almost exclusively made up of young, white males'.[82]

As for the Anti-Racist Alliance, aside from the charge that the Anti-Nazi League was a front for the Socialist Workers' Party, recited by ARA co-chair Ken Livingstone in his column in the *Sun*, the ANL was judged 'a typical white-led attempt to steal the thunder from a black-led initiative'.[83] The ANL was branded an 'exercise in nostalgia', with Holborrow, Hain and Roberts the 'three white men telling anti-racists what to do'.[84] For many in the ARA, the ANL's refrain of 'Never Again' with images of concentration camps was predicated on an 'old, historical fascism' when the focus should be, as *CARF* had already recognised, the fight against new forms of state and institutionalised racism. But according to Lindsey German, editor of *Socialist Review*, the strength of the Anti-Nazi League was precisely its broad appeal, which through mobilising mass opposition to the Nazis necessarily 'means *undercutting* other levels of racism'. Indeed, with some justification, Lindsey German identifies the problem with ARA-type campaigns: they 'attempt to mobilise around twenty different aspects of racism [and] often find themselves incapable of mobilising round any, and are consequently less effective'.[85] On the ANL's other flank, Anti-Fascist Action held the SWP responsible for recklessly abandoning the anti-fascist struggle over a decade earlier and with a smile of contempt, ridiculed the SWP for having to call *Searchlight* 'to try and get some information on the fascists because they didn't know what was happening'.[86] An additional sore point was that the SWP had previously rejected AFA's approach for a militant united front against fascism in 1989–90 and had boycotted a meeting organised by AFA on 13 February 1992 intended to consider ways in which the various newly emerging anti-fascist groups could work together with existing organisations.[87] Moreover, AFA believed that the ANL had also been somewhat disingenuous about the reasons for its relaunch with the SWP having resurrected the Anti-Nazi League largely because of pressure from the grassroots activists who were being regularly attacked 'on the streets' by groups of street-hardened fascists.[88]

Nevertheless, the popularity that the ANL had acquired in the 1970s worked to its obvious advantage and these criticisms were brushed aside. Early publicity material shows that the Anti-Nazi League won endorsements from numerous Labour MPs and MEPs (Tony Benn, Frank Cook, Joan Lestor, Tony Banks, Chris Smith, Glenys Kinnock), trade unionists, local councillors, media personalities (Julian Clary,

Stephen Fry, Jonathan Ross) and rock stars (Sinead O'Connor, Paul Weller).[89] *Searchlight* claimed that this publicity material contained purported supporters, such as Ray Hill, who 'have neither signed nor have been invited to sign' and this was not a careless mistake but a deliberate 'political con trick' designed to give the impression of the widest possible support.[90] All the same, even if some 'names' were misappropriated, the ANL's later literature confirms that it registered the support of over 100 MPs, numerous media personalities, certain trade unions, such as the National Union of Teachers and the National Union of Mineworkers, and thousands of individual members.[91]

On the organisational side, as with the 1970s original, there was to be a national steering committee to provide the ANL with overall direction, though unsurprisingly, this time a representative from *Searchlight* was not asked to join. Day-to-day co-ordination of activities was to be the responsibility of the national office in London, but though centrally run, emphasis was still placed on non-militant, locally oriented activity. At this level, the ANL encouraged groups to leaflet and petition shopping areas and housing estates, paint out racist and fascist graffiti, organise anti-fascist concerts, expose Nazi sympathisers in the workplace, lobby local councils and organise counter-marches.[92] But at the outset, given that the SWP had not seriously monitored fascism for many years, first indications were that it was ill-prepared. In its first forays into Rochdale, for instance, the ANL distributed anti-BNP leaflets on Asian rather than white housing estates. At Welling, a coach carrying ANL members to protest against the BNP's headquarters was ambushed by the BNP whilst a similar fate awaited a group of ANL activists on a leafleting drive in Tower Hamlets which resulted in three BNP activists being charged with grievous bodily harm.[93] But that said, in advance of the May 1992 general election, the ANL claims to have distributed over one million leaflets. According to ANL sources, it also sold over 500,000 badges and put up 250,000 posters. During the 1992 general election campaign itself, a total of 250,000 election leaflets were said to have been distributed specifically in constituencies contested both by the British National Party and the National Front. And in the ANL's view, the result of this anti-fascist propaganda drive was 'the electoral breakthrough which the Nazis hoped for was not achieved'.[94]

Standing 13 candidates at the 1992 election, the BNP polled some 7,000 votes, whereas the National Front fared worse with around 4,800 votes for its 14 candidates. No National Front candidate polled more than 1.5 per cent of the vote and the highest score for the British

National Party was a very modest 3.6 per cent. However, as AFA discerned, the 2,500 votes for the BNP combined from two constituencies in Tower Hamlets confirmed that the BNP had secured a local support base and this marked 'a qualitative breakthrough for the fascists'.[95] Accordingly, AFA warned against demobilisation of anti-fascist activity yet in the period between the 1992 general election and the election of the BNP councillor in September 1993, Tower Hamlets appears to have been largely abandoned by the anti-fascist opposition. When BNP candidate, Barry Osborne, polled 20 per cent of the vote at the Millwall by-election on the Isle of Dogs in October 1992, the highest fascist vote for over a decade, AFA maintained that the ANL had dismissed it as a 'freak result due entirely to low turn-out'[96] (down from 42 per cent in 1990 to just 33 per cent in 1992). Yet in all fairness, the Millwall by-election had not been entirely disregarded by the ANL. Locally, an 'Island Against the Nazis' group had formed after the October 1992 by-election whilst campaign work against the BNP did take place during September 1993. A rally was held at Millwall Park, a leaflet drive was undertaken and there was opposition to the BNP paper sale at Brick Lane, though this was, it has to be said, a case of 'too little, too late'.

But equally, Anti-Fascist Action was also at fault. When it should have been concentrating efforts on Millwall, it was diverted by Blood and Honour's attempt to re-establish itself in London. On 12 September 1992, Anti-Fascist Action mobilised some 1,000 anti-fascists to confront Blood and Honour concert-goers at their assembly point at Waterloo railway station.[97] What followed was dubbed the 'Battle of Waterloo' by AFA, with 44 people arrested as anti-fascists clashed with Blood and Honour supporters.[98] Whilst this clearly set back Blood and Honour, the more significant point was that it was Blood and Honour and not the BNP that 'got smashed'. Even so, it was still a major victory for AFA not least because it finally substantiated its claim to the radical anti-fascist tradition. Though drawn away by Blood and Honour, AFA argued that there were other reasons why it lost its grip on East London during 1992–3. The first was that Workers' Power deserted its ranks in the hope of 'radicalising' the Anti-Nazi League. The second was the intervention of the ANL in East London in early 1992 when, as previously mentioned, its badly organised leafleting session resulted in the ANL contingent 'getting battered and run all over the place', so boosting confidence on the fascist side. A further factor was that the BNP switched tactics and rather than hold 'mass rallies' which gave AFA the opportunity to ensure that the BNP was

'Waterlooed', the BNP focused on canvassing in small teams of 20–30 activists instead.[99] Clearly, at least part of the reason for the BNP's electoral emergence in Tower Hamlets in the early 1990s was the failure of anti-fascist opposition. Despite the founding of a variety of new groups dedicated to fighting fascism and racism, the anti-fascist opposition was set against itself and, most significantly, anti-fascists largely withdrew from East London after the 1992 general election. This allowed the BNP space in which to develop local appeal in an area made fertile by a Liberal Democrat council whose policies and election literature encouraged popular racism within the white community and so awarded the BNP much coveted political respectability.[100]

IV

After the supposedly woeful performance of the BNP at the 1992 general election, the victory of the BNP's candidate at the Millwall by-election in September 1993 took most anti-fascists by surprise. This was the first time that a candidate from an extreme-Right political party had won any type of election since the election of two National Party candidates at local elections in Blackburn in 1976. What further deepened concerns was that this election victory was widely interpreted as part of the broader electoral rise of the extreme Right in Europe. This generated rather alarmist predictions that what was happening in Europe could well happen in Britain and with anti-fascist tabloid headlines such as 'SIEG HEIL ... and now he's a British Councillor' (*Daily Mirror*, 18 September 1993), a wave of popular anti-fascism was sparked, not seen since mass opposition to the National Front in the 1970s. Mainstream politicians swiftly condemned the result, whilst more than 350 local council workers in Tower Hamlets took immediate strike action. Within the anti-fascist movement itself, following a number of snap mobilisations at Brick Lane, where on one occasion police arrested over 50 BNP supporters, calls were made for the disparate anti-fascist organisations to pull together. The Anti-Nazi League took the lead and proposed that a march against the BNP's headquarters in Welling scheduled for 16 October 1993 should be turned into a mass demonstration of popular anti-fascist unity, a proposal described by the ANL's Steering Committee as the 'best response possible' to developments in East London.[101]

Not surprisingly, given the shock wave that the BNP's local election victory caused, the ANL's appeal for a show of unity did strike a responsive chord with the majority of Britain's anti-fascists. Most of

Britain's anti-fascist and anti-racist groups agreed to sponsor this demonstration, with support coming from *Searchlight* (which had decided to put past differences with the ANL to one side) as well as AJEX, TWAFA, Youth Against Racism in Europe (a sizeable 'front' organisation of Militant set up in October 1992), *CARF*, the Indian Workers' Association, various locally based anti-racist groups, the NUS and many trade unions.[102] However, it was noticeable that despite the BNP's by-election victory, support was not forthcoming from either Anti-Fascist Action or the Anti-Racist Alliance. AFA held that the proposed march served little purpose as there had already been six marches against the BNP's headquarters and 27 lobbies of the local council to no effect. For AFA, the problem was that this demonstration was purely symbolic and would do nothing to counter deep-rooted racism in south London where fascist influence had grown not as a consequence of the BNP's headquarters, 'but from an ability by their activists to exist anonymously and operate with impunity' within the local community.[103] Meanwhile, the Anti-Racist Alliance predicted violence and supported by *The Guardian*, Marc Wadsworth, in rather sectarian manner, urged his supporters to avoid Welling and instead attend the ARA's demonstration at Trafalgar Square on the same day. But whereas only 3,500 gathered in central London, an estimated 40,000–60,000 people converged on Welling in easily the largest anti-fascist demonstration since the 1970s.

The initial plan for the Welling demonstration, agreed by police in June, was to march past the BNP headquarters. But five days before the march was due to take place, the route was altered by police. Consequently, once the protesters arrived at the crossroads where the march was to be diverted away from the BNP headquarters, the leaders of the march, including Leon Greenman, a Holocaust survivor, tried to persuade police to allow them to pass. It was at this point that initial altercations between police and demonstrators broke out before police horses rode into the crowd followed by riot police. With lead protesters separated from the rest of the march, all possible exit routes were blocked by lines of police and so penned in and subjected to repeated baton charges, the crowd was forced against a cemetery wall which then collapsed. At this point, a small number of angry demonstrators picked up bricks and proceeded to throw them at police. Metropolitan Police Commissioner, Paul Condon, subsequently blamed the disorder on this 'mob of extremists' who had worn ski-masks and scarves over their faces and had come to Welling determined on violence. According to the police version, these 'extremists' had triggered the police response by using the ruins of the wall against police ranks. Anti-fascists, though, were all too aware that the incident had happened *after* the police had charged into the crowd. Moreover, some of those that had pelted the police with missiles had themselves been victims of seemingly indiscriminate police charges.[104] Although there were few arrests, over 60 people were hospitalised with head injuries.[105] For the Anti-Nazi League, Welling had been a 'police riot', a view supported by Steve Platt of the *New Statesman and Society*, present on the demonstration and unfortunate enough to have had a thumb broken by a police riot shield. Perceptively, the conclusion that Platt draws is that the squabbling within the anti-fascist movement that resulted in the holding of two separate demonstrations allowed for the 'demonisation of those who chose to go to Welling rather than Trafalgar Square; and this as much as anything, was what sowed the seeds for such a disastrous and brutal, policing operation'.[106]

With the mainstream media accepting the official version of events, condemnation of 'professional troublemakers' quickly followed, with the *Sun* kindly offering a £1,000 reward for anyone who could provide information on the rioters. As expected, even though it had not sponsored the march, Anti-Fascist Action/Red Action was suspected of being responsible for the violence. This view was supported by the London *Evening Standard*, which reported that information gathered by MI5 and police surveillance units on the march would soon result in arrests of extremists from two organisations, one of which was Red Action.[107] Moreover, despite a record of anti-fascist investigative reporting, which had been revisited earlier in the year when Combat 18,[108] a shady neo-Nazi group, had been exposed, *World in Action* gave further credence to the line that the Welling demonstration had been manipulated by a hard core of extremists. In a subsequent documentary it turned on anti-fascist militancy, presented AFA as a paramilitary conspiracy and screened footage of violence at the 'Unity' march to imply that AFA had deliberately planned disorder. The underlying message from the programme was that the anti-fascist movement and especially AFA should be avoided. The point made was that racist violence could be effectively managed by both legislation and the police; thus anti-fascism was not necessary. And since violent anti-fascism did nothing to stop racist violence, anti-fascism was also said to be counter-productive.[109] But if the aim of this programme was to expose the 'sinister side' of anti-fascism and thereby discredit the anti-fascist movement, it failed dismally. Even before the Anti-Nazi League held its carnival in Brockwell Park on 28 May 1994 which attracted over 150,000 people, the ANL possibly had as many as 60,000 members.[110] This easily corresponds to numbers drawn to the Anti-Nazi League in the 1970s and shows the continuing significance and resilience of popular anti-fascism. Even the militant wing of the anti-fascist movement did not suffer for *World in Action's* treatment – AFA expanded to over 30 branches in 1994, rising to over 40 in 1995.[111]

After Welling and following a brief pause in anti-fascist activity, the attention of anti-fascists was soon drawn towards the May 1994 local elections. The TUC led the way with its 'Unite against Racism' demonstration through the East End in March 1994 which saw 50,000 people turn out.[112] This demonstration, initially proposed by Tower Hamlets Trades Council,[113] looked to forge unity between the trade union movement, the Anti-Racist Alliance, the Anti-Nazi League and various locally based anti-fascist and anti-racist groups ahead of the local elections. Wider still, the Board of Deputies decided to act, and initiated the formation of the United Campaign Against Racism (UCAR), which followed the model of the Joint Committee Against Racialism in the 1970s. This looked to attract broad support from across the political mainstream as well as from Christian, Muslim, Hindu and Jewish leaders. The UCAR organised a public meeting where pledges were made to oppose racism and keep the race issue out of electoral politics. This meeting brought together the then Home Secretary, Michael Howard, Shadow Home Secretary, Tony Blair, and the Liberal Democrat Home Affairs spokesperson, Baroness Sear.[114] Yet when it comes to political expediency, pledges are not necessarily honoured and in Newham, for instance, five Conservatives played the race card and stood as 'Conservatives Against Labour's Unfair Ethnic Policies'.[115] But the major weakness of the BoD's initiative was that although the UCAR did publish a number of anti-BNP leaflets, it had little grass-roots presence. According to one observer, the UCAR's meeting at Central Hall, Westminster had more people on the platform than in the audience.[116]

Whilst broad campaigns against racism have their place, it was all too clear that the focus for anti-fascists had to be on grass-roots activity in Tower Hamlets. Menacingly, the BNP was not only confident of retaining its seat but also of capturing two more seats, thereby securing control over the Isle of Dogs community council with its budget of some £23 million. In concentrating its efforts on the Isle of Dogs, the BNP, which at the time probably had no more than 2,000 members, was forced to import activists from outside East London. So as not to give the BNP free rein, anti-fascists reciprocated with a show of force.

However, even though the Anti-Nazi League's membership far exceeded that of the BNP, the ANL still had to 'parachute' activists into East London because even though the ANL claimed a membership of tens of thousands, the number of committed activists prepared to work the ground fell far short of this 'paper' figure.

With priority on the East End of London, the ANL launched a 'Don't Vote For Nazis' campaign and this saw teams of ANL activists on the Isle of Dogs in regular leafleting drives, flyposting and canvassing. Over the weekend prior to the local elections on 5 May 1994, 200 ANL members worked the ground leafleting, flyposting and canvassing voters backed by a number of local council workers, teachers and students.[117] Certainly, the impression from ANL sources is that its activities were enthusiastically supported by the local community but the Vicar of Christ Church on the Isle of Dogs strikes a cautionary note. In his view, the ANL's tactics were 'extremely destructive':

> Like the BNP, they brought in large numbers of people from outside this well-boundaried and insular community to canvas door to door. On weekends near to the May elections there were running battles between rival groups. Islanders hated it, and the Anti-Nazi League got the reputation of being worse than the BNP who had done their best throughout to seem respectable and to appear as a party of law and order.[118]

These comments are interesting not least because they reinforce the claim that confrontational anti-fascism can backfire and alienate anti-fascists from the wider community. Ironically, the SWP's official line recognised this point when, in *Killing the Nazi Menace*, Bambery makes it clear that the SWP was 'for confrontation, but only through mobilising large numbers of people'.[119] This rule supposedly set the ANL apart from Anti-Fascist Action which, according to the SWP, had substituted 'mass action' with the 'squadist' tactics of 'isolated confrontation'. Following on from this and assuming that the ANL adhered to the SWP's official line, the opinion on the ground must have been that sufficient local support on the Isle of Dogs had been built up to justify a more confrontational approach. Indeed, in his review of the May local elections, Chris Bambery maintains that prior to these elections in Millwall, the SWP/ANL had won over local civil servants, firefighters and health workers and had also built up a network of *Socialist Worker* readers.[120] Nevertheless, it seems that outside these pockets of local support, the Anti-Nazi League probably damaged the anti-fascist cause by giving credence to the BNP's claim that the ANL were violent and 'unwelcome outsiders'.

Surprisingly, the most effective local response to fascism on the Isle of Dogs actually developed within the local churches and was separate from the Anti-Nazi League.[121] Following Beackon's by-election victory, a number of concerned Christians came together to form an *ad hoc* churches' group determined on drawing up a coherent anti-fascist response from the local churches. Although this response had many elements to it, the most important part was the campaign to increase the size of electoral turn-out at the 1994 local elections and, in particular, to raise the ethnic minority vote. The BNP had emerged victorious in September 1993 by the narrowest of margins – just seven votes ahead of the Labour candidate on a 42 per cent turn-out. Hence if turn-out could be maximised this would, in all probability, ensure the BNP's defeat, especially if voters could be encouraged to vote tactically. Thus, when the Institute of Community Studies, based in Bethnal Green and headed by Lord Young of Dartington, published an opinion poll which showed that Labour's support was well ahead of the Liberals', the message was clear: vote Labour to keep out the BNP. With financial support from the Rowntree Trust, the local churches set about encouraging people to exercise their right to vote. Electoral information was specifically translated for ethnic minorities and, following a meeting with church representatives and Bangladeshi groups, both Labour and the Liberals agreed to translate their election literature. The local churches also helped housebound voters to register for postal votes and, in conjunction with local Bangladeshi community organisations, organised minibuses to transport voters to polling stations where independent observers from Liberty (and some 80–100 ANL activists) ensured that voters were free from BNP intimidation. As a further guarantee, there was also a relatively large police presence – all deemed necessary following complaints that skinheads with pit bull terrier dogs had scared ethnic minority voters away from polling booths in September 1993.[122] In the event, the churches' broad alliance with local community groups proved decisive despite having played what appeared to be a secondary role to the ANL. Voter turn-out was over 67 per cent, extraordinary for a local election, and the BNP lost its seat even though it captured more than 550 extra votes.

By siding with the anti-fascist cause, another possible reason why the British National Party failed to retain its council seat was the hostility of the local media. Of the two main local newspapers, the *Docklands Recorder* (circulation 28,000) and the *East London Advertiser*

(circulation 24,000), the latter had gained something of a reputation
for being not entirely unsympathetic to certain aspects of the BNP's
agenda. After the 1993 by-election, it had described BNP voters as
'decent law abiding folk who turned to the BNP simply because they
had nowhere else to turn', and although racism was said to be 'evil',
the *Advertiser* stressed that 'it isn't just whites who do it. And the
quicker this message sinks home with all the thick-headed, do-
gooding, politically correct dopes who've been sounding off last week,
the quicker we'll beat the problem'.[123] Aware that this editorial line
helped construct political legitimacy for the BNP, the churches'
responded by pressing the *East London Advertiser* to become more critical and, to this end, Lord Young held a meeting with the editor in the
week before the May local elections. This had the desired result: on
5 May, under the headline 'IT'S TIME TO FACE FACTS', the *East
London Advertiser* changed tack and clearly associated the BNP with
fascism and the Holocaust, suggesting to readers that they should 'go
and see *Schindler's List*, and see if you feel quite so content to vote for
a party of the far right'. Since throughout, the *East London Advertiser*
had sought to reflect the opinions of its local readers (and not the
opinions of 'unwelcome outsiders'), once the *East London Advertiser*
had finally made a stand, one would espect that the BNP would have
been divested of at least some of its remaining local legitimacy.

However, we should not lose sight of the fact that Beackon captured
more votes in May 1994 than in September 1993, an increase of over
one third; whilst other BNP candidates in Millwall and neighbouring
Globe Town polled an average of 25 per cent of the vote. Given this
growth in local support, the main conclusion that needs to be drawn
is that the key to the defeat of the BNP in Tower Hamlets was not the
impact that anti-fascist propaganda had on white voters but clearly the
unusually high electoral turn-out. Thus, the drive to encourage as
many people as possible to vote, especially from the ethnic minorities,
proved of more consequence than traditional leaflet-based anti-fascist
campaigning. In the case of the latter, the effectiveness of the
ANL's 'Don't Vote Nazi' campaign was probably impaired by the ANL's
growing reputation for violence. And, as AFA argued, it may well have
been the case that the ANL's anti-fascist message of 'anything but the
fascists' was also suspected by local residents of being 'a spoiling tactic'
carried out in an effort to maintain the local political status quo.[124]
The obvious lesson from Tower Hamlets, therefore, was that anti-
fascists had to adopt new forms of community-based campaigning.
Fortunately, this was a lesson learnt quickly by other community

groups in East London, such as the Newham Monitoring Project (NMP).[125] At a by-election contested by the BNP in January 1995, the NMP organised a broad-based campaign which called on people to 'vote for equality, not hatred'. This appeal for local unity secured wide support from Labour and Liberal Democrat candidates, as well as former boxing champion Terry Marsh, the Bishop of Barking and Beckton Community Association. On election day itself, so as to ensure maximum turn-out, the NMP visited residents in their homes whilst also providing transport to polling stations. In an area that had seen the BNP capture 33 per cent of the vote in a neighbouring ward in May 1994, the BNP finished behind both Labour and Conservatives with just 12 per cent of the poll, a result which saw many BNP activists expecting an electoral breakthrough understandably demoralised.[126]

V

As a matter of course, following Beackon's failure to hold his seat and thereafter, the inability of the BNP to build on its local election scores and so break through into mainstream political respectability, anti-fascism lost impetus and the anti-fascist movement experienced both a diminution in size and activity. The Anti-Nazi League gradually wound down and membership was under 10,000 by January 1996.[127] But whilst the ANL was determined to stay afloat just in case fascism re-emerged from political isolation, the Anti-Racist Alliance disintegrated amidst internal factional warfare and disagreements over money. In December 1994, a breakaway grouping, the National Black Alliance, was established from a coalition of black and Asian organisations – the National Black Caucus, Tower Hamlets Anti-Racist Committee, the Society of Black Lawyers and the Indian Workers' Association – which led to the launch of the National Assembly Against Racism in February 1995. The effective end of the ARA came the following month when a national demonstration against racism, held by the remnants of ARA in central London, attracted fewer than 200 people. The militant wing of the anti-fascist movement was also in decline and, in an attempt to prevent AFA from atrophying, a new departure was proposed. In a strategy document endorsed by London AFA in May 1995, a programme was drawn up for the creation a new organisation that would work alongside AFA. The objective of this organisation – the Independent Working-Class Association – was to offer working-class voters a radical alternative to the politics of the Labour Party.[128]

Elsewhere, with its February 1995 issue celebrating '20 Fighting Years', *Searchlight* reaffirmed its determination to stand its ground and continue the anti-fascist struggle. As the editorial from the November 1996 issue explained, 'We have never believed that winning battles means that one can retire from the fray. Short term gains do not equate with winning a war against fascism.'[129] For *Searchlight*, the ultimate objective was still the total eradication of fascism from society. Yet with this an arguably impossible task, critics allege that *Searchlight's* enduring presence is more readily explained by the fact that its team has invested significant effort in, and built its livelihood around, the existence of a fascist 'threat'. And hence, when no fascist 'threat' exists, *Searchlight* merely invents one. In this respect, its arch-critic has been Larry O'Hara, an independent researcher, who went on the offensive against *Searchlight* in the early 1990s. Later, in his highly speculative *Searchlight for Beginners* (1996), O'Hara accuses *Searchlight* of deliberately 'manufacturing' scare stories and exaggerating anti-Semitism in order to win financial support from the Jewish community.[130] O'Hara even suggests that *Searchlight* has worked alongside state intelligence agencies to publicise and hype up certain far-Right organisations, such as the violent Combat 18 group which, after Millwall, served to divide and weaken the BNP by drawing away those street-hardened activists disillusioned and frustrated by failing electoral activity. Thus, O'Hara pours scorn on *Searchlight's* claim that it is an independent source of anti-fascist intelligence but rather, according to O'Hara, *Searchlight* works closely with state intelligence to which it not only supplies information on the extreme Right but also information on the radical Left. In return, *Searchlight's* 'key personnel', such as Gerry Gable and Ray Hill, are said to receive state protection. Moreover, since *Searchlight* monopolises information on the extreme Right and is the chief source of media stories on British fascism, O'Hara concludes by calling on anti-fascists to 'destroy' *Searchlight* as soon as possible and to replace it with an independent anti-fascist intelligence body that is not compromised by its relationship with the state.[131]

Naturally O'Hara's claims were welcomed by fascists; *Searchlight* was furious and proceeded to vilify O'Hara. The ferocity of *Searchlight's* attack on O'Hara, carried in numerous issues of the magazine in 1993, even exceeded earlier attempts to cut both the ANL and the ARA down to size. By playing to a fascist tune, *Searchlight's* primary riposte was that O'Hara was not an 'independent researcher' but was close to leading fascists and a fellow traveller of the extreme Right, 'a political errand boy for Patrick Harrington'.[132] Predictably, O'Hara faced a further onslaught following publication of *Searchlight for Beginners* and in January 1997 was dismissed as a 'paranoid conspiracy theorist' and 'an intellectual solipsist'.[133] From one angle, O'Hara appears to have touched a raw nerve as *Searchlight's* character assassination was certainly excessive. But conversely, to have dismissed such accusations lightly or to have ignored them altogether may have sent out signals that there was something to hide. At least initially, O'Hara's thesis won some converts on the Left,[134] though favourably for *Searchlight*, it gained little credibility with the wider anti-fascist movement. *CARF* and the Anti-Nazi League both appear to have ignored it (Gerry Gable being invited to the ANL's conference in 1994), whilst Anti-Fascist Action refused to be drawn into the ongoing dispute.[135] Thus despite O'Hara's denigration of *Searchlight*, its respected position amongst anti-fascists was never seriously challenged.

In fact, any status that *Searchlight* may have lost was more than compensated by the deserved praise it won for the publication of its ground-breaking 'Community Handbook' in November 1995. Published by the Searchlight Educational Trust,[136] the handbook, *When Hate Comes to Town*, provides practical information and advice on how best to respond to fascism and racism. Of particular note here was that in the wake of Millwall, *Searchlight's* analysis had seemingly altered. Where on previous occasions it had called for, and supported, national anti-fascist organisations (the ANL in the 1970s; AFA in the 1980s/early 1990s); it now appeared convinced that contemporary anti-fascist activity had to be rooted in community based self-organisation. The problem with national anti-fascist/anti-racist organisations, the handbook says, is their inability to put down local roots and though not always, 'All too often they are seen by local people as 'parachuting' into areas with serious problems of racial violence, gaining some publicity and moving on again.'[137] Sivanandan refers to this as 'floating' anti-fascism where:

> its actions tend to be reactive and follow a pre-set formula, organising around a specific threat or eventuality. But such floating anti-fascism renders local communities mere venues for disconnected actions, and prey to the fascist backlash once the marchers have gone.[138]

Thus the work of local groups based in the community, such as Tyne and Wear Anti-Fascist Association and the Newham Monitoring Project, are singled out for special attention in *Searchlight's* handbook, whilst national organisations such as the Anti-Nazi League are alluded to only briefly. More consistently, *Searchlight* did not waver from its line that the state and the forces of 'law and order' should play a more active role in countering fascist activity and so the types of responses recommended by the handbook fall within the general scope of 'legal' anti-fascism.[139]

In a further new departure, *Searchlight* launched 'Trade Union Friends of Searchlight' (TUFS) in the autumn of 1996. O'Hara conspiratorially sees this venture as a way of both raising money from, and gathering information on, the working class.[140] More likely, it was an attempt to restore the confidence of trade unionists in anti-fascist/anti-racist activity following the demise of the Anti-Racist Alliance. The ARA had been backed heavily by TUC money and according to AFA, the only 'success' that the ARA had was 'in convincing large numbers of trade unionists not to involve themselves ever again in anti-racist/anti-fascist activities'.[141] Apparently, thousands of pounds were made available to the ARA to produce an anti-racist exhibition as part of the TUC's 'Unite against Racism' campaign, but no exhibition ever materialised. It was therefore a measure of the respect that *Searchlight* retained that, within its first year, TUFS secured the support of over 100 affiliated trade union branches.[142] Where these newly established links with trade union branches proved especially useful was in monitoring fascist candidates at the 1997 general election. In what was described by *Searchlight* as its 'largest and most successful election information gathering exercise for many years',[143] a two-way process emerged whereby local trade unionists supplied *Searchlight* with information on fascist candidates once *Searchlight* had distributed a list alerting trade union affiliates of those constituencies where fascists intended to stand.

In the event, four extreme-Right organisations contested the 1997 general election.[144] The BNP put up 56 candidates and supplied the largest proportion, followed by the National Democrats,[145] formerly the National Front, with some 21 candidates. Not surprisingly, given that by standing over 50 candidates, the BNP qualified for a five-minute TV broadcast and free distribution of over two million leaflets by the Royal Mail, the BNP's electoral intervention generated foremost attention. But the BNP's strategy did raise problems for organised anti-fascists as it desisted both from canvassing and holding election meetings. In keeping with tactics employed at Millwall, high-profile public activity was avoided and this both denied anti-fascists a focal point for counter-mobilisation whilst also circumventing the negative association with violence and 'extremism' that typically resulted from street confrontations with anti-fascist opponents.

Accordingly, the Anti-Nazi League, alongside the National Assembly Against Racism, put their efforts into pressing the broadcasting networks not to screen the BNP's election broadcast. The ANL's 'Media Workers Against the Nazis' sub-section, founded in 1994, was activated and this collected hundreds of signatures from BBC employees calling on the BBC not to transmit the BNP's broadcast.[146] Yet despite receiving over 1,000 complaints, the BBC (and ITV) transmitted the broadcast, insisting that it could not be pulled because it was neither libellous nor contravened race relations legislation. Channel Four, on the other hand, did win praise from anti-fascists for 'pulling the plug' on the BNP's broadcast, though this decision appears to have been made not 'on principle' but because the BNP was unable to edit part of the programme within a given timescale. Therefore, as with 'No Plugs for Nazi Thugs' in the 1970s, efforts by anti-fascists to deny fascism this specific platform once again proved futile. Meanwhile, denied the opportunity to confront the BNP physically, Anti-Fascist Action concentrated on a leafleting the BNP's strongholds in east London, where some 20,000 leaflets were distributed. Interestingly, these leaflets departed from traditional anti-fascist approaches. There was no photograph of Tyndall in Nazi regalia; the BNP was pictured as 'Tories in Flight Jackets' instead. By identifying the BNP as 'ultra-conservatives', the aim was to use the unpopularity of John Major's Conservative government against the BNP. As a pre-election *Fighting Talk* made clear, AFA anticipated a Labour election victory and was determined that any future political challenge to Labour did not come from the extreme Right.[147] None the less, in relative terms, AFA distributed less than 1 per cent of the total of the BNP's election literature output and this, alongside the ANL's failure to 'silence' the BNP, shows that the impact of organised anti-fascism on the 1997 general election was minimal.

Regardless, the average BNP vote was still only 1.35 per cent. The highest scores the BNP recorded were in its East London 'fiefdoms' of Bethnal Green and Bow (7.5 per cent), and Poplar and Canning Town (7.26 per cent).[148] So why, in the absence of a substantive anti-fascist challenge, did the BNP not do better? Thurlow has argued that since the early 1990s the BNP's strategy had been to target disillusioned Tory voters; in 1997, 'New Labour' attracted many disaffected Conservative voters whilst more nationalist-inclined Tories opted for respectable non-fascist anti-European parties, such as the UK Independence Party and James Goldsmith's Referendum Party.[149] A further decisive factor, strangely omitted by Thurlow, was that race, though clearly having local resonance in places like East London, was not a major electoral issue during the 1997 general election campaign – even at the point of impending defeat John Major did not resort to playing the 'race card' despite the efforts of a number of West Midlands Tory MPs led by Nicholas Budgen.

Undoubtedly, in the sense that 'white' citizens accept it as such, British society has become progressively more multicultural, a process of acceptance reinforced by the greater prominence of black and Asian personalities in sport and the media. None the less, a culture of popular racism still exists. One indicator is racially motivated criminal incidents. In the mid-1990s, the Home Office estimated a figure 130,000 incidents for 1994 based on an under-reporting rate of one in ten.[150] In many inner-city areas, as Favell and Tambini recognise, 'Behind the figures is an everyday reality of fear for many immigrants and minorities.'[151] A second indicator is potential electoral support for anti-immigrant politics. An ICM opinion poll in the *Daily Express* (8 August 1995) found that 26 per cent of its sample would definitely or would seriously consider voting for a far-Right party of the Le Pen type. Society is not static, there is generational change, but clearly anti-immigrant racial populism still holds significant residual appeal. Yet in 1997, given Major's decision not to play the 'race card', there was little opportunity for the BNP to impact on mainstream political debate and convince voters that the mainstream parties were 'soft' on immigration.

Furthermore, although there were claims that the BNP received 3,500 enquiries following its election broadcast, this initial interest was not converted into active support.[152] Consequently, despite having little influence on the 1997 general election, anti-fascists could take comfort in the fact that the BNP had not expanded its membership and remained cut off from the political mainstream. Outside East London and with the possible exception of West Yorkshire where a deposit had been saved in Dewsbury, the BNP was left languishing on the very margins of British political life. At local elections in 1998, a further positive sign came when in its East London stronghold of Tower Hamlets, the BNP's average vote fell to just 4.53 per cent.[153] Hence, as the 1990s draw to a close, barring an improbable reversal in fortunes at the 1999 European elections, the BNP's bid for electoral credibility looks almost certain to have ended in comprehensive failure.

In this final chapter of this twentieth-century history of British anti-fascism, we have seen how, once again, the fluctuating fortunes of British fascism give life to, and take life from, anti-fascism. In the early 1980s, following the electoral collapse of the National Front and with fascism no longer such a visible threat to mainstream society, the ANL and its popular anti-fascism faded. In the early 1990s, especially after the BNP's shock by-election victory, fascism's public profile increased and so popular anti-fascism briefly re-emerged in a size and form equal to the 1970s. But recall that Anti-Fascist Action emerged in 1985 at a time when fascism was marginalised electorally and when its public profile had visibly declined. Did the formation of AFA therefore break with this historical pattern? No, and the point that needs to be made here is that anti-fascism reacted to a perceived change in fascism where fighting fascism in the 1980s was not so much a case of fighting fascism as an electoral force but as a threat to those black and Asian communities 'hidden' from mainstream society.

As this chapter has documented, a further recurring feature was anti-fascist sectarianism. This reached a peak in the early 1990s when opposition groups with their own political agendas insisted on quarrelling with one another rather than achieving broad unity. More traditional disagreements over anti-fascist strategy also re-emerged in the early 1990s with the militant wing of the anti-fascist movement now represented by Anti-Fascist Action insisting on physical confrontation, whilst others, such as the Anti-Racist Alliance, opting for a more moderate legal response. Whilst this debate is likely to run and run, the potential weakness of militant anti-fascism clearly emerges from the experience of Millwall. Although anti-fascist militancy can undoubtedly disable the street operations of fascist groups, a problem obviously arises when adversaries change tactics and adopt campaigning methods that avoid the possibility of confrontation. A further problem, as the ANL appears to have found to its cost, is that confrontational anti-fascism risks isolating anti-fascists from the local community.

As for elements of discontinuity in the history of anti-fascism in the 1980s and 1990s, the founding of the ARA clearly stands out. Although it soon collapsed, the Anti-Racist Alliance was none the less an attempt to build a broad national anti-fascist and anti-racist response around black and Asian leadership. The fate of the ARA shows, however, that this approach is fraught with difficulties and seems to confirm that fascism needs to be fought collectively by all sectors of society, even if through racial violence it impacts on society unequally. Moreover, as

Millwall reveals, and as *Searchlight* has now recognised, any collective anti-fascist response must be rooted firmly in the local community. This is the practical lesson for anti-fascists today. Whether it will be accepted by all remains to be seen.

Conclusion

This book has unearthed a much under-studied and absorbing area of British political history. Considering the imbalance in existing literature and anti-fascism's historical significance, this was long overdue. In this book, anti-fascism was seen in both active and passive terms and it was from this broad definition that the wider development of British anti-fascism over the course of the twentieth century was documented. Within this frame of reference, our particular concerns were the range of anti-fascist opposition, its organisation, strategic positions and the contribution of anti-fascism to the political weakness of British fascism.

As we have seen, the anti-fascist tradition in Britain dates as far back as the 1920s when it first established itself as a reactive phenomenon. Ever since, the pattern of anti-fascism's historic development has been determined by this overarching characteristic. This means quite simply that the scale of response has been defined by the nature of its stimulus. Accordingly, responses to the relatively insignificant forerunners to Mosley's Blackshirts were small-scale, restricted to London and largely exclusive to the radical Left. The scope of opposition to British fascism only assumed wider dimensions when, after the Nazi seizure of power in 1933, the stimulus hardened. In consequence, the labour movement isolated Oswald Mosley's British Union of Fascists as a serious threat especially after Mosley received influential backing from the Rothermere press. All the same, the Labour Party dismissed out of hand joint action with the radical Left and as a result the British labour movement, like its German counterpart, failed to form a solid, unbroken anti-fascist front. None the less, left-wing militants and moderates still came together in grassroots *ad hoc* committees and thus a locally oriented popular anti-fascism emerged as multiple examples from 1934 show. This was the case despite an organisational structure to anti-fascism which remained loose and ill-defined particularly when for a variety reasons which we will not be rehearsed here, the Communist-sponsored Co-ordinating Committee for Anti-Fascist Activities wound down in 1935.

Thereafter, what widened the scope of activist-oriented anti-fascism was the emergence of fascist-related anti-Semitism. This extended anti-fascist activity beyond radical-Left groups to involve Jewish groups in a bloc of militant opposition. Though not exclusively focused on the East End, it was in East London where concerted opposition to Mosley's fascism peaked at the 'Battle of Cable Street' in October 1936. After 1936–7, the scale of anti-fascist activity diminished, but opposition lasted to the outbreak of war and, following a brief pause, resumed in 1943 with popular hostility to Mosley's release. It should also be borne in mind that after 1935 what widened opposition to Mosley still further was the intervention of another important actor in the anti-fascist arena – the state. Its open intervention came about first through the Public Order Act, which attempted to contain the threat of fascist (and left-wing) extremism, before assuming greater force in 1940 when the British Union of Fascists was proscribed and internment introduced.

As the beginning of chapter 3 shows, the breadth of active anti-fascist opposition was then cut by fascism's post-Holocaust cultural antipathy which made the possibility of Mosleyite fascism reviving to any significant degree in the immediate postwar period negligible. In these circumstances, the scope of opposition initially narrowed to a core of militant Jewish anti-fascists who, post-Holocaust, were understandably angered when Mosley's followers resumed activity in their districts. Between 1947 and 1948, and then again during 1962–3 as Mosley's profile was raised, opposition extended to numerous other objectors, but even then opposition remained localised and largely confined to London. It was the 1970s before popular anti-fascism re-emerged on a national scale – the point at which the National Front seemed to be breaking out of the fascist fringe and into mainstream political respectability. Undoubtedly, the main vehicle for popular participation was the Anti-Nazi League, for the first time in anti-fascist history, a union of the radical and moderate Left in one national organisation. But as we have stressed, opposition to the National Front involved more than the ANL and in this respect, the intervention of the media in the anti-fascist arena was also of major significance. Where previously the media had responded to fascism largely through publicity boycotts of Mosley, in the 1970s the national and local media more actively embraced the anti-fascist cause and did so to marked effect.

Following the electoral collapse of the Front in 1979 and the general fall in fascist activity thereafter, the relative quantity of anti-fascist activity diminished in the 1980s though campaigns such as 'Harrington Out' and the formation of Anti-Fascist Action indicated a continuing resilience. The short-lived success of the British National Party in 1993–4 against the backdrop of sizeable electoral support for extreme-Right parties in continental Europe provided the stimulus for a further resurgence of popular anti-fascism in the 1990s. Yet in line with the historical pattern, once the British National Party had lost its council seat and fascism returned to its customary political isolation, the stimulus was removed and popular anti-fascism subsequently abated. What clearly emerges from this study therefore is a cyclical pattern to anti-fascist activity where in terms of popular participation, anti-fascism has undergone periodic highs and lows. The 1930s, the 1970s and the early to mid-1990s were all periods when public partici-pation peaked and drew in tens of thousands of people. It should not be forgotten, however, that even in the absence of mass displays of popular anti-fascism, anti-fascist activity has been ever present in Britain since the 1920s.

In further reviewing the history of this activity, it would be wrong to see anti-fascism simply in terms of mass mobilisations and physical confrontations. Evocative images of fascist and anti-fascist street confrontations dominate everyday perceptions, but as this study has shown, the operation of anti-fascism has been subject to far more vari-ation. Whilst mass demonstrations and militant confrontations have been important recurring features, we must remember that when pieced together, the overall picture of anti-fascism has been compli-cated by many different activities and strategies. This picture has been further differentiated by a plurality of organisations and marked disagreements of tactical approach. As we have seen, the primary divi-sion has been between radical anti-fascism and 'legal' anti-fascism which in the 1930s separated the militant Left from the official line of the Labour Party and which during the 1930s, 1940s and early 1960s, divided Jewish anti-fascist groups from those bodies sponsored by the leaders of Anglo-Jewry. However, this strategic division was often blurred. Some ostensibly 'radical groups' (for example, the 43 Group) have called on the state to legislate against fascism/racism whilst other more 'moderate' anti-fascist organisations (for example, the postwar

Communist Party) have had grassroots activists engage in militant opposition. Moreover, the question of opposing fascism with violence has not only set one organisation apart from another, it has also resulted in conflict and division within organisations as the experience of the Communist Party in the 1930s and Anti-Fascist Action in the 1980s reveal. It may well have been the case that anti-fascism came across as a unified whole to its fascist antagonists, but as this book shows, the fact remains that opposition to British fascism has been far from homogeneous.

This brings us to our final area for review: what impact has anti-fascism had on British fascism? Clearly anti-fascism exerted considerable impact on the fortunes of British fascism in the pre-1945 era. By actively disrupting fascist activities, militant anti-fascism restricted the BUF's capacity to propagate its ideology and invited fascist opponents to discredit themselves by engaging in confrontational disorder. Negative association with violence and extremism denied the British Union of Fascists political legitimacy and discouraged potential support. The BUF then had to fall back on visceral anti-Semitism, which merely contained its support to east London where anti-Semitism had some degree of local legitimacy. Second, the Labour Party's 'legal' anti-fascism reinforced the existing liberal-democratic consensus and helped sustain the prevailing cultural exclusion of political extremism and violence. Here, we should not forget the contribution made by anti-fascist Labour-controlled public authorities, which additionally helped isolate Mosley by denying the BUF public space to disseminate its ideology. Third, the anti-fascist activity of the state also played its part in marginalising the Blackshirts, first by pressuring the media not to give Mosley undue publicity, second by curbing fascist activity through the Public Order Act, and finally, albeit on national security grounds, by proscribing the BUF and interning its leading members.

After 1945, the incorporation of anti-fascism into British national identity proved the most decisive factor in fascism's continued marginalisation. This was the overarching context in which Mosleyite fascism made efforts to rebuild and so it is in this context that the role of active anti-fascism in the immediate postwar era must equally be judged. We therefore concluded that what active anti-fascism achieved between 1946 and 1966 was further marginalisation of a political ideology that was already contained by the strength of passive anti-fascist feeling in postwar British nationalism. But, as we saw, the problem is that this anti-fascist side to British nationalism can easily coexist within a culture of popular racism and, in the 1970s, the respectability of anti-black racism provided the National Front with a cloak to hide its Nazism. Yet by variously exposing the Front as a 'front for Nazis', a message channelled through the mainstream media and through activist groups, anti-fascism successfully appealed to popular anti-Nazi sentiment and so dispossessed the National Front of political and social legitimacy. However, popular racism went largely unchallenged and, having supplanted the National Front, the British National Party was able to exploit this culture of 'respectable' racism in the 1990s. Rather predictably, the BNP's election victory was met yet again by appeals to popular anti-Nazism, but as the example of Tower Hamlets shows, alternative community-based anti-fascist strategies were employed to greater effect and suggest that local initiatives are the way forward.

In the last instance, this underlines the point that tried-and-tested methods of anti-fascist campaigning can no longer be relied upon. At this point, we will leave with a number of questions for contemporary anti-fascists to ponder: what happens if an extreme-Right party emerges, like the French Front National in the 1980s, that immunises itself against charges of Nazism? Even if a 'hidden core' of fascism can be exposed, what happens when, with generational shift, the strength of anti-Nazi feeling and the memory of war fades? There is no denying that anti-fascists have had much success in restricting space for fascists to disseminate their ideology, but what of fascist propaganda on the Internet? How are anti-fascists to respond to the potential that this rapidly growing medium offers fascists for spreading their message of hate? These are clearly disconcerting questions which demand much closer reflection. However, our last words strike a more optimistic note: will the public's ever wider acceptance of multiculturalism – by no means a certainty – marginalise fascism to the point that the need for anti-fascist activity will eventually disappear altogether?

Notes

Introduction

1 See L. Kibblewhite and A. Rigby, *Fascism in Aberdeen – Street Politics in the 1930s* (Aberdeen: Aberdeen People's Press, 1978); N. Todd, *In Excited Times: The People Against the Blackshirts* (Whitley Bay: Bewick Press, 1995); D. Turner, *Fascism and anti-Fascism in the Medway Towns 1927–1940* (Kent: Kent Anti-Fascist Action Committee, 1993); and D. Renton, *Red Shirts and Black: Fascists and Anti-Fascists in Oxford in the 1930s* (Oxford: Ruskin College Library Occasional Publication, No. 5, 1996). See also S. Gewirtz, 'Anti-Fascist Activity in Manchester's Jewish Community in the 1930s', *Manchester Region History Review*, Vol. 4, No. 1 (1990) 17–27; and N. Barrett, 'A Bright Shining Star: The CPGB and Anti-Fascist Activism in the 1930s', *Science and Society*, Vol. 61, No. 1 (1997) 10–26.
2 See J. Jacobs, *Out of the Ghetto* (London: Janet Simon, 1978); and M. Beckman, *The 43 Group* (London: Centerprise, 1993).
3 See N. Branson, *History of the Communist Party of Great Britain 1927–1941* (London: Lawrence and Wishart, 1985).
4 See R. Benewick, *The Fascist Movement in Britain* (London: Allen Lane The Penguin Press, 1972); D. S. Lewis, *Illusions of Grandeur* (Manchester: Manchester University Press, 1987); and S. Taylor, *The National Front in English Politics* (London: Macmillan, 1982).
5 R. Thurlow, *Fascism in Britain*, 2nd rev. edn (London: I.B. Tauris, 1998).
6 C. Bambery, *Killing the Nazi Menace* (London: Socialist Workers' Party, 1992) pp. 29 and 34.
7 See Lewis, *Illusions of Grandeur*, esp. ch. 5.
8 Thurlow, *Fascism in Britain*, p. 256.
9 R. Griffin, 'British Fascism: The Ugly Duckling', in M. Cronin (ed.) *The Failure of British Fascism* (Basingstoke: Macmillan, 1996) p. 162.
10 D. Renton, *The Attempted Revival of British Fascism* (University of Sheffield, PhD thesis, 1998) p. 97.
11 Renton, *The Attempted Revival of British Fascism*, p. 98.
12 For the purpose of this study, what is determined as 'fascism' relies entirely on anti-fascism. The definition of fascism is therefore implicit to anti-fascism.

Chapter 1

1 [P]ublic [R]ecord [O]ffice CAB 24/162/153, 433 and 577.
2 See for instance, R. Thurlow, *Fascism in Britain: A History 1918–85* (Oxford: Blackwell, 1987) p. 68. An exception is K. Lunn, 'The Ideology and Impact of the British Fascists in the 1920s', in T. Kushner and K. Lunn (eds) *Traditions of Intolerance* (Manchester: Manchester University Press, 1989) pp. 140–54. Lunn attempts to provide a corrective to the prevailing view

that the British Fascists were a highly insignificant forerunner to Mosley's British Union of Fascists. This perspective has been most recently countered by D. Baker in his chapter 'The Extreme Right in the 1920s: Fascism in a Cold Climate or "Conservatism with Knobs on"?', in M. Cronin (ed.) *The Failure of British Fascism* (Basingstoke: Macmillan, 1996) pp. 12–28.

3 See R. Bosworth, 'The British Press, the Conservatives, and Mussolini, 1920–34', *Journal of Contemporary History*, Vol. 5 (1970) 163–81; and R. Palme Dutt, 'Notes of the Month', *Labour Monthly*, Vol. 7 (7 July 1925), p. 390.

4 This has been suggested by J. Hope, in a footnote to his article, 'Fascism and the State in Britain: The Case of the Britsh Fascists, 1923–31', *Australian Journal of Politics and History*, Vol. 39, No. 3 (1993) 367–80.

5 PRO CAB 30/69/220. New Scotland Yard Special Branch Reports on Revolutionary Organisations in the United Kingdom, Report No. 241, 31 January 1924.

6 The National Unemployed Workers' Committee was a Communist ancillary organisation. Formed in 1921, it became the National Unemployed Workers' Movement in 1929.

7 PRO CAB 30/69/220: New Scotland Yard Special Branch Reports on Revolutionary Organisations in the United Kingdom, Report No. 241, 31 January 1924.

8 PRO CAB 30/69/220: New Scotland Yard Special Branch Reports on Revolutionary Organisations in the United Kindom, Report No. 270, 4 September 1924.

9 The *Daily Herald*, 5 June 1925.

10 *Fascist Bulletin*, 12 September, 1924, p. 3.

11 There were clashes between left-wing militants and fascists in Hyde Park in July 1924 and at Clapham Common in August 1924.

12 The Plebs League originated at Ruskin College, Oxford. Its function was to popularise Marxist education within the labour movement.

13 The Plebs League, *Fascism: Its History and Significance* (London: Plebs, 1924), p. 34.

14 See K. Lunn, 'The Ideology and Impact of the British Fascists in the 1920s', esp. pp. 145–6. Lunn does point out that social and leisure activities could assume politicising roles.

15 Palme Dutt, 'Notes of the Month', p. 395.

16 See T. Bell, *British Communist Party: A Short History* (London: Lawrence and Wishart, 1937) pp. 107–8.

17 Described as such by Herbert Morrison in a letter to the Prime Minister, see *Daily Herald*, 10 November 1925.

18 According to BF sources, many fascists did co-operate with the OMS as 'British Fascists' during the General Strike, see PRO HO 144/19069/34–5.

19 PRO HO 144/13864/31–2.

20 PRO HO 144/13864/31–2.

21 PRO HO 144/13864/31–2, 43–4 and 47–9.

22 PRO HO 144/13864/81–5.

23 PRO HO 144/19069/154.

24 F. G. Portsmouth in *The Fascist Gazette*, 8 November 1926.

25 PRO HO 144/19069/85, 9, 19 and 81.

26 The *Daily Herald*, 21 October 1925.
27 The *Daily Herald*, 7 and 11 November 1925.
28 PRO HO 144/16069/211–12. Also see *Labour Monthly*, Vol. 7 (7 July 1925), p. 385.
29 R. Benewick, *The Fascist Movement in Britain* (London: Allen Lane The Penguin Press, 1972) p. 38.
30 See Introduction to Cable Street Group, *The Battle of Cable Street 1936* (London: Cable Street Group, 1995).
31 See R. Skidelsky, *Oswald Mosley* (London: Macmillan, 1981) pp. 355–7.
32 The organisation that Mosley formed in early 1931 following his break with the Labour Party over its refusal to accept his proposal for a radical Keynesian solution to the economic crisis.
33 For a comprehensive list of disruptions, see D. S. Lewis, *Illusions of Grandeur* (Manchester: Manchester University Press, 1987) p. 20.
34 N. Mosley, *Rules of the Game* (London: Secker and Warburg, 1982) p. 184.
35 Skidelsky, *Oswald Mosley*, p. 356.
36 John Strachey had resigned from the Parliamentary Labour Party in 1931. He was later to return to the Labour Party and was adopted Labour candidate for Dundee in 1943 and served in the Labour administration of 1945–51.
37 *The Blackshirt*, No. 3, 18 March 1933.
38 Skidelsky, *Oswald Mosley*, p. 353.
39 Skidelsky, *Oswald Mosley*, p. 358.
40 *The Blackshirt*, 18 March 1933.
41 *The Blackshirt*, 17 April 1933.
42 H. Pelling, *The British Communist Party: A Historical Profile* (London: Adam and Charles Black, 1975) p.77.
43 Pelling, *The British Communist Party*, p. 76.
44 For an overview of the Labour Party's policy on British fascism, see M. Newman, 'Democracy versus Dictatorship: Labour's Role in the Struggle against British Fascism, 1933–1936', *History Workshop*, No. 5 (1978) 67–88.
45 See R. Griffin, 'British Fascism: The Ugly Duckling', in M. Cronin (ed.) *The Failure of British Fascism* (Basingstoke: Macmillan, 1996) pp. 141–65.
46 R. Palme Dutt, *Democracy and Fascism* (London: Communist Party of Great Britain, 1933) p. 7.
47 D. Renton, *Red Shirts and Black: Fascists and Anti-Fascists in Oxford in the 1930s* (Oxford: Ruskin College Library Occasional Publications, No. 5, 1996), p. 21, D. Turner, *Fascism and anti-Fascism in the Medway Towns 1927–40* (Kent: Kent Anti-Fascist Action Committee, 1993) pp. 18–19; and N. Todd, *In Excited Times: The People Against the Blackshirts* (Whitley Bay: Bewick Press, 1995) p. 14.
48 F. Mullally, *Fascism Inside England* (London: Claud Morris, 1946) p. 30.
49 Mullally, *Fascism Inside England*, p. 30.
50 See N. Branson, *History of the Communist Party of Great Britain 1927–41* (London: Lawrence and Wishart, 1985) pp. 115–17.
51 *The Fascist Week*, 2–8 March 1934.
52 For reports of disorders during 1933, see PRO HO 45/25386/25–7. Also see *The Blackshirt*, 1–7 July 1933.
53 PRO MEPO 2/3069/91.

54 See W. F. Mandle, *Anti-Semitism and the British Union of Fascists* (London: Longmans, Green and Co. Ltd, 1968) pp. 2–6.

55 Anon., *Mosley's Blackshirts: The Inside Story of the British Union of Fascists* (London: Sanctuary Press, 1986) p. 51; and *The Blackshirt*, 16–22 September 1933.

56 PRO HO 144/19070/5, PRO HO 144/19070/8–10.

57 S. Cullen, 'Political Violence: The Case of the British Union of Fascists', *Journal of Contemporary History*, Vol. 28 (1993) 260. Also see PRO HO 144/19070/29.

58 On the role of the *Daily Mail* as a 'recruiting agent' for British fascism, see R. Griffiths, *Fellow Travellers of the Right: British Enthusiasts for Nazi Germany 1933–39* (London: Constable, 1980) p. 107.

59 Lewis, *Illusions of Grandeur*, p. 134.

60 H. Thomas, *John Strachey* (London: Eyre Methuen, 1973) p. 130.

61 Printing and Allied Trades Anti-Fascist Movement, *Printers and the Fascist Menace* (London: Printing and Allied Trades Anti-Fascist Movement, 1934).

62 Douglas argued that economic depression could be overcome by increasing mass purchasing power through the creation of public credit, that is 'social credit'.

63 Figures given in the *Daily Express*, 21 February 1934. On background to the Green Shirts, see J. L. Finlay, 'John Hargrave, the Green Shirts, and Social Credit', *Journal of Contemporary History*, Vol. 5 (1970) 53–71. Also see M. Drakeford, *Social Movements and their Supporters: The Green Shirts in England* (Basingstoke: Macmillan, 1997).

64 See PRO HO 144/19070/239–41 and Drakeford, *Social Movements and their Supporters: The Green Shirts in England*, pp. 123–24, 142 and 154.

65 See *The Blackshirt*, 16 November 1934 and PRO HO 144/20140/117 and 135–8.

66 *The Fascist Week*, 23 February–1 March 1934.

67 PRO HO 144/20140/267–8, 20143/393, 390 and 389.

68 PRO HO 144/19070/16–18.

69 See Todd, *In Excited Times*, esp. pp. 54–9.

70 'The Struggle against Fascism in the Thirties', *Bulletin of the North East Labour History Society*, No. 18 (1984) 22.

71 John Beckett had been Labour MP for Gateshead between 1924 and 1929 before becoming a Labour MP for Peckham between 1929 and 1931.

72 PRO HO 144/20140/58–9 and 376–7.

73 See Labour Party Archive [LPA] LP/FAS/34/218.

74 See I. Montagu, *Blackshirt Brutality: The Story of Olympia* (London: Workers Bookshop Ltd, 1934) p. 8.

75 PRO HO 144/20140/29–34.

76 R. Thurlow, *Fascism in Britain*, 2nd rev. edn (London: I. B. Tauris, 1998) p. 71.

77 See M. Pugh, 'The British Union of Fascists and the Olympia Debate', *Historical Journal*, Vol. 41, No. 2 (1998) 529–42.

78 *Daily Mail*, 12 June 1934.

79 PRO HO 144/20141/85. According to *Who's Who* (1962), the background of Maggs does not suggest that he was Jewish. His family base was Melksham in Wiltshire, where Blackshirts had been subjected to local hostility.

80 PRO HO 45/25386/279–89.
81 See *Anti-Fascist Special* (1934) p 3.
82 See *Fight*, July 1934 and Aug 1934. On meetings of New World Fellowship, see PRO HO 144/20143/363, 364, 366, 372 and 382.
83 See *Fight*, July 1934 and PRO HO 144/20143/378 and 374.
84 H. Maitles, 'Fascism in the 1930s: The West of Scotland in the British Context', *Scottish Labour History Society Journal*, Vol. 27 (1992) 7–22.
85 PRO HO 144/20143/379–80.
86 PRO HO 144/ 20143/376.
87 See *Leicester Evening Mail*, 15 June 1934.
88 PRO HO 144/20141/38, 46–8 and 238.
89 *Fight*, August 1934.
90 *Daily Worker*, 27 July 1934.
91 PRO HO 45/25388/400–404 and 25383/685.
92 PRO HO 45/25383/421–3.
93 LPA ID/CI/24/9i and ii.
94 LPA ID/CI/24/12i and ii.
95 For instance, one pamphlet produced by the Labour Research Department in 1934 entitled 'Who Backs Mosley?' portrayed Mosley as a 'Toff' – an aristocratic enemy of the working class.
96 See TUC, *United Against Fascism!* (1934) pp. 25–8.
97 PRO HO 45/25383/442–47.
98 Branson, *History of the Communist Party of Great Britain 1927–41*, p. 123.
99 For a selection of these leaflets, see PRO HO 45/25383/569, 570 and 575–77.
100 J. Jacobs, *Out of the Ghetto* (London: Janet Simon, 1978) p. 145.
101 See CPGB, *Drowned in a Sea of Working-Class Activity – September 9th* (1934) and PRO HO 45/25383/602–17.
102 PRO HO 45/25383/602–17.
103 *Fight*, September 1934.
104 See *The New Statesman and Nation*, 8 September 1934, pp. 283–5.
105 See PRO HO 45/25383/602–17.
106 Quoted in M. Power, *The Struggle against Fascism and War in Britain 1931–39* (History Group of the Communist Party, Our History Pamphlet No. 70, n.d.) p. 16.
107 E. Trory, *Between the Wars: Recollections of a Communist Organiser* (Brighton: Crabtree Press, 1974) p. 46.
108 G. Allison, 'The Next Steps in the Fight against Fascism', *Labour Monthly*, Vol. 16 (December 1934) p. 730.
109 From resolution of the Central Committee of the CPGB, August 1934, quoted in J. Strachey, 'The Prospects of the Anti-Fascist Struggle', *Labour Monthly*, Vol. 16 (October 1934) p. 609.
110 Strachey, 'The Prospects of the Anti-Fascist Struggle', pp. 610–11.
111 Strachey, 'The Prospects of the Anti-Fascist Struggle', p. 611.
112 Allison, 'The Next Steps in the Fight against Fascism', p. 732.
113 See N. Barrett, 'A Bright Shining Star: The CPGB and Anti-Fascist Activism in the 1930s', *Science and Society*, Vol. 61, No. 1 (1997) 10–26.
114 See S. Gewirtz, 'Anti-Fascist Activity in Manchester's Jewish Community in the 1930s', *Manchester Region History Review*, Vol. 4, No. 1 (1990) 23.

115 PRO HO 144/20143/41 and 353.
116 PRO HO 144/20143/49–50 and 68–9.
117 Jacobs, *Out of the Ghetto*, p. 146.
118 See Thomas, *John Strachey*, pp. 139–40.
119 PRO HO 20143/332.
120 See Cullen, 'Political Violence: The Case of the British Union of Fascists', footnote 22, p. 266.
121 M. Newman, *John Strachey* (Manchester: Manchester University Press, 1989) p. 52.
122 Quoted in *Labour Monthly*, Vol. 16, December 1934, p. 732.
123 See G. C. Webber, 'Patterns of Membership and Support for the British Union of Fascists', *Journal of Contemporary History*, Vol. 19 (1984) 575–606.
124 See Cullen, 'Political Violence: The Case of the British Union of Fascists', 249. These figures appear to be largely derived from meetings held in the Metropolitan Police District. As Cullen notes, provincial Fascist meetings were only recorded if there was serious disorder or if they were on a large scale.
125 It appears that the Anti-Fascist League was defunct by mid-1935. See Todd, *In Excited Times*, pp. 79–80.
126 Thurlow, *Fascism in Britain: A History, 1918–1985*, p. 126.

Chapter 2

1 See G. C. Lebzelter, *Political Anti-Semitism in England 1918–1939* (London: Macmillan, 1978) p. 158.
2 See E. Smith, 'Jewish Responses to Political Antisemitism and Fascism in the East End of London, 1920–1939', in T. Kushner and K. Lunn (eds) *Traditions of Intolerance* (Manchester: Manchester University Press, 1989) esp. pp. 60–1.
3 See PRO HO 144/20147/263, 269 and 271.
4 PRO HO 144/20147/400.
5 On Thurloe Square, see S. Scaffardi, *Fire under the Carpet: Working for Civil Liberties in the 1930s* (London: Lawrence and Wishart, 1986) pp. 123–32.
6 On the NCCL, see R. Thurlow, *The Secret State* (Oxford: Blackwell, 1994) pp. 169–72 and Scaffardi, *Fire under the Carpet*, esp. p. 112. Scaffardi, a companion of Ronald Kidd and an assistant secretary of the NCCL, denies that links with the CPGB were strong.
7 J. Jacobs, *Out of the Ghetto* (London: Janet Simon, 1978) p. 199.
8 R. Benewick, *The Fascist Movement in Britain* (London: Allen Lane/The Penguin Press, 1972) p. 204.
9 H. Pelling, *The British Communist Party: A Historical Profile* (London: Adam and Charles Black, 1975) p. 97.
10 See N. Barrett, 'A Bright Shining Star: The CPGB and Anti-Fascist Activism in the 1930s', *Science and Society*, Vol. 61, No. 1 (1997) 10–26.
11 See S. Gewirtz, 'Anti-Fascist Activity in Manchester's Jewish Community in the 1930s', *Manchester Region History Review*, Vol. 4, No. 1 (1990) 17–27.
12 PRO HO 144/21060/244, 245 and 248–9.
13 D. Cesarani in his contribution to P. Catterall (ed.), 'Witness Seminar: The Battle of Cable Street', *Contemporary Record*, Vol. 8, No. 1 (1994) 124.

14 On the BUF in south Wales, see S. Cullen, 'Another nationalism: The British Union of Fascists in Glamorgan, 1932–40', *Welsh History Review*, Vol. 17, No. 1, (1994) 101–14.

15 See H. Francis, *Miners against Fascism* (London: Lawrence and Wishart, 1984) pp. 92–4.

16 See PRO HO 144/21060/141–44.

17 Anon., *Mosley's Blackshirts: The Inside Story of the British Union of Fascists* (London: Sanctuary Press, 1986) p. 35.

18 J. Charnley, *Blackshirts and Roses* (London: Brockingday, 1990) p. 72.

19 See S. Cullen, 'Political Violence: The Case of the British Union of Fascists', *Journal of Contemporary History*, Vol. 28 (1993) 259.

20 D. Renton, *Red Shirts and Black: Fascists and Anti-Fascists in Oxford in the 1930s* (Oxford: Ruskin College Library Occasional Publication, No. 5, 1996) pp. 38 and 42.

21 See G. C. Webber, 'Patterns of Membership and Support for the British Union of Fascists', *Journal of Contemporary History*, Vol. 19 (1984) esp. 585–6.

22 Charnley, *Blackshirts and Roses*, p. 76.

23 R. Skidelsky, *Oswald Mosley* (London: Macmillan, 1981) p. 361.

24 See K. Morgan, *Against Fascism and War* (Manchester: Manchester University Press, 1989) pp. 33–55.

25 Comprised of former members of the ILP that remained within the Labour Party following the ILP's disaffiliation.

26 See P. Piratin, *Our Flag Stays Red* (London: Thames Publications, 1948) pp. 17–18.

27 Piratin, *Our Flag Stays Red*, p. 18.

28 See Gewirtz, 'Anti-Fascist Activity in Manchester's Jewish Community in the 1930s', esp. 24–6.

29 On the defence debate, see D. Cesarani, *The Jewish Chronicle and Anglo-Jewry 1841–1991* (Cambridge: Cambridge University Press, 1994) pp. 149–51; and D. Rosenberg, *Facing up to Antisemitism: How Jews in Britain Countered the Threats of the 1930s* (London: JCARP Publications, 1985) pp. 46–60.

30 See PRO MEPO 2/3043/253–61.

31 K. Newton, *The Sociology of British Communism* (London: Allen Lane/The Penguin Press, 1969) p. 21.

32 PRO HO 20147/32. Also see Benewick, *The Fascist Movement in Britain*, p. 221.

33 See C. Rosenberg, 'The Labour Party and the Fight against Fascism', *International Socialism*, Vol. 2, No. 39 (1988) 55–93.

34 D. S. Lewis, *Illusions of Grandeur* (Manchester: Manchester University Press, 1987) p. 123.

35 B. Burke, *Rebels with a Cause: The History of Hackney Trades Council* (London: Hackney Trades Council and Hackney Workers Educational Association, 1975) p. 44.

36 F. Mullally, *Fascism Inside England* (London: Claud Morris, 1946) p. 71.

37 See T. P. Linehan, *East London for Mosley: The British Union of Fascists in East London and South-West Essex 1933–40* (London: Frank Cass, 1996) p. 60.

38 PRO MEPO 2/3043/289–94.

39 PRO MEPO 2/3043/276.
40 This had been formed in November 1934 at a conference of left-wing Jewish trade unionists who were committed to fighting fascism and anti-Semitism.
41 PRO HO 144/21060/314.
42 Smith, 'Jewish responses to political antisemitism and fascism in the East End of London, 1920–1939', p. 64.
43 PRO HO 144/21060/316.
44 A. Harris in the Foreword to A. C. Miles, *Mosley in Motley* (London: A. C. Miles, 1937).
45 See PRO MEPO 2/3043/289–94.
46 PRO HO 144/20143/258.
47 Lebzelter, *Political Anti-Semitism in England 1918–1939*, pp. 162–3.
48 See F. Renton, *Jewish Defence Campaign: Speakers' Handbook* (London: Woburn Press, 1937?) p. 9.
49 See Scaffardi, *Fire under the Carpet*, p. 140.
50 See PRO HO 144/21060/307, 309 and 316.
51 R. Thurlow, *The Secret State*, p. 198.
52 Jacobs, *Out of the Ghetto*, p. 238.
53 These figures are cited in Smith, 'Jewish Responses to Political Antisemitism and Fascism in the East End of London, 1920–1939', p. 61.
54 CPGB London District Committee, *District Bulletin*, No. 24, 1 October 1936.
55 See Jacobs, *Out of the Ghetto*, pp. 246–8.
56 See Catterall (ed.), 'Witness Seminar: The Battle of Cable Street', 112.
57 See Jacobs, *Out of the Ghetto*, p. 249. Jacobs complains that the *Daily Worker* on 3 October carried no reports on preparations for the following day's mobilisation. However, there was a special supplement to the *Daily Worker* circulated on 3 October which contained a map and instructions on where to assemble. It is not clear how widely this was distributed and Jacobs claims that he does not remember seeing a copy of this supplement.
58 F. Brockway, *Inside the Left* (London: Allen and Unwin, 1942) p. 271.
59 The ILP did hold some bases of local support, especially Clydeside and Derby.
60 Brockway, *Inside the Left*, p. 271.
61 See ILP, *THEY DID NOT PASS – 300,000 Workers Say NO to Mosley* (1936), pp. 5–6.
62 See PRO HO 144/21060/360 and 361.
63 Quoted in N. Branson, *History of the Communist Party of Great Britain 1927–1941* (London: Lawrence and Wishart, 1985) p. 163.
64 See contribution by C. Goodman in P. Catterall, 'The Battle of Cable Street', 118–20.
65 C. Rosenberg, 'The Labour Party and the fight against fascism', 62–3.
66 L. Susser, *Fascist and Anti-Fascist Attitudes in Britain Between the Wars* (University of Oxford, DPhil thesis, 1988) p. 302.
67 Piratin, *Our Flag Stays Red*, p. 23.
68 See PRO HO 144/21061/102–12.
69 See R. Bellamy, *We Marched with Mosley* (Unpublished official history of the BUF, condensed version, University of Sheffield Library) pp. 182–3.
70 N. Deakin, 'The Vitality of a Tradition', C. Holmes (ed.) *Immigrants and*

Minorities in British Society (London: Allen and Unwin, 1978) p. 167.

71 See contribution of Smith in Catterall (ed.), 'Witness Seminar: The Battle of Cable Street', 126.

72 N. Deakin, 'The Vitality of a Tradition', p. 167.

73 Piratin, *Our Flag Stays Red*, pp. 23–4.

74 C. Goodman in his contribution to Catterall (ed.), 'Witness Seminar: The Battle of Cable Street', 120.

75 See S. Rawnsley, 'The membership of the British Union of Fascists', in K. Lunn and R. Thurlow (eds) *British Fascism* (London: Croom Helm, 1980) pp. 150–65.

76 See Chapter 6 in *The Battle of Cable Street* (London, Cable Street Group, 1995).

77 See Barrett, 'A Bright Shining Star, 10–26.

78 See PRO HO 144/21061/287.

79 See T. Gallagher, *Edinburgh Divided* (Edinburgh: Polygon, 1987) p. 109. On the BUF and Ireland, see J. Loughlin, 'Northern Ireland and British fascism in the inter-war years', *Irish Historical Studies*, Vol. 29, No. 116 (1995) 537–52.

80 See PRO MEPO 2/3043/253–61.

81 R. Thurlow, *Fascism in Britain: A History, 1918–1985* (Oxford: Basil Blackwell, 1987) p. 111.

82 See Linehan, *East London for Mosley*, pp. 202–3.

83 W. F. Mandle, *Anti-Semitism and the British Union of Fascists* (London: Longmans, Green and Co. Ltd, 1968) p. 55.

84 Susser, *Fascist and Anti-Fascist Attitudes in Britain Between the Wars*, p. 303.

85 See J. Stevenson and C. Cook, *Britain in the Depression: Society and Politics, 1929–1939* (London: Longman, 1994) p. 231.

86 J. Hamm, *Action Replay* (London: Howard Baker, 1983) pp. 211–12.

87 See Jacobs, *Out of the Ghetto*, pp. 262–3.

88 See PRO MEPO 2/3043/253–61.

89 Jacobs, *Out of the Ghetto*, p. 263.

90 See PRO HO 144/21061/318: Extract from *Morning Post*, 14 October 1936.

91 See Thurlow, *The Secret State*, pp. 173–213.

92 See for instance, D. S. Lewis, *Illusions of Grandeur*, pp. 145–80.

93 Lewis, *Illusions of Grandeur*, p. 160.

94 Lewis, *Illusions of Grandeur*, p. 160.

95 See Thurlow, *The Secret State*, esp. pp. 201–2; and G. C. Lebzelter, *Political Anti-Semitism in England 1918–1939*, esp. p. 130.

96 In a speech in the House of Commons in 1943. Quoted in M. Newman, 'Democracy versus Dictatorship: Labour's role in the Struggle against British Fascism, 1933–1936', *History Workshop*, Issue 5 (1978) 73.

97 See J. Stevenson and C. Cook, *Britain in the Depression: Society and Politics, 1929–1939* (London: Longman, 1994) p. 231.

98 See Linehan, *East London for Mosley*, pp. 10–13.

99 See G. C. Webber, 'Patterns of Membership and Support for the British Union of Fascists', *Journal of Contemporary History*, Vol. 19 (1984) 575–606. The BUF's membership for the period 1938–40 has been the subject of some debate. It is clear that support for Mosley in the East End fell, but this was offset by new recruits from the 'respectable' middle class in other areas

of London. Indeed, Webber argues that BUF membership reached 22,500 by the end of September 1939.

100 See PRO HO 144/21086/69–70.
101 See PRO HO 144/21086/98.
102 See PRO HO 144/21086/141–7.
103 Lewis, *Illusions of Grandeur*, p. 127.
104 See PRO HO 144/21086/141–7.
105 See PRO HO 144/21086/167A and 203–11.
106 London Labour Party circular re: Bermondsey, 20 September 1937.
107 See PRO HO 144/21087/69–78.
108 See Branson, *History of the Communist Party of Great Britain 1927–1941*, p. 169.
109 The figure of 50,000 is suggested by Lewis, *Illusions of Grandeur*, p. 127. For the Special Branch estimate, see PRO HO 144/21087/69–78.
110 The Federation of Democrats appear to have originated in the East End from an amalgamation of the British Union of Democrats, the British Democratic Association and the Legion of Democrats.
111 N. Todd, *In Excited Times: The People against the Blackshirts* (Whitley Bay: Bewick Press, 1995) p. 111.
112 Lewis, *Illusions of Grandeur*, p. 128.
113 See PRO HO 144/21087/69–78.
114 Branson, *History of the Communist Party of Great Britain 1927–1941*, p. 171.
115 PRO HO 144/21281/6. This figure precedes the launch of Mosley's anti-war policy in March 1938.
116 Lewis, *Illusions of Grandeur*, p. 128.
117 See Barrett, 'A Bright Shining Star', 10–26.
118 *Daily Worker*, 30 March 1938.
119 See D. Turner, *Fascism and anti-Fascism in the Medway Towns 1927–1940* (Kent: Kent Anti-Fascist Action Committee, 1993) pp. 34–5.
120 See L. Kibblewhite and A. Rigby, *Fascism in Aberdeen – Street Politics in the 1930s* (Aberdeen: Aberdeen People's Press, 1978).
121 Kibblewhite and Rigby, *Fascism in Aberdeen*, p. 27.
122 *Evening Dispatch* (Edinburgh), 21 June 1937 and *East End News*, 24 June 1938.
123 PRO MEPO 2/3043/71–2.
124 See PRO MEPO 2/3043/59–61.
125 Piratin, *Our Flag Stays Red*, p. 32.
126 Piratin, *Our Flag Stays Red*, p. 44.
127 H. F. Srebrnik, *London Jews and British Communism 1935–1945* (Ilford: Valentine Mitchell, 1995) p. 56.
128 It blamed precarious finances, apathy and the growth of smaller anti-fascist groups for its demise.
129 [B]oard of [D]eputies, C6/1/1/1, Report on conference between LAC and the JPC held on 26 April 1938.
130 BD, C6/1/1/1, JDC minutes, 13 January 1939.
131 BD, C6/1/1/1, Vigilance Committees in Great Britain. A General Survey (1936).
132 BD, C6/1/1/1, Report on Outdoor Meetings of the London Area Council by I. Gellman (1939).

133 See PRO HO 144/21281/150–4.
134 Lewis, *Illusions of Grandeur*, p. 138.
135 R. Bellamy, *We Marched with Mosley* (unpublished official history of the BUF, condensed version, University of Sheffield Library) p. 226.
136 See PRO HO 144/21281/142–6 and 150–4.
137 See *News Chronicle*, 6 November 1939.
138 Communist Party membership temporarily fell from 18,000 in 1939 to 12,000 in June 1941. It revived with the entry of the Soviet Union into the war and subsequently peaked at 64,000 in September 1942. J. Callaghan, *The Far Left in British Politics* (Oxford: Basil Blackwell, 1987) p. 48
139 R. Thurlow, *Fascism in Britain: A History, 1918–1985* (Oxford: Basil Blackwell, 1987) pp. 211–12.
140 See T. Kushner, *The Persistence of Prejudice. Antisemitism in British Society during the Second World War* (Manchester: Manchester University Press, 1989) p. 167.
141 See D. Hyde, *I Believed* (London: Reprint Society, 1950) p. 178.
142 See D. Renton, *The Attempted Revival of British Fascism* (University of Sheffield, PhD thesis, 1998) pp. 50–1; and Branson, *History of the Communist Party in Britain 1941–1951*, pp. 77–9.
143 Hyde, *I Believed*, p. 178.
144 See Stevenson and C. Cook, *Britain in the Depression: Society and Politics 1929–39* (London: Longman, 1994) pp. 154–5. On the East End, see H. Srebrnik, 'The British Communist Party's National Jewish Committee and the Fight against Anti-Semitism during the Second World War', in T. Kushner and K. Lunn (eds) *The Politics of Marginality* (London: Frank Cass, 1990) pp. 82–96.
145 See E. Allen, *It Shall Not Happen Here: Anti-Semitism, Fascists and Civil Liberty* (London: Walthamstow Press, 1943) pp. 29–31.
146 See Kushner, *The Persistence of Prejudice*, p. 182.
147 R. Skidelsky, 'Reflections on Mosley and British Fascism', in K. Lunn and R. Thurlow (eds) *British Fascism* (London: Croom Helm, 1980) p. 86.
148 Skidelsky, 'Reflections on Mosley and British Fascism', p. 87.
149 This was suggested to Harry Pollitt by Neville Laski following the 'Battle of Cable Street'; see C. Holmes, 'East End Anti-Semitism 1936', *Society for the Study of Labour History*, Vol. 32 (1976) 26–33.

Chapter 3

1 R. Eatwell, *Fascism: A History* (London: Chatto and Windus, 1995) p. 14.
2 Mullally was a journalist for the *Sunday Pictorial*.
3 F. Mullally, *Fascism Inside England* (London: Claud Morris, 1946) p 88.
4 Mullally, *Fascism Inside England*, p. 88.
5 This had in the region of 6,000 members in London.
6 M. Beckman, *The 43 Group* (London: Centerprise, 1993) p. 16.
7 Beckman, *The 43 Group*, pp. 21–2.
8 Morris Beckman to author, 29 May 1998.
9 Len Rolnick to author, 7 July 1998.
10 See *The 43 Group Fights Fascism Today* (43 Group leaflet, Zaidman Papers, University of Sheffield).

11 Over its four-year life, perhaps 60 Gentiles were associated with the 43 Group.
12 Morris Beckman to author, 29 May 1998. According to Beckman, Bud Flanagan contributed £30 a month to the 43 Group. Flanagan was the son of Jewish immigrants from Poland.
13 A. Hartog, *Born to Sing* (London: Dennis Dobson, 1978) p. 77.
14 Beckman, *The 43 Group*, p. 31.
15 *Socialist Review*, No 162, March 1993, p. 23.
16 Beckman, *The 43 Group*, p. 51.
17 At this time the *Sunday Pictorial* was estimated to have had a weekly circulation of five million.
18 See D. N. Pritt, *Autobiography of D. N. Pritt, Part 2, Brasshats and Bureaucrats* (London: Lawrence and Wishart, 1966) pp. 52–7.
19 See T. Kushner, 'Anti-Semitism and Austerity: The August 1947 riots in Britain', P. Panayi (ed.) *Racial Violence in Britain 1840–1950* (Leicester: Leicester University Press, 1993) pp. 149–68.
20 See L. Rose, 'Survey of Open-Air Meetings held by Pro-Fascist Organisations, April–October 1947', *Factual Survey No. 2*, April 1948.
21 National Museum of Labour History, [C]ommunist [P]arty [A]rchives, CP/CENT/SPN/1/7.
22 E. P. Thompson, *The Fascist Threat to Britain* (London: CPGB, 1947) pp. 14–15.
23 See Rose, 'Survey of Open-Air Meetings'.
24 CPA CP/CENT/ORG/12/7.
25 Len Rolnick to author, 7 July 1998.
26 See R. West (pseud.), 'A reporter at Large: Heil Hamm!', *New Yorker*, 14 August 1948, pp. 26–44.
27 Len Rolnick to author, 7 July 1998.
28 A similar pattern of activity took place in neighbouring Bethnal Green. The Communist Party was also involved in the Bethnal Green NCCL Area Committee. However, anti-fascist activity was stronger in Hackney. The reason for this, according to the NCCL, was that the Jewish population was smaller in Bethnal Green and workers were not as well organised.
29 Brynmor Jones Library, University of Hull, [N]ational [C]ouncil for [C]ivil [L]iberties papers, DCL 42/2b.
30 See R. C. Thurlow, *The Secret State* (Oxford: Basil Blackwell, 1994) pp. 276–7.
31 See Pritt, *Autobiography*, pp. 56–7 and p. 75.
32 See D. Renton, 'An Unbiased Watch? The police and fascist/anti-fascist street conflict in Britain, 1945–51', *Lobster*, No. 35 (Summer 1998), 12–19.
33 The RCP was formed in 1944 from a merger of the Trotskyist Workers' International League and the Revolutionary Socialist League. By 1950, however, the RCP had disbanded as a consequence of an 'entrist' strategy whereby members had been encouraged to join the Labour Party.
34 According to M. Crick, *The March of Militant* (London: Faber and Faber, 1986), p. 29.
35 Grant, *The Menace of Fascism, What it is and How to Fight it* (London: Militant, 1978), p. 72.
36 See L. Trotsky, *Fascism. What it is and How to Fight it* (New York: Pathfinder, 1993).

37 Grant, *The Menace of Fascism*, p. 74.
38 See Rose, 'Survey of Open-Air Meetings'.
39 See J. Hamm, *Action Replay* (London: Howard Baker, 1983) pp. 144–5; and *Searchlight*, No. 273, March 1998, pp. 12–13.
40 See D. Renton, *The Attempted Revival of British Fascism* (University of Sheffield, PhD thesis, 1998) p. 170.
41 A. Hartog, *Born to Sing*, pp. 75–6.
42 Beckman, *The 43 Group*, p. 95.
43 See *On Guard*, Vol. 2, No. 1 (December 1949).
44 *On Guard*, No. 1 (July 1947), p. 2.
45 Driberg also authored an anti-fascist pamphlet which called for a ban on fascist activity and fascist propaganda. See T. Driberg, *Mosley? No!* (London: W. H. Allen, n.d.) pp. 17–19.
46 See *Searchlight*, No. 257 (November 1996) p. 16.
47 *On Guard*, No. 3 (September 1947) p. 3.
48 Beckman, *The 43 Group* p. 95, and *On Guard*, No. 3, September 1947, p. 3.
49 Beckman, *The 43 Group*, p. 61.
50 See Rose, 'Survey of Open-Air Meetings'.
51 Beckman, *The 43 Group*, p. 177.
52 BD C6/4/2/3.
53 BD C6/1/1/3. JDC minutes, 30 July 1947.
54 NCCL DCL/42/1.
55 Described as such by Morris Beckman to author, 29 May 1998.
56 See *Concord*, No. 3 (November 1943) p. 4.
57 See BD C6/2/1/5. Survey of the work of the Jewish Defence Committee of the Board of Deputies 1945–1948. Also see S. Salomon, *Anti-Semitism in Post-War Britain: The Work of the Jewish Defence Committee* (London: Woburn Press, 1950).
58 See *On Guard* (March 1948), p. 3 and for outlandish devotion to Mosley, see T. Grundy, *Memoir of a Fascist Childhood* (London: Heinemannn, 1998).
59 L. Rose, 'Fascism in Britain', *Factual Survey No. 1* (April 1948), p. 8.
60 On Mosley's postwar philosophy, see A. Poole, 'Oswald Mosley and the Union Movement: Success or Failure?', in M. Cronin (ed.) *The Failure of British Fascism* (Basingstoke, Macmillan, 1996) pp. 53–80.
61 See CPA CP/CENT/ORG/12/7: Report on May Day agitation (1948).
62 M. Walker, *The National Front*, 2nd rev. edn (London: Fontana, 1978) p. 26.
63 See Beckman, *The 43 Group*, pp. 131–9.
64 Beckman, *The 43 Group*, p. 134.
65 See *Searchlight*, No. 262 (April 1997), pp. 10–11.
66 MUJEX newsletter, Vol. 2, No. 4 (March 1948).
67 MUJEX newsletter, Vol. 2, No. 6 (May–June 1948).
68 See CPA CP/CENT/ORG/12/7: Report on Fascist activities in the Lancashire and Cheshire District (May 1948).
69 See CPA CP/CENT/ORG/12/7: Letter from Leeds Area Committee of the CPGB (May 1948).
70 *On Guard*, No. 9 (April 1948) p. 1.
71 See *On Guard*, No. 13 (September 1948) p. 2.
72 *On Guard*, No. 16 (December 1948) p. 3.
73 Michael McLean also distributed his own anti-fascist literature, e.g. *Mosley*

Exposed: The Union Movement from Within.

74 Report on the National Anti-Fascist League by Michael McLean, Board of Deputies, October 1948.

75 Over 1,000 people were said to have attended an outdoor rally held by the NAFL and 43 Group at Bethnal Green in July 1948. The pre-publicity for this meeting had promised 'the most sensational meeting since the War'.

76 See BD C6/1/1/3, JDC minutes, 15 July 1948 and 2 September 1948.

77 BD C6/1/1/3. JDC minutes, 30 September 1948.

78 See BD C6/4/2/3. The fact that MUJEX received a substantial grant from the Board of Deputies probably accounts for why the JDC secured the support of MUJEX for this particular plan.

79 See BD C6/1/1/3, Chairman's Statement, 16 February 1949.

80 *On Guard*, No. 18, February 1949, p. 1.

81 See *On Guard*, No. 20, April 1949, p. 1, and Beckman, *The 43 Group*, pp. 188–9.

82 By banning all political processions in London, the Labour government also prohibited left-wing May Day parades. This meant that the only two capitals in Europe where May Day marches were banned were London and Madrid.

83 Beckman, *The 43 Group*, p. 196.

84 *On Guard*, Vol. 2, No. 1, December 1949, p. 1.

85 Len Rolnick to author, 7 July 1998. Lack of funds also explains the non-appearance of *On Guard* in June and August 1948.

86 BD C6/1/1/3. JDC minutes, 5 April 1950.

87 Morris Beckman to author, 29 May 1998.

88 Jeffrey Hamm, *Action Replay* (London, Howard Baker, 1983), p. 150.

89 Len Rolnick to author, 7 July 1998. Also see Beckman, *The 43 Group*, p. 177.

90 See Beckman, *The 43 Group*, p. 177.

91 Jeffrey Hamm, *Action Replay* (London: Howard Baker, 1983), p. 150.

92 D. Renton, *The Attempted Revival of British Fascism*, p. 52.

93 See R. C. Thurlow, 'The Guardian of the "Sacred Flame": The Failed Political Resurrection of Sir Oswald Mosley after 1945', *Journal of Contemporary History*, 33 (1998) 241–54.

94 See A. Graham, *Fascism in Britain* (Pharos Press, 1966) in National Museum of Labour History.

95 BD C6/1/1/3. JDC current notes, September–October 1959.

96 See BD C6/1/1/3. JDC minutes, 8 and 16 September 1959.

97 Hamm, *Action Replay*, p. 184.

98 O. Mosley, *My Life* (London: Nelson, 1968) p. 453.

99 This followed an attack in the paper *Unità* triggered by the Venice Conference.

100 Walker, *The National Front*, p. 39.

101 *The Times*, 2 July 1962.

102 See G. Ashe, 'Yellow Star-Retrospect and Query' (1), *Institute of Race Relations Newsletter*, April 1964, pp. 26–9.

103 See *Daily Worker*, 6 July and 18 July 1962.

104 *Daily Worker*, 21 July 1962.

105 *Daily Worker*, 21 July 1962.

106 *Daily Worker*, 23 July 1962.

107 See *Action*, No. 97, 1 August 1962, pp. 10-11.
108 See *Action*, No. 97, 1 August 1962, p. 18.
109 For details, see Walker, *The National Front*, pp. 42–3.
110 See Ashe, 'Yellow Star-Retrospect and Query' (1), p. 27 and *The Times*, 3 September 1962.
111 The Board of Deputies and AJEX jointly collected 150,000 signatures.
112 On mainstream depoliticisation of race, see A. Messina, *Race and Party Competition in Britain* (Oxford: Clarendon Press, 1989) pp. 21–52.
113 See G. Thayer, *The British Political Fringe* (London: Anthony Blond, 1965) p. 87.
114 G. Ashe, 'Yellow Star-Retrospect and Query' (1), p. 28.
115 See BD C6/1/3/4, JDC minutes, 12 September 1962.
116 See *Spearhead*, April 1965, p. 6.
117 *Searchlight*, No. 281, November 1998, p. 16.
118 See G. Ashe, 'Yellow Star-Retrospect and Query' (2), *Institute of Race Relations Newsletter*, May 1964, pp. 11–14.
119 See Thayer, *The British Political Fringe*, p. 88.
120 These convictions had resulted from activities at a National Socialist Movement summer camp held in the Cotswolds in 1962.
121 *Action*, No. 99 (1 October 1962).
122 See *Action*, No. 101 (1 November 1962) p. 9.
123 See *Fighting Talk*, Issue 5, p.16.
124 D. S. Lewis, *Illusions of Grandeur* (Manchester: Manchester University Press, 1987) p. 247
125 Walker, *The National Front*, p. 43.
126 According to JDC records, in order to deny Mosley an indoor hall, authorities usually insisted on prohibitively large insurance premiums to cover damages; alternatively, the Union Movement was refused because it was deemed racist, and in a small minority of cases, no reason was given for the denial of halls. See BD C6/1/3/4, JDC Provincial Liaison Committee minutes, 14 July 1963.
127 BD C6/1/3/4, JDC minutes, 11 December 1962.
128 G. Ashe, 'Yellow Star-Retrospect and Query' (1), p. 29.
129 See NCCL DCL/611/10.
130 See *Spearhead*, April 1965, p. 6.
131 Jewish Defence Committee, *Defence with Responsibility* (1966), p. 14.
132 For a list see *Searchlight*, No. 2, 1966.
133 BD C6/1/2/4, JDC minutes, 17 August 1965.
134 Jewish Aid Committee of Britain, *With a Strong Hand* (March, 1966), p. 7.
135 See Jewish Aid Committee of Britain, *With a Strong Hand*, p. 9.
136 See Jewish Aid Committee of Britain, *With a Strong Hand*, p. 13.
137 Jewish Defence Committee, *Defence with Responsibility*, p. 10.
138 Jewish Defence Committee, *Defence with Responsibility*, p. 13.
139 Jewish Aid Committee of Britain, *With a Strong Hand*, p. 11.
140 Jewish Aid Committee of Britain, *With a Strong Hand*, p. 12.
141 On the same grounds, the Conservative government refused to give permission to the Yellow Star Movement to hold an anti-fascist meeting in Trafalgar Square.
142 On Chesterton, see D. Baker, *Ideology of Obsession, A. K. Chesterton and*

British Fascism (London: I. B. Tauris, 1996).
143 A. K. Chesterton's address to the first AGM of the National Front, reproduced in *Candour*, Vol. XVIII, No. 469 (October 1967).

Chapter 4

1 A. Messina, *Race and Party Competition in Britain* (Oxford: Clarendon Press, 1989) pp. 118–19.
2 See C. Rosenberg, 'The Labour Party and the Fight against Fascism', *International Socialism*, Vol. 2, No. 39 (1989) 55–93. In 1992, anti-fascists from Britain handed out thousands of leaflets at an anti-FN demonstration in Paris offering advice on how French anti-fascists could use the Anti-Nazi League as a model to defeat Jean-Marie Le Pen, head of the Front National.
3 See *Spearhead*, No. 129, July 1979, pp. 10–12.
4 See M. Walker, *The National Front*, 2nd rev. edn (London: Fontana, 1978) p. 92.
5 CP/CENT/SUBJ/OG/18, Communist Party Memo dated May 1969.
6 On Powellism and the response of the Left, see D. Widgery, *The Left in Britain 1956–68* (London: Penguin, 1978) pp. 407–13.
7 J. Spiers, A. Sexsmith and A. Everitt, *The Left in Britain* (Hassocks: Harvester Press, 1976) p. 21.
8 See Anti-Fascist Research Group, *Facts on Fascism*, Bulletin No. 3 (n.d.) and Bulletin No. 5 (n.d.) included in the *The Left in Britain* (Harvester/Primary Social Sources Microform Collection, 1976).
9 See *Red Mole*, April 1971.
10 Anti-Fascist Research Group, Bulletin No. 5.
11 *Spearhead*, No. 39 (January 1971), p. 15.
12 Anti-Fascist Research Group, Press Release, 31 October 1971. Brynmor Jones Library, University of Hull, National Council for Civil Liberties papers, DCL/611/10.
13 Trade Unions Against Fascism (1972) included in the *The Left in Britain* (Harvester/Primary Social Sources Microform Collection, 1976).
14 According to *Searchlight* figures in *From Ballots to Bombs. The Inside Story of the National Front's Political Soldiers* (London: Searchlight Publishing Ltd, 1984) p. 4.
15 S. Taylor, *The National Front in English Politics* (London: Macmillan, 1982) p. 34.
16 See Transport and General Workers' Union, *Racialism, Fascism and the Trade Unions* (1974).
17 Walker, *The National Front*, p. 157.
18 See Jewish Defence Committee, *It can happen here – if you let it!* (n.d.).
19 *State Research Bulletin*, No. 7, August-September 1978, p. 126.
20 Brockway became a Labour MP in 1956 before becoming a Labour peer in 1964. Brockway had introduced a Bill in the House of Commons to outlaw racial hatred eight times before the Race Relations Act was finally passed in 1965.
21 Kay Beauchamp became a member of the Communist Party in the 1920s and later was very active in the Movement for Colonial Freedom/Liberation as well as in the Hackney borough organisation of the

CPGB. Her spouse, Tony Gilbert, fought in the International Brigades and was also active in the Communist Party and Movement for Colonial Freedom/Liberation.

22 See *The Red Lion Square Disorders of 15 June 1974*, Report of Inquiry by the Rt Hon. Lord Justice Scarman (London, HMSO, 1975).

23 Walker, *The National Front*, p. 163.

24 R. Clutterbuck, *Britain in Agony: The Growth of Political Violence* (London: Faber and Faber, 1978) p. 163.

25 S. Taylor, 'Race, Extremism and Violence in Contemporary British Politics', *New Community*, Vol. 7 (1978–9) 59.

26 *Fighting Talk*, Issue 16, p. 18 and *Morning Star*, 4 October 1974.

27 See *A Well-Oiled Nazi Machine: An Analysis of the Growth of the Extreme Right in Britain* (A.F. and R. Press, 1974).

28 See *Searchlight*, No. 1, Spring 1965, No. 2, 1966, No. 3, Spring 1967 and No. 4 (n.d).

29 Gerry Gable was a former member of the Young Communist League and former CPGB candidate in Stamford Hill, North London in 1962. He was also associated with the Yellow Star Movement (see *The Times*, 3 September 1962) and an intelligence officer for the 62 Group.

30 See *Searchlight*, No. 73 (July 1981).

31 *The Guardian*, 24 August 1974.

32 Walker, *The National Front*, p. 163.

33 Walker, *The National Front*, p. 149.

34 Although it should not be forgotten that literature exposing the fascist pasts of Front leaders distributed by anti-fascists helped sow the seeds of this division in the first place.

35 In 1976, the National Party had two of its representatives elected to Blackburn District Council, although one had to resign for not declaring a criminal record. Amidst mutual recriminations (Kingsley-Read was later exposed as having secured links with neo-Nazi groups abroad) the National Party collapsed in the late 1970s.

36 Walker, *The National Front*, p. 181.

37 On these incidents, see *Searchlight*, June and July 1975, Walker, *The National Front*, p. 181 and *Fighting Talk*, Issue 16, p. 19.

38 *Morning Star*, 13 October 1975.

39 Walker, *The National Front*, p. 195.

40 Taylor, *The National Front in English Politics*, p. 102.

41 Labour Research Department, *The National Front Investigated* (London, LRD publications, 1978) p. 7.

42 *CARF*, No. 6, 1978, p. 15.

43 A central figure in AFFOR was the Rev. John Hick, Professor of Theology at Birmingham University. See for instance, Rev. J. Hick, *The New Nazis of the National Front: A Warning to Christians* (1976) and *The New Nazism of the National Front and National Party* (1977). Also see Rev. T. Holden, *So What are You Going to Do about the National Front?* (1978?).

44 See Z. Layton-Henry, *The Politics of Race in Britain* (London: Allen and Unwin, 1984) pp. 99–100.

45 See Taylor, *The National Front in English Politics*, pp. 111–15.

46 Jenny Bourne (*CARF*) to author, 14 May 1997.

47 See *CARF*, No. 2, October–November 1977, p. 15.
48 *CARF*, the paper of the Kingston Campaign Against Racism and Fascism, had an initial print run of 500 copies.
49 D. Widgery, *Beating Time* (London: Chatto and Windus, 1986) p. 43.
50 Widgery, *Beating Time*, p. 45.
51 For details of anti-fascist responses at local level, see *CARF*, August–September 1977, p. 11 and October–November 1977, p. 14.
52 See M. Steed, 'The National Front Vote', *Parliamentary Affairs*, Vol. 31, No. 3 (1978) 282–93.
53 See *Socialist Worker*, 28 May 1977.
54 See *CARF*, No. 2, October–November 1977, p. 10.
55 See commentary on Lewisham in *CARF*, No. 2, October–November 1977.
56 *CARF*, No. 2, October–November 1977, p. 7.
57 Taylor, *The National Front in English Politics*, p. 133.
58 See D. Cook, *A Knife at the Throat of Us All*, CPGB pamphlet (n.d.).
59 *Morning Star*, 26 August 1977.
60 See *Socialist Worker*, 18 June and 9 July 1977.
61 *International Socialism*, Vol. 94, 1977, p. 13.
62 *Socialist Worker*, 13 August 1977.
63 See Big Flame, *The Past against our Future: Fighting Racism and Fascism* (n.d.), p. 35.
64 Clutterbuck, *Britain in Agony*, p. 216.
65 *Socialist Worker*, 20 August 1977.
66 Steve Radford, Secretary of the Southwark Campaign against Racism and Fascism, in *CARF*, October–November 1977, p. 10.
67 See *CARF*, October–November 1977, p. 11.
68 On the press and Lewisham, see *CARF*, October–November 1977, p. 7.
69 See A. Callinicos, 'In Defence of Violence', *International Socialism*, Vol. 101 (September 1977), pp. 24–8.
70 See S. Taylor, 'Race, Extremism and Violence in Contemporary British Politics', 62.
71 On the Ladywood by-election, see Z. Layton-Henry and S. Taylor, 'Race and Politics in Ladywood', *New Community*, Vol. 6, Nos. 1 and 2 (1977–8) 130–42.
72 C. Bambery, *Killing the Nazi Menace* (London: Socialist Workers' Party, 1992) p. 33.
73 See *State Research Bulletin*, No. 7 (August–September 1978) p. 127.
74 Big Flame, *The Past against our Future*, p. 36.
75 Nona Peras, in *CARF*, October–November 1977, p. 11.
76 Widgery, *Beating Time*, p. 49.
77 Taylor, *The National Front in English Politics*, p. 136.
78 See *Founding Statement of the Anti-Nazi League* (1977) for full list of sponsors.
79 *New Society*, 11 May 1978, p. 294.
80 *Founding Statement of the Anti-Nazi League* (1977). This is partly reproduced in Taylor, *The National Front in English Politics*, p. 137.
81 *Socialist Worker*, 19 November 1977.
82 *CARF*, No. 3, n.d., p. 5.
83 See *CARF*, No. 6, 1978, p. 14.

84 Taylor, *The National Front in English Politics*, p. 139.
85 See *Searchlight*, No. 31, 1978, pp. 10–11.
86 *The Guardian*, 8 December 1977.
87 *The Times*, 11 December 1977.
88 *The Daily Mirror*, 9 December 1977.
89 *The Sun*, 9 December 1977.
90 A Messina, *Race and Party Competition in Britain*, p. 120.
91 Big Flame, *The Past against our Future*, p. 36.
92 National Front Ex-Servicemen's Association, *Lifting the Lid off the Anti-Nazi League* (NFN Press, 1978) p. 6.
93 *Socialist Worker*, 12 August 1978.
94 J. Tomlinson, *Left, Right: The March of Political Extremism in Britain* (London: John Calder, 1981) p. 85.
95 *Searchlight*, No. 100 (October 1983) p. 3.
96 Taylor, *The National Front in English Politics*, p. 103.
97 P. Gilroy, *There Ain't No Black in the Union Jack* (London: Routledge, 1995) pp. 131–2.
98 An offshoot from the International Socialists.
99 M. Williams/Revolutionary Communist Group, *The Anti-Nazi League and the Struggle against Racism* (RCG Publications, 1978) p. 9.
100 Quoted in Z. Layton-Henry, *The Politics of Race in Britain* (London: Allen and Unwin, 1984) p. 104.
101 Gilroy, *There Ain't No Black in the Union Jack*, p. 134.
102 Widgery, *Beating Time*, p. 62. By 1979, *Temporary Hoarding* was selling 12,000 copies.
103 C. Rosenberg, 'The Labour Party and the Fight against Fascism', *International Socialism*, Vol. 2, No. 39 (1988) 80.
104 See T. Cliff, 'Build the Anti Nazi League', *Socialist Worker*, 13 May 1978.
105 Tomlinson, *Left, Right*, p. 79. The Workers' Revolutionary Party was formerly the Socialist Labour League.
106 The Trotskyist Militant Tendency followed an entrist strategy and probably had between 1,000 and 2,000 members in the mid- to late 1970s.
107 See *CARF* , No. 6 (1978) p. 16.
108 Arthur Merton, in letter to *Fighting Talk*, Issue 3 (Summer 1992) p. 19.
109 A black 'self-defence' organisation formed following three racially motivated murders in East London.
110 See *CARF*, No. 7 (1978) p. 7.
111 *Forewarned Against Fascism*, No. 4 (1978).
112 See *Forewarned Against Fascism*, No. 5 (1978); also see Taylor, *The National Front in English Politics*, pp. 152–3.
113 *CARF*, No. 7 (1978) p. 2.
114 *CARF*, No. 8 (1979) p. 2.
115 *Searchlight*, No. 100 (October 1983) p. 2.
116 See *Unity Against Fascism*, No. 1 (1976); and *Forewarned Against Fascism*, No. 4, 1978.
117 Anti-Fascist Democratic Action circular, dated 26 May 1978.
118 Press Statement by Anti-Fascist Democratic Action, dated November 1978.
119 See *Forewarned Against Fascism*, No. 5 (1978).
120 *Forewarned Against Fascism*, No. 5 (1978) p. 14.

121 See *Searchlight*, No. 100 (October 1983) p. 3.

122 *Forewarned Against Fascism*, No. 5 (1978).

123 Graeme Atkinson in *Searchlight*, No. 74 (August 1981) p. 8.

124 C. T. Husbands, *Racial Exclusionism and the City* (London: Allen and Unwin, 1983) p. 273.

125 See P. Wilkinson, *The New Fascists* (London: Grant McIntyre, 1981) pp. 169–70.

126 See B. Troyna, 'The Media and the Electoral Decline of the National Front', *Patterns of Prejudice* Vol. 14, No. 3 (1980) 25–30.

127 See Troyna, 'The Media and the Electoral Decline of the National Front', 29.

128 R. Eatwell, 'Why has the Extreme Right Failed in Britain?', in P. Hainsworth (ed.) *The Extreme Right in Europe and the USA* (London: Frances Pinter, 1992) p. 187.

129 This was an offshoot of the All London Anti-Racist, Anti-Fascist Co-ordinating Committee.

130 *CARF*, No. 1 (May 1977) p. 4.

131 *Socialist Worker*, 16 September 1978,

132 See P. Cohen and C. Gardner, *It Ain't Half Racist Mum* (London: Comedia, 1982) pp. 12–13.

133 See *Hornsey Journal*, April 29 1977.

134 *South East London and Kentish Mercury*, 5 May 1977.

135 See *East Ender*, 11 August 1977.

136 For examples, see *Camden Journal*, 20 April 1979, *Southall Gazette*, 20 April 1979, *East Ender*, 14 April 1979 and 5 May 1979, *Rochdale Observer*, 28 April 1979 and *Wolverhampton Express and Star*, 24 April 1979.

137 See comments made by Ian Trethowan, BBC Director General in *Yorkshire Post*, 21 September 1978.

138 *Spearhead*, No. 129 (July 1979) p. 11.

139 See Statement by the Labour Party's National Executive Committee, *Response to the National Front*, September 1978, p. 3.

140 J. Tyndall, *The Eleventh Hour* (London: Albion Press, 1988) p. 230.

141 See National Council for Civil Liberties, *Southall 23 April 1979, Report of the Unofficial Committee of Enquiry* (London: NCCL, 1980) p. 121.

142 Board of Deputies Memorandum: *The Board's Programme for Combating the National Front during the General Election* (n.d.).

143 National Front Ex-Servicemen's Association, *Lifting the Lid off the Anti-Nazi League*, p. 3.

144 *Socialist Worker*, 13 May 1978.

145 Big Flame, *The Past against our Future*, p. 36.

146 *Spearhead*, No. 129 (July 1979) p. 10.

147 National Council for Civil Liberties, *Southall 23 April 1979, Report of the Unofficial Committee of Inquiry* (London: NCCL, 1980) p. 190.

148 A mobile unit of the Metropolitan Police that had gained a reputation for heavy-handed policing.

149 See Campaign Against Racism/Southall Rights, *Southall: The Birth of a Black Community* (London: Institute of Race Relations and Southall Rights, 1981).

150 *CARF*, No. 9 (1979) p. 2.

151 The first to vacate the NF was the National Front Constitutional

214 Anti-Fascism in Britain

Movement. This was followed by the British Democratic Party, which was the old Leicester branch of the NF. Both of these were short-lived and came to nothing. The final break came in 1980 when John Tyndall left to form the New National Front, which became the British National Party in 1982.

152 See M. Harrop, J. England and C. T. Husbands, 'The Bases of National Front Support', *Political Studies*, Vol. 28, No. 8 (1980) esp. 279–82.

153 R. Griffin, 'British Fascism: The Ugly Duckling', in M. Cronin (ed.) *The Failure of British Fascism* (Basingstoke: Macmillan, 1996) pp. 162–3.

154 *Workers' Action*, 25 March–8 April 1978, quoted in National Front Ex-Servicemen's Association, *Lifting the Lid off the Anti-Nazi League*, p. 7.

Chapter 5

1 For a summary of ANL activities during 1980, see C. Bambery, 'Euro-fascism: The Lessons of the Past and Current Tasks', *International Socialism*, Autumn 1993, p. 67.

2 See interview with Peter Hain, *Searchlight*, No. 68 (February 1981) pp. 16–17.

3 *Searchlight*, No. 76 (October 1981) p. 2.

4 The *Guardian*, 30 May 1984.

5 Alan Howarth, *New Society*, 11 October 1984, p. 56.

6 *The Times*, 18 May 1984.

7 This figure was claimed by John Marks, a physics lecturer at the polytechnic who co-wrote *The Rape of Reason*, a history of the polytechnic in the 1970s.

8 *Times Higher Education Supplement*, 14 December 1984.

9 *The Guardian*, 23 May 1984.

10 *The Guardian*, 12 October 1984. See questionnaire circulated by second-year sociology students in University of North London, Patrick Harrington File.

11 University of North London, Patrick Harrington File: Dr David MacDowall, Announcement of Resignation, 16 October 1984.

12 See *Daily Telegraph*, 29 November 1984.

13 Harrington was also provided with 250 library books and his own refreshment facilities.

14 See *The Guardian*, 11 January 1985. The '90 per cent victory' verdict was the official line of the Polytechnic Students' Union Executive, see *Time Out*, 24–30 January 1985.

15 *The Times*, 18 June 1984.

16 R. Thurlow, *Fascism in Britain*, 2nd rev. edn (London: I.B. Tauris, 1998) p. 260.

17 *Daily Mail*, 13 December 1984. The author would like to reassure readers that as a former student at the Polytechnic of North London, he is not a 'graduate in the art of anarchy'.

18 Andrew Lightfoot, a British National Party activist, encountered student opposition at Royal Holloway and Bedford New College in the early 1990s. The discovery of Troy Southgate, a leading member of the minuscule 'English Nationalist Movement', at the Univerity of Kent at Canterbury sparked opposition from the Kent Anti-Fascist Committee in 1996.

19 Ray Hill was a former member of the National Socialist Movement in the 1960s who had been recruited by *Searchlight* following his return from South Africa in the late 1970s.
20 See R. Hill with A. Bell, *The Other Face of Terror* (London: Grafton Books, 1988). At this time, Joe Pearce was the leading figure in the Young National Front.
21 Hill with Bell. *The Other Face of Terror*, p. 291.
22 Larry O'Hara has speculated that this story was fabricated by *Searchlight,* see *Lobster*, No. 24 (1992) 17–18.
23 Hill with Bell, *The Other Face of Terror*, p. 138.
24 *Spearhead*, No. 177, July 1983, pp. 11–13.
25 L. Fekete, 'The Anti-fascist Movement: Lessons We Must Learn', *Race and Class*, Vol. 28 (Summer 1986) p. 82.
26 Fekete, 'The Anti-fascist Movement', p. 80.
27 *Searchlight*, No. 136, October 1986, p. 17.
28 See Anti-Fascist Action, *An Introduction to London AFA* (1991) p. 3.
29 *Searchlight*, No. 125 (November 1985) p. 8.
30 Originally the strong-arm wing of the Socialist Workers' Party.
31 A Trotskyist offshoot from the International Socialists.
32 A street activist anarchist group that played a central role in the 'Stop the City' demonstrations in London in 1985.
33 *Searchlight*, No. 126 (December 1985) p. 2.
34 See *Searchlight*, No. 138 (December 1986) pp. 6–7.
35 See *Searchlight*, No. 136 (October 1986) pp. 18–20.
36 L. O'Hara, *Turning up the Heat* (London: Phoenix Press, 1994) p. 36.
37 See *Red Action*, Issue 75, Autumn 1997.
38 On the ideological side to National Front split in 1986, see R. Eatwell, 'The Esoteric Ideology of the NF in the 1980s', in M. Cronin (ed.) *The Failure of British Fascism* (Basingstoke: Macmillan, 1996) pp. 96–117.
39 Anti-Fascist Action, *An Introduction to London AFA* p. 3.
40 See *Fighting Talk*, Issue 7, p. 17.
41 See *Searchlight*, No. 173 (November 1989) p. 4.
42 For a summary of the work of Tyne and Wear Anti-Fascist Association, see Searchlight, *When Hate Comes to Town: Community Responses to Racism and Fascism* (London: Searchlight Educational Trust, 1995) section 8.4.
43 *Fighting Talk*, Issue 9, p. 4.
44 See Anti-Fascist Action, *An Introduction to London AFA* p. 11.
45 See Anti-Fascist Action, *An Introduction to London AFA* pp. 3–4 and *Searchlight*, No. 174 (December 1989) p. 5.
46 *Fighting Talk*, Issue 7, p. 6.
47 L. O' Hara, *Searchlight for Beginners* (London: Phoenix Press, 1996).
48 *Fighting Talk*, Issue 7, p. 6.
49 See *Fighting Talk*, Issue 3 (Summer 1992) p. 18.
50 *Fighting Talk*, Issue 7, p. 12.
51 *Fighting Talk*, Issue 3 (Summer 1992) p. 16.
52 Anti-Fascist Action, *An Introduction to London AFA* p. 4.
53 See *Fighting Talk*, Issue 3 (Summer 1992) p. 16.
54 For an overview of the BNP in the 1980s, see N. Copsey, 'Contemporary Fascism in the Local Arena: The British National Party and Rights for

Whites', in M. Cronin (ed.) *The Failure of British Fascism* (Basingstoke: Macmillan, 1996) pp. 118–40.

55 Anti-Fascist Action, *An Introduction to London AFA* p. 12.
56 See Anti-Fascist Action, *An Introduction to London AFA* p. 5.
57 Anti-Fascist Action, *An Introduction to London AFA* p. 14.
58 *Fighting Talk*, Issue 1 (September 1991) p. 2.
59 See *Fighting Talk*, Issue 2 (Spring 1992) p. 2.
60 It donated £1,000 towards the first issue.
61 Letter to *Searchlight*, *CARF*, No. 1 (February/March 1991) p. 2.
62 Letter to *Searchlight*, *CARF*, No. 1 (February/March 1991) p. 2.
63 *CARF*, No. 1 (February/March 1991) p. 2.
64 *Searchlight*, No. 199 (January 1992) p. 2.
65 *Times Higher Education Supplement*, 7 December 1984.
66 *The Guardian*, 30 March 1992.
67 See *Anti-Racist Alliance Bulletin*, March/April 1994.
68 See Anti-Racist Alliance, *Building an Anti-Racist Alliance* (1992).
69 *CARF*, No. 10 (September–October 1992) p. 16.
70 *Searchlight*, No. 199 (January 1992) p. 2.
71 See *New Statesman and Society*, 6 March 1992, p. 35 and 13 March 1992, p. 92.
72 See *Fighting Talk*, Issue 3 (Summer 1992) pp. 15–16.
73 See *Searchlight*, No. 200 (February 1992) p. 2.
74 See Anti-Nazi League, *Fighting the Nazi Threat*, p. 2.
75 See *Searchlight*, No. 200 (February 1992) p. 2.
76 See *New Statesman and Society*, 20 March 1992, p. 36.
77 C. Bambery, *Killing the Nazi Menace* (London: Socialist Workers' Party, 1992) pp. 45–6.
78 Bambery, *Killing the Nazi Menace*, p. 45.
79 C. Bambery, 'Planning the Party', *Socialist Review*, Issue 169 (November 1993) p. 12.
80 Bambery, *Killing the Nazi Menace*, p. 45.
81 See Bambery, 'Planning the Party', pp. 12–13.
82 Bambery, *Killing the Nazi Menace*, p. 44.
83 See *New Statesman and Society* (15 October 1993) pp. 18–19.
84 See *New Statesman and Society* (28 February 1992) pp. 12–13.
85 L. German, 'Return of the Anti Nazi League', *Socialist Review*, Issue 150 (February 1992) p. 10.
86 *Fighting Talk*, Issue 2 (Spring 1992) p. 7.
87 *Fighting Talk*, Issue 2 (Spring 1992) p. 7.
88 *Fighting Talk*, Issue 10 (January 1995) p. 13.
89 Anti-Nazi League, *Sign up against the Nazis* (1992).
90 *Searchlight*, No. 202 (April 1992) p. 14.
91 See Anti-Nazi League, *Fighting the Nazi Threat Today*, p. 16.
92 See Anti-Nazi League, *Fighting the Nazi Threat Today*, p. 17.
93 See *Searchlight*, No. 202 (April 1992) p. 14. For a description of the attack on the ANL in Tower Hamlets, see Searchlight, *At War with Society* (London: Searchlight, 1993) p. 36.
94 Anti-Nazi League leaflet, *Invest in a Nazi Free Future* (1992).
95 *Fighting Talk*, Issue 3 (Summer 1992) p. 2.

96 See *Fighting Talk*, Issue 7 (1994) p. 12.
97 The ANL did claim that it had a contingent present at Waterloo.
98 See *Searchlight*, No. 208 (October 1992) pp. 4–5.
99 *Fighting Talk*, Issue 10 (January 1995) p. 12.
100 On the electoral emergence of the BNP in Tower Hamlets, see Copsey, 'Contemporary Fascism in the Local Arena', pp. 118–40, and R. Eatwell, 'The Dynamics of Right-wing Electoral Breakthrough', *Patterns of Prejudice*, Vol. 32, No. 3 (1998) 3–31.
101 See *ANL Newsletter*, Issue 4 (October 1993) p. 2.
102 For full list of sponsors, see *ANL Newsletter*, Issue 4 (October 1993) p. 5.
103 *Fighting Talk*, Issue 7 (1994) p. 14.
104 See *Searchlight*, No. 221 (November 1993) p. 3.
105 ANL Open Letter – Welling Demonstration.
106 S. Platt, in *New Statesman and Society*, 22 October 1993, p. 13.
107 O'Hara, *Turning Up the Heat*, p. 41.
108 The orgins of Combat 18 have been the matter of some debate as well as inconsistent analysis. AFA maintains that Combat 18 emerged as a direct consequence of its confrontations with the BNP in the early 1990s (see *Fighting Talk*, Issue 16 [March 1997] p. 11). At first, *Searchlight* saw Combat 18 as a group inspired by a US neo-Nazi, Harold Covington. In April 1995 its position changed, with Combat 18 now said to be the creation of MI5.
109 See *Fighting Talk*, Issue 7 (1994) p. 18.
110 *Fighting Talk*, Issue 13 (March 1996) p. 15.
111 See *Fighting Talk*, Issue 8 (1994) p. 2 and Issue 12 (November 1995) p. 15.
112 See *Searchlight*, No. 227 (May 1994) p. 9.
113 See *Tower Hamlets Trades Union Council*, Bulletin No. 1 (November 1993), and Tower Hamlets Trades Union Council, *No More Blood on the Streets, How to Fight Fascism and Racism* (1994).
114 See Institute of Jewish Affairs and American Jewish Committee, *Antisemitism World Report 1995* (London: IJA, 1996) p. 244.
115 See *CARF*, No. 20 (May/June 1994) p. 3.
116 G. Gable, Foreword to N. Holtam and S. Mayo, *Learning from the Conflict* (London: Jubilee Group, 1998).
117 See ANL, *Fighting the Nazi Threat Today*, 2nd edn (May 1994) p. 16.
118 N. Holtman, 'The BNP on the Isle of Dogs: Developing a Church Response', in Holtman and Mayo, *Learning from the Conflict*, p. 12.
119 Bambery, *Killing the Nazi Menace*, p. 44.
120 See *Socialist Review*, Issue 176 (June 1994) p. 10.
121 See Holtman and Mayo, *Learning from the Conflict*.
122 *East London Advertiser*, 23 September 1993.
123 *East London Advertiser*, 23 September 1993.
124 *Fighting Talk*, Issue 12 (November 1995) pp. 16–17.
125 Formed in 1980 to monitor and campaign against racial violence.
126 See Newham Monitoring Project, *The Enemy in Our Midst* (London: Newham Monitoring Project, 1995) pp. 20–1 and *Searchlight*, No. 237 (March 1995) p. 3.
127 *Searchlight*, No. 247 (January 1996) p. 2.
128 See *Fighting Talk*, Issue 12 (November 1995) pp. 15–17.
129 *Searchlight*, No. 257 (November 1996) p. 2.

130 See O'Hara, 'Searchlight and the Jewish Community', *Searchlight for Beginners*.

131 O'Hara, final page of *Searchlight for Beginners*.

132 See especially, *Searchlight*, No. 218 (August 1993) p. 12.

133 See *Searchlight*, No. 259 (January 1997) pp. 14–15.

134 See *Lobster*, No. 26 (1993) 19–20.

135 On AFA's position, see *Fighting Talk*, Issue 14, July 1996, p. 4. It did, however, stop advertising *Searchlight* and also criticised *Searchlight* for exaggerating the threat from Combat 18.

136 Founded in 1992, the Searchlight Educational Trust has charitable status and its primary function is to educate young people about fascism and racism. According to *Searchlight*, it addresses over 200 meetings at schools, synagogues, youth groups and churches every year.

137 Searchlight Educational Trust, *When Hate Comes to Town* p. 3.1–4.

138 *New Statesman and Society*, 15 October 1993, p. 17.

139 See Searchlight Educational Trust, *When Hate Comes to Town*, Section Four.

140 See 'Is the Writing on the Wall?', in O'Hara, *Searchlight for Beginners*.

141 *Fighting Talk*, Issue 13 (March 1996) p. 15.

142 *Searchlight*, No. 267 (September 1997) p. 12.

143 *Searchlight*, No. 267 (September 1997) p. 12.

144 These were the BNP, the National Democrats, the National Front, and the Third Way (formed in 1990 by Patrick Harrington).

145 In May 1995 the National Front changed its name to the National Democrats. A minority of the party centred in the West Midlands refused to accept this and continued as the National Front.

146 *The Guardian*, 10 April 1997.

147 See *Fighting Talk*, Issue 16 (March 1997) pp. 12–15.

148 For a comprehensive list of far-Right election results, see *Searchlight*, No. 264 (June 1997) p. 4.

149 See Thurlow, *Fascism in Britain*, p. 275.

150 Institute of Jewish Affairs and American Jewish Committee, *Antisemitism World Report 1995* (London: IJA, 1995) p. 236.

151 A. Favell and D. Tambini, 'Great Britain: Clear Blue Water Between Us and Europe?', in A. Favell and B. Baumgartl (eds) *New Xenophobia in Europe* (London: Kluwer Law International, 1995) p. 155.

152 *Searchlight*, No. 276 (June 1998) p. 3.

153 CST Elections Research Unit for Board of Deputies of British Jews, Local Elections 7 May 1998, p. 5.

Index